CUSTOMER SERVICE

S/NVQ LEVEL 2

Candidate Handbook

Sally Bradley

Heinemann
Inspiring generations

Heinemann Educational Publishers
Halley Court, Jordan Hill, Oxford OX2 8EJ
Part of Harcourt Education

Heinemann is the registered trademark of
Harcourt Education Limited

First published 2003

08 07 06 05 04 03
10 9 8 7 6 5 4 3 2 1

British Library Cataloguing in Publication Data is available
from the British Library on request.

ISBN 0 435 45169 3

Typeset by Techtype, Abingdon, Oxon

Printed in Great Britain by Scotprint

Please note that the examples of websites suggested in this book were up to
date at the time of writing. It is essential for tutors to preview each site before
using it to ensure that the URL is still accurate and the content appropriate. We
suggest that tutors bookmark useful sites and consider enabling students to
access them through the school or college intranet.

Acknowledgements
With thanks to Neil Black for making this book possible.

The author and publishers would like to thank the following individuals and
organisations for permission to reproduce photographs and screen shots:

Alamy/ ImageSource page 42; Alamy/Imagestate page 182; Alamy/Indiapicture page
239; Alamy/Photofusion page 120; Corbis pages 58, 76, 124, 144, 228, 256 and 284;
Harcourt page 94; Harcourt/Trevor Clifford page 33 and Topham page 200

Every effort has been made to contact copyright holders of material published
in this book. We would be glad to hear from any unacknowledged sources at
the first opportunity, and any omissions will be rectified in subsequent
printings.

Tel: 01865 888058 www.heinemann.co.uk

Contents

Foreword

Knowing how to deliver high standards of customer service is a major challenge facing all organisations, whether in the private, public or voluntary sectors. Customers are much more demanding than they were, are less likely to tolerate poor service and are more likely to articulate any complaints. Recent research by the Institute of Customer Service indicates that customers' willingness to complain about poor products or service had increased by 12% in only one year.

Excellent customer service is all about "being easy to do business with". From the customer's perspective this involves the organisation delivering the promise, providing a personal touch, going the extra mile and resolving problems well.

The demand from employers for staff in customer-facing roles who have the right mix of skills to deliver customer service, to the right standards is growing rapidly. For those who can acquire and use these skills effectively there are many opportunities to pursue a rewarding and satisfying career as a **customer service professional**.

If you believe you have what it takes to become a customer service professional, the National Occupational Standards in Customer Service at Level 2 are designed to help you. They are detailed statements of what individuals must be able to do to deliver customer service effectively at that level. The Standards have been written by the Institute in response to what employers have told us they need from customer-facing staff and are designed to challenge individuals to raise their customer service performance by thinking reflectively about **what** they do to deliver customer service and, just as important, **how** they do it.

If you can demonstrate that you can work to these Standards you can obtain a Scottish or National Vocational Qualification in Customer Service at Level 2. Over 80,000 people have already achieved one of these qualifications placing them among the most highly used vocational qualifications in the UK.

This handbook has been written by Sally Bradley who is a widely respected customer service professional herself and who played a significant role in helping the Institute of Customer Service write the Standards. This handbook is designed to help you work with the Standards and give you support and guidance in preparing for assessment for the SVQ or NVQ.

Delivering customer service to a high standard is important, challenging and satisfying work, which can also be fun! Good luck with your journey towards becoming a customer service professional.

David Parsons

Chief Executive, Institute of Customer Service

Introduction

Whether you have been in your role for some time or are new to the world of customer service, you are one of many people who have chosen to use this book to help achieve your S/NVQ in Customer Service.

Achieving your S/NVQ in Customer Service will demonstrate to your organisation, your colleagues and yourself, that you are committed to consistently delivering good customer service and that you want to develop and improve what you do.

As far as your customers are concerned, customer service is important because they want a positive experience when dealing with you. They want you to make life easy for them. In doing so, you will make your life easier too. A happy customer will come back time and time again and you will enjoy dealing with them.

Your organisation knows it is the way in which it delivers customer service that makes the difference between success and failure. It is you who can make the difference between mediocre customer service and service that delights the customer.

'Best practice organisations listen to their customers and exceed their expectations.'

Fit for the Future Guide to Best Practice

Customers will often deal with organisations that may not necessarily be the cheapest, simply because they enjoy the customer service they get. This means they value the level of service given by employees, i.e. you.

Being good at your job can give you:

♦ increased confidence
♦ job satisfaction
♦ respect for your colleagues and employer
♦ greater flexibility within your role
♦ better prospects
♦ recognition of what you do well by your organisation, your colleagues and your customers.

Helping to keep customers happy will also help keep you happy in your job

Getting started

There are many ways of working towards an S/NVQ, so talk to the individuals who are supporting you to find the best way of using this book. For instance, there is no real need to start at Unit 1 and work through in a logical order. You can dip in and out as best suits you.

For all the units in this book, you will need to relate what you are reading to your own role, the environment in which you work and the types of customers you deal with. Do not forget to consider what your organisation expects you to do, how your colleagues fit in to your work and how you fit in with theirs.

Whether you work in the public sector or the private sector, you will probably have noticed that customers are becoming ever more demanding.

Positive and negative comments can be made by anybody you come into contact with, i.e. not just your customers but also people you work with or suppliers or other people from your organisation whom you may not deal with very often. Customer service is all about everyone getting it right first time; not just you, but all those who work with you as well.

As you work through the units in this book, keep asking yourself the following important questions:

1 What do I need to do?
- How will I prove I meet the requirements of my S/NVQ?
- What support will I get from my S/NVQ assessor/advisors?
- What do I need to do to gain the support of my colleagues in helping me achieve my S/NVQ?
- What do I need help with?
- How will I ensure I know what is required of me?

2 What do I need to know and understand?
- Looking through the knowledge requirements, I realise I don't know enough about

  _____

- I will sort this out by

  _____

- I will need the support of

  _____ to do this.

3 How do I relate this to what I do and the way in which I do it?
- What standards am I expected to reach?
- Is what I do good enough or can I improve on it?
- Who will help me?

UNIT 1 Give customers a positive impression of yourself and your organisation

Getting it right first time is very important in customer service, as it will create that all-important positive impression of both yourself and your organisation.

The elements for this unit are:

♦ 1.1 Establish effective relationships with customers
♦ 1.2 Respond appropriately to customers
♦ 1.3 Communicate information to customers.

If you were able to make a video recording of one day in your working life, how would you like to appear? How would you react to what you see yourself doing, what you look like and how you talk? What would you do when faced with a difficult situation? You may not get the chance of seeing a video of yourself, but think what it would be like if you were able to be a fly on the wall and observe yourself working. You would learn a great deal about how you work. In particular, you would be able to see how you behave with other people and how your behaviour affects how they behave with you. You would be able to see and hear what sort of an impression you create.

In this unit you will learn to look at yourself in your job objectively. This way you will see what you do right and what areas need to be worked on so that you get it right first time, every time.

1.1 Establish effective relationships with customers

WHAT YOU NEED TO KNOW OR LEARN

♦ What you can do to create a positive impression of yourself and your organisation.
♦ Why your behaviour can affect how other people behave with you.
♦ How to get off to a good start with customers.
♦ What you can do to maintain your good start.

What you can do to create a positive impression of yourself and your organisation

Even though they may not be keen to admit it, most people do judge a book by its cover. Like it or not, you are in control of what other people think about you, and therefore how good or not they think you might be at your job. In judging you, your customers will also be automatically creating an image – a perception – of your organisation. The image you project is complex and will be perceived in different ways by different people. For instance, what you see as an appropriate standard of dress might seem quite inappropriate to others.

Picture a hot summer's day. You might find it more comfortable to go to work without wearing tights or without a tie. However, is this in keeping with your organisation's dress code? Does it look right? Does it create the wrong image? Some customers might not even notice the difference, some will consider it scruffy, and some might prefer it. Clearly, it is impossible to ensure everyone sees you in the same light, so it is best to stick to your organisation's standards for appearance.

Standards for appearance might include the following:

♦ wearing a uniform
♦ following health and safety practices, e.g. having hair tied back or covered in the food industry
♦ a casual-wear day on a Friday
♦ adhering to certain colours
♦ guidelines on use of make-up and jewellery
♦ following your organisation's smoking policy.

Creating the right image is not just about what you look like. It is also about the tools with which you work. Take a look around the environment in which you work and at the equipment you use. How much is visible to customers? What kind of image is created? Think about the following:

♦ Premises: are they clean and tidy or is the paint peeling off the walls?
♦ Equipment: is it in working order and safe?
♦ Information: is it up-to-date? Is it dog-eared?
♦ Tools: do the pens provided for customers actually work?

– When you write to customers do you hand write or use a computer printout?
– What does the letterhead look like?
– Does it convey the right image?

Did you know

Research carried out in the early 1970s showed that when you are dealing face-to-face with someone, your words comprise just 7 per cent of your communication, quality of voice 38 per cent and your appearance and body language 55 per cent.

Creating a positive impression

| Appearance (you and your surroundings) | + | Body language | + | Behaviour | = | Customer service professional |

Figure 1.1 *Effective communication is not only about what you say, it's also about how you say it*

Remember that you will also communicate an image to customers via the five senses. Take a look at the table below and think about what you feel when forming an impression of people and places using your senses. Remember, what pleases you may not be to someone else's liking.

The five senses	Making a positive impression
SIGHT	Good signage in hospitals. Correct spellings on posters on notice boards. Appropriately dressed customer service people. Fresh flowers in a motorway service station toilet.
HEARING	Music in lifts (this may or may not please people). Accurate announcements on a railway platform. Audible announcements on a train.
SMELL	The smell of freshly baked bread wafting out from the bakers. No smell at all coming from the customer service people.
TOUCH	Comfortable chairs in waiting rooms/buses/trains/planes. Clean and tidy work surfaces in a bank.
TASTE	Hot food served hot in a restaurant. Wine served at the right temperature in a bar.

It is important that you are aware of how each of the five senses can contribute to creating a positive impression of yourself and your organisation.

Always try to create a positive impression

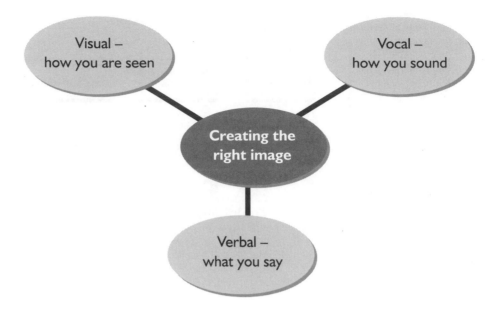

Figure 1.2 The three Vs of creating the right image

Creating the right impression involves three elements: how you are seen, how you sound and what you say. These are the three Vs of creating the right image.

These three areas combined are what creates the image other people have in their minds of you and your organisation.

The visual area

You and your body

How you convey messages to other people through your body language, i.e. what you do with your hands, your feet and your overall posture, is important. The way you dress is also important. Looking sloppy will convey an image that you don't care. Appearing hunched up will make you look as if you are lacking in confidence and therefore unable to help. Looking away when the customer approaches might make the customer feel unwanted or he or she might think you don't know what you are doing.

If you pay attention to your posture, e.g. do what your mother always told you to do and 'stand up straight', dress in a style that is appropriate to your job and maintain eye contact, then you are more likely to be creating a positive impression and to appear professional and credible.

We don't always get out of bed feeling full of the joys of spring before going off to work. If you are not careful your body language will tell your customer you would rather be back at home. This is because your emotional state will show through your body language.

Think about what impression you give customers if you do the following:

♦ Look tense, e.g. stiff, wrinkled forehead, hands clasped tightly to your body. This might mean you are lacking in confidence or unduly worried. You might feel tense simply because you are aware you have a great deal of work to get through. It still means your customer can see all is not well.
♦ Fidgeting, e.g. moving around unnecessarily, playing with a pen or jewellery, drumming fingers on your desk or table. This might mean you are bored, nervous or are losing patience.
♦ Leaning far back on a chair. Unless you know your customer very well, he or she might feel you want to take control or that you feel you are in a position of power over your customer. It is an arrogant position to adopt.
♦ Yawning. Again, this is a sign of boredom, or perhaps you are just very tired. Either way, it does not look good.
♦ Wandering eyes. Are you bored with your customer?
♦ No eye contact. This shows you lack confidence or that you do not trust your customer or yourself to do the right thing.
♦ Sloppy posture, e.g. slumped positions. It looks far too casual and as if you do not care. Do something about it. You will feel much better and so will your customer, because a good posture shows you care and are confident in your job.

 Keys to good practice

Improving your posture

Imagine you have a string coming out from the top of your head and into the ceiling, now:
✓ Stand up straight.
✓ Sit up straight in a chair with your shoulders back. Do this without looking false.
✓ Be comfortable in your new position.
✓ Regularly check out what you look like in the mirror.

You and your working environment

Your working environment, if it is visible to your customers, also has its part to play in the image you create. Take responsibility (or make someone responsible) for making sure everything is where it should be, that it is neat and tidy and that equipment works. Look around at any product displays; are they neat and tidy, is any literature up-to-date or is it dog-eared?

Overleaf are some suggestions for making a good impression in the workplace. Not all may be applicable to where you work.

Figure 1.3 Creating a good impression in the workplace

Your organisation is also responsible for portraying the right image. It may have its own values, which it needs you to demonstrate. These values might include the following:

♦ trust
♦ openness
♦ honesty
♦ creativity
♦ reliability.

If you uphold these values, you will be creating an image that is professional. This is very important in the world of customer service. Indeed, many organisations spend millions of pounds each year on creating their image – this is called their brand. Think about all the advertising you see on a daily basis. This has the effect of creating expectations and an image in the customers' minds. It is likely your customers will have a mental picture of you based upon their understanding of what your organisation is all about. Rightly or wrongly, customers already think they know what you might look like and how you might behave with them, even before you deal with them. To meet their expectations and to exceed them, you will clearly need to match your image to your organisation's brand.

Active knowledge

Think about the type of organisation you work for. What does it stand for? What values does it have? For instance, would it look appropriate if a nurse dressed like an accountant? Would it feel right if you went to a restaurant and were served by someone who was wearing a lot of jewellery and smelling of strong perfume or aftershave, or worse, body odour?

The vocal area

You will clearly not create a positive impression if you cannot be heard, if you use inappropriate language or if you do not listen. Below are some tips to improve the way you sound.

♦ Remember to breathe! The deeper you breathe, the firmer your tone will be.
♦ Try to make sure your facial gestures match what you are saying; smile at the right time.
♦ Vary your voice to avoid speaking in one way; a flat voice is very dull to listen to and your customer will soon switch off. Even though your customer cannot see you, smiling as you speak when you are on the telephone will really make your voice sound much better. Your customers will pick up on you wanting to talk with them.
♦ Learn how loudly or how softly you speak. Ask a friend to give you some feedback. Perhaps tape yourself and listen to it.
♦ Do not drop the start and end of words, e.g. words starting with 'h' or ending with 'ing'. The sentence 'I am helping you as quickly as I can' should not sound like 'I am 'elpin' you as quickly as I can'. This is not about talking posh, it is all about paying attention to what you sound like in order not to appear sloppy.

Keys to good practice

Improving your vocal skills

✓ Keep to a steady pace.
✓ Speed up or slow down to emphasise a point.
✓ Pronounce any technical words very clearly.
✓ If you think you are going too fast or too slowly, ask.
✓ Encourage your customer to give you the information you need to help him or her.

The verbal area

There is little point getting your image and the way you sound right if the words you use let you down. The vocal area dealt with what you sound like. The verbal area deals with the words you use. Below are some tips to help you improve what you say.

♦ Using dull, nondescript language will make even the most exciting product seem boring or will make you sound as if you do not want to help. Bring some colour into what you say, but do not go over the top.
♦ If you are in a sales role, find different ways of saying the same thing. Instead of saying 'You may be interested to know about …' you could try 'You may be fascinated to know about …'.
♦ Avoid using jargon. What you understand as everyday language may be completely alien to your customers.
♦ Do not swear.
♦ Think about what you really want to say and then say exactly what you mean.
♦ Ask a friend to tell you if there are any words that you use frequently, e.g. 'actually', 'basically' and 'you know', which are often slotted in over and over again. They become what are called verbal mannerisms and can be very annoying to the listener.
♦ Say what you can do, not what you cannot do.

Pulling it all together

Creating that all-important positive first impression will mean that you are more likely to go on to be successful at delivering fantastic customer service. People are likely to make up their minds about you in an incredibly short period of time, in fact, just a few seconds is all that is needed for a judgement to be made.

A genuine smile will always create a good impression

Active knowledge

♦ Find out what your organisation expects from you in terms of standards for appearance and behaviour.
♦ Check out whether there are written guidelines.
♦ Check out whether the standards are informal.
♦ Either way, do you conform to these standards?
♦ What do you need to do, if anything, to follow the standards more effectively?

Case study

Joe works as a security officer in the reception area at the local council offices. The public space is large, has a customer waiting area, a reception desk staffed by a team of people who work four-hour shifts, and there are various information boards around the walls. Council information leaflets and tourist information leaflets are available for customers to pick up. There are also what Joe calls 'extravagant plant displays that make the place look like a jungle'. Joe thinks that most customers believe all he does is stand around all day looking at people come and go.

What can Joe do to create a positive impression of himself and his organisation?

Why your behaviour can affect how other people behave with you

Establishing an effective relationship with customers is all about your behaviour towards your customers and their behaviour towards you. You should always behave in a manner that shows you care. Think back to what we said about body language and how the way you feel can translate into your actions. If you are feeling bored you might seem uninterested in your customer. If you are feeling angry because you are having to miss out on a night out with your friends, you might unwittingly take out this frustration on those around you, including your customers. This will not create a good image. Behaviour refers to everything you do and say. People will draw conclusions about you, based on your behaviour with them.

Face-to-face
Face-to-face behaviour occurs when your customer can see you and you can see them. Even if you work in a call centre you will still be in situations where face-to-face behaviour is important, e.g. with your colleagues and with your internal customers.

Here your customer has access to all your behaviour patterns. He or she can both see and hear you. You know you have done well when a customer starts to copy your behaviour. This is called mirroring. When people do this it means they like you and respect you. It is all done subconsciously; people do not normally set out to mirror another person's actions, it just happens when they are comfortable with the person they are with. For instance, if you lean your head to one side while talking to a customer, this shows you are listening carefully. If your customer starts to do the same, it shows he or she is mirroring your behaviour and is therefore comfortable with the situation. You will be able to spot this happening on TV. Watch out for it in interviews: when the interviewer and the interviewee are getting on really well they will copy each other's body language.

On the telephone

On the telephone, the attitude you get back from the caller is a direct result of the attitude you give out. If you are polite, respectful, show you are listening and are confident in what you say, then you are more likely to be seen as being a true customer service professional. Even the most irate of callers is likely to come round to your way of thinking. However, if you are rude and abrupt then your caller is likely to be so too.

Case study

Sheila has just dealt with a queue of customers waiting at her reception desk at the local council offices. Just before Sheila is about to go for lunch, the telephone rings. She is a bit annoyed, but takes the call.

Sheila: Hello, Hartson Town Council. Can I help?

Customer: Yes. I'm from Hartson Hospital Press Relations. I need to check what time the Mayor is visiting the hospital tomorrow.

Sheila: I didn't know he was. Hang on, I'll put you through to his secretary. *Sheila tries to connect the caller but the telephone line is engaged.*

Customer: Are you there?

Sheila: Yes, I'm still here. The line is engaged. You'll have to call back later.

Customer: Just a minute! Don't you think you should be calling me back or at least telling me who I need to speak to?

Sheila: It's not my fault you've rung through to reception. I'm not responsible for the Mayor's diary and I'm just off to lunch. You'll have to ring back. Goodbye.

1 What image has Sheila given of:
   ♦   herself?
   ♦   her organisation?
2 How should Sheila handle this call in order to create the right impression?

The written word

The impact of your behaviour on the customer through the written word must also be considered, even though you will not be physically present or on the telephone. If your mind is distracted and your attention to detail suffers, you might find yourself sending letters or emails that are not up to your usual standard. The customer will see spelling mistakes and poor grammar as sloppy behaviour.

How to get off to a good start with customers

As we have seen, your behaviour is very important in creating a good image and a good first impression. What your customers think about you in those all-important first few seconds of dealing with you will influence their entire experience of dealing with you and your organisation. Little things really do count when it comes to giving a positive impression. You would be amazed at how many people pay attention to small details. Trying to avoid all pitfalls will help you get off to a good start.

You may find yourself doing some of the things below when you start to deal with your customers. Figure 1.4 illustrates how each action might be interpreted by a customer even though it may not be your intention to be seen in that way.

You do this:	Your customer might think you are:
No eye contact	Not interested, untrustworthy, not friendly, not confident, new to job
Frown	Unhappy, angry, disagreeing, disapproving
Fidget and fiddle, e.g. with hair, coins, pen, glasses	Nervous
Overuse of hand gestures/pointing fingers/tapping fingers	Aggressive, impatient, bored
Cross arms	Defensive, unwilling to listen
Slouch	Too casual, have no respect
Wear snagged tights/dirty shoes/are generally dirty and unkempt	Unprofessional, uncaring, not fit for the job
Have bad breath/body odour	Stay away from me!
Have badly applied make-up	Tries hard but could do better!
Speak very loudly and quickly	Aggressive
Raise your voice during a conversation	Stressed, angry
Speak very softly	Not confident, unsure of your facts
Work in an untidy way	Uncaring of yourself and your customers
Use out-of-date literature	Untrustworthy – incorrect information
Use faulty equipment/materials	Paying no attention to detail, your organisation doesn't care enough/has no money to put things right

Figure 1.4 Behaviours and their possible impact on your customers

All these behaviours apply just as much throughout a customer transaction as they do at the beginning. However, if you do not get off to a good start, it is much more difficult to recover the situation later.

Keys to good practice

Creating a positive image

✓ Watch your posture. Sit upright, not slumped or slouched.
✓ Use good eye contact. Look at the other person 60 per cent of the time.
✓ Use open and warm facial expressions.
✓ Smile often.
✓ Listen and show you are listening by nodding your head or leaning forward.
✓ Watch your hands; have them open and uncrossed.
✓ Pay attention to personal grooming.
✓ Be sincere.
✓ Ensure your workspace also creates the right image.

Remember

If you do not have many dealings face-to-face with a customer (perhaps you deal solely on the telephone), you may think that your posture does not matter as the customer cannot see you. But it does matter. Your colleagues are important too. You will not be playing your part as a member of a team if you do not also consider your colleagues in what you do. Think about it, do you really want to work with someone who sits slouched over a desk all day or with someone who always looks miserable?

How was it for you?

1 Next time you go into a shop and before you speak with anyone, make a mental note of what impressed you the most about:
   ♦ the people working there
   ♦ the shop itself.

2 After you have made a purchase and left, make a mental note of how you felt about the individual who dealt with you.

3 Was your initial impression correct?

Active knowledge

- Think about the way in which you behave with customers.
- List what you do which seems to have a positive impact.
- Now list what you do which appears to provoke a negative reaction in your customers.
- What can you do to change those negative behaviours?
- How might you set about receiving feedback from your colleagues?

What you can do to maintain your good start

We have looked at those first important few seconds when you start to deal with customers. You need to keep up the good work by building on your good start. This is known as developing and maintaining rapport.

Rapport is that sense of being comfortable with someone, however well or not you may know him or her. Without rapport there will be no trust. Without trust, your customer service will not be what it should be.

There will be some people who you meet in both your personal and work life who you instantly hit it off with. You may warm to others over a period of time, but there will also be some people who you simply do not like. Much of this 'like/dislike' judgement will stem from those all important initial impressions and what happens immediately after, to either confirm your judgement or to help you to change your mind.

To maintain your good start it is essential that you treat each customer as an individual. If you do not, they will not feel that you respect and value them. This will involve you recognising that everyone will have different needs. In the same way that customers will want different things from you, you will need to adjust the way you behave with each customer.

Building rapport

Building rapport can be seen as an extension of creating a positive impression. The key areas for you to think about are described below.

Face-to-face

◆ Eye contact: ensure you give the right amount of eye contact. If you give too much, you may appear to be staring; too little and you will come across as uninterested.
◆ Smiling: smile warmly when it is appropriate for the occasion. But be genuine; everyone can see through a smile that is fake.
◆ Touch: sometimes a handshake will be appropriate. If so, make sure it is firm enough to convey confidence and interest.
◆ Posture: think about standing up to greet a customer, particularly if you are seeing someone by appointment. Do not invade their personal space: if you are too close you will make someone feel uncomfortable.
◆ If you are sitting down, do not slouch. Not only does it look bad, it will also affect the quality of your voice.
◆ Mirroring: you are really in rapport with someone when you both mirror each other's body posture. If you are sitting down, you may find suddenly that you are both leaning towards each other or both nodding at the same time. Do not copy what your customer is doing! That would be disrespectful. Unless you are a very highly skilled communicator, it is perhaps best to let it happen naturally.

On the telephone

Increasingly, customers do not have a choice as to whether they deal face-to-face or on the telephone. For instance, transactions that would routinely have taken place at the enquiries counter of a bank are now dealt with via customer service representatives based in a call centre. If working over the telephone applies to you, then you do not have the advantage of being able to observe your customers' behaviour, nor are they able to observe you. You both have to rely solely on what you hear.

Keys to good practice

Building rapport on the telephone

✓ Greet callers with courtesy and warmth.

✓ You may need to use your organisation's standard form of greeting; be sincere in the way that you say it.

✓ Do not sound as if you are reading from a script.

✓ Answer as promptly as possible.

✓ Remember you may have said the same thing tens of times that day, but the customer will be hearing it for the first time.

✓ Watch your posture. Sit upright to sound alert and remember to smile. Your customer will be able to hear if you are smiling or not.

✓ Be patient.

✓ Mirror the language your customer uses.

✓ If you feel under pressure, watch the speed of your voice. If you speak too quickly, you will only end up having to repeat yourself and you may also confuse the customer.

Whether face-to-face or on the telephone, once you have got past the initial greeting, you will need to find out what it is the customer wants. He or she may tell you directly or it may be necessary for you to ask questions. You will need to be watching for signs – both verbal and non-verbal – that the customer will give you about how he or she is feeling.

Maintaining rapport in difficult situations

How do you handle situations where you have an angry or confused customer? Do you just carry on in your normal way, or would it be better to change your own behaviour to reflect the nature of the situation?

When things go wrong from their point of view, customers often instinctively become angry and sometimes even aggressive. Their behaviour might include pointing at you, shouting and swearing, sighing, threatening some sort of action or simply keeping silent. If you are face-to-face with customers you are likely to see faces redden as blood pressure rises. This, in turn will have an effect on you and your behaviour and you must ensure you deal with this in order to maintain rapport and to bring the situation to a satisfactory conclusion for all concerned. It is difficult not to react, you will naturally want to. However, getting it right means learning to recognise and control these reactions.

The natural response from anyone when faced with an angry or confused customer is to behave in the same way. However, your voice is the most powerful tool you have for generating emotions in someone else. Used effectively, your voice can help you to control a difficult situation. When used with appropriate body language, it will help you to give people positive feelings about yourself and your organisation.

Think back to the case study on page 10. Imagine what Sheila sounded like to her caller. Her voice would have been getting more and more tense as she realised her lunch hour was disappearing and all because she was taking a call that wasn't even her responsibility! Sheila probably raised her voice and sounded abrupt. She clearly wasn't listening and was preoccupied with one thought only, her lunch.

Keys to good practice

Maintaining your good start when the situation becomes difficult

✓ Put yourself in the customer's shoes and remember that emotions will be running high. You will not have long to recover the situation.
✓ Listen actively.
✓ Control your tone of voice and body language.
✓ Show some understanding of the situation.
✓ Show you want to help.
✓ Ask questions to get to the facts.
✓ Summarise the situation.
✓ Say what you can do.
✓ Suggest options to your customer.
✓ Follow things through to completion.
✓ Check the customer is satisfied.

Did you know?

♦ If you can solve the problem quickly and efficiently, and your organisation is in the wrong, it might cost your organisation £50.
♦ If you need to refer the issue to a Service Manager it might cost your organisation £100 to resolve it.
♦ If the customer is still not happy and refers the matter to 'the top', it might cost the organisation double again, i.e. £200.

Remember

You will establish effective relationships with customers when you view problems and difficulties as opportunities to put things right.

Test your knowledge

Think about how you behave with customers over a specified hour every day for a week. For example, you might select from 10.00–11.00am for the first week of next month.

- ◆ What worked well in the way in which you used your voice?
- ◆ What didn't go so well?
- ◆ Did what you wear make any difference?
- ◆ What happened that made you feel good?
- ◆ How does your working environment help you?
- ◆ Can you make any improvements to it?

1.2 Respond appropriately to customers

- ◆ What your organisation expects from you when recognising customers' needs and expectations.
- ◆ How to select the right method of communicating with customers.
- ◆ How to communicate with people in a clear, polite and confident way.
- ◆ How to deal with customers' questions and comments.

What your organisation expects from you when recognising customers' needs and expectations

What makes your organisation different from its competitors? You! Service failings frequently revolve around employees and their attitudes and behaviour. Staff who are helpful, willing to take responsibility and have the right level of knowledge to help customers will be on their way to providing the right level of customer service.

You, your colleagues and the systems and processes that support customer service in your organisation, are what make or break the customer service experience. You have an enormous part to play in ensuring that customers are dealt with properly and to everyone's satisfaction.

Every organisation will expect different things from its customer service employees. Every organisation will expect people to perform to different standards. Some organisations will tell employees what should be said when the telephone is answered, while others will leave it up to employees. Some might let you know they expect calls to be answered within five rings. Others will have a dress code, e.g. how a uniform must be worn.

Active knowledge

♦ Find out now about your own organisation's customer service standards and procedures.
♦ Keep copies of these handy in order to refer to them as you work through your S/NVQ.

The behaviours and attitudes expected from employees will be similar across organisations. Most organisations will expect employees to display the behaviour shown below.

Figure 1.5 Recognising customer needs and expectations

It's not just what you do that counts when responding to customers' needs and expectations, the way in which you do it is also important. If you are answering a query from a customer who is anxious to sort out a problem, not only should you sort the problem out, but you should also consider your customer's feelings in doing so and adapt your behaviour accordingly. For example, if a travel agent wants to go the extra mile in sorting out a flight for someone who is going to a funeral abroad, he or she would need to adapt their behaviour accordingly and not treat this customer as if he or she was off on holiday. If you do not recognise customers' needs and expectations appropriately, you may be committing a 'service sin'.

The seven service sins

Customer feedback tells us there are seven deadly sins that customer service people commit that consistently anger and frustrate customers.

1 No eye contact

How are customers supposed to feel wanted if the person they are dealing with cannot even be bothered to look at them? Making eye contact costs nothing. Failing to make eye contact is inexcusable; it is therefore one of the worst sins to commit.

Make sure you look at your customers. Do not stare, just show them you are interested in them as individuals by looking into their eyes from time to time.

Eye contact is vital, it shows you care

2 Being insincere

'Have a nice day.' This phrase is often perceived to be irritating, insincere and shows you are talking from a script. Nothing is guaranteed to annoy customers more than being spoken to by someone who is less than genuine. It is important to be genuine in what you say and do. If you are not, a customer will not trust you.

When you smile at someone it should be a genuine smile because you want to help your customer. If your work involves you reading from a script (e.g. in a call centre where you are required to read from a standard script laid down by your organisation) you should try your best to let the customer believe you have not been saying the same thing over and over again. It is very easy to sound bored and your customer will pick up on this. Do not forget you need to treat each customer as an individual, not one in a long line of other people. Try listening to the customer's voice as he or she speaks to you and imagining what he or she might look like. Make him or her real; have a little picture in your head and talk to that person!

Active knowledge

It is very easy to sound false, whether you are in a face-to-face situation or on the telephone. Try practising some sentences with a friend or colleague. Ask him or her to give you feedback on how genuine they feel you are. Ask for feedback on what you sound like, what your facial expressions are like and how your body language appears to match what you are saying.

3 Bouncing customers around your organisation

'I'll put you through to someone else.' Bouncing customers around your telephone system and expecting him or her to explain everything again and again will make anyone's blood pressure rise. This is one of the most frequent causes of complaint.

No one expects you to be able to help all the time. There is nothing wrong in not having the authority to act or to complete a customer's query. The secret in providing good service is the way in which you let the customer know you need to transfer him or her or find somebody else to help. This means taking the time yourself to explain to your colleague what the customer has already told you.

4 Policy restrictions

'It's not our policy to do that.' Your organisation will have guidelines such as the following, within which you are expected to work:

♦ when to give a discount in a shop
♦ accepting credit card payments below a certain limit
♦ when to give a gesture of goodwill in order to say sorry
♦ health and safety guidelines that must not be breached.

Which of the seven sins is being broken?

Telling your customer 'It's not our policy to take credit cards for payments under £10' is not the best way of dealing with it. Your customer will not necessarily understand why you cannot help. You will need to explain the reasons for the policies being in place. In this instance it is because the credit card company charges your employer for each transaction, making it costly to offer the facility for small transactions.

5 Being distracted by colleagues

If you work on the front line and can be seen by customers, it is unprofessional to be holding a conversation with a colleague while your customer is waiting to be served.

Imagine a situation where a personal trainer (Jon) is working with his client (Tracy) in the gym. While Tracy is pedalling furiously on the bike with Jon watching over her, one of the other personal trainers walks over and starts a conversation with Jon. Soon they are deep in discussion while poor Tracy pedals her heart out. Bearing in mind that Tracy is paying Jon by the hour, it does not take long before she becomes disgruntled. Jon must pay attention to his client and not be distracted by his colleagues.

6 Lack of knowledge

Lack of knowledge about products and services, and showing no desire to find out, will not be welcomed by your customers. You will come across as not being good at your job and your customer will soon lose confidence in you and your organisation. At worst he or she will find another organisation where the people are more helpful. Your organisation will therefore lose business. It might also be risky from a safety point of view to not know enough about your products or services. For example, if you sell electrical equipment and fail to tell customers about safety aspects they query, there might be serious consequences.

Saying 'I don't know anything about that' tells the customer you are not interested in them, nor do you have any respect for yourself. After all, why do you do this job if you do not know about the products or services your organisation offers? You are not expected to carry all the information around in your head. You will need to know where to find the information easily and who to ask for help and assistance for those products or services that are outside your area of responsibility.

Researching your products or services means you will be more confident in your job. Your life will be made easier and your customers will benefit greatly. This will help you to create a good impression with them.

7 Waiting times

Increasingly, customers are no longer prepared to wait, either on the telephone or face-to-face. You may find the customer puts the telephone down after a few rings if it is not answered. Your organisation may have guidelines for you to follow when responding to a customer. These can include the guidelines given in the table overleaf. As you can see, these are all operational guidelines and so will vary between organisations.

How was it for you?

1 Over the past three weeks how much time have you spent waiting in queues?

♦ How much time have you spent waiting in shops, banks, supermarkets, doctors', and dentists' surgeries, airports and railway stations?

♦ How much time have you spent waiting on the telephone?

♦ How much time have you spent waiting for an Internet connection to work?

2 Add it up. What could you have achieved if you hadn't been in those queues?

3 How did waiting make you feel? If you were kept waiting on the telephone, were you made to listen to music? Was that welcome or not?

TIME	How many rings of the telephone before it must be answered?
ACKNOWLEDGEMENTS	Acknowledging letters/emails within a set timescale. Sending an acknowledgement, e.g. a letter/email to confirm safe receipt with a full response to follow
USE OF NAMES	What to call the customer, i.e. first name or surname or neither. Giving your own name to the customer
LEGISLATION & REGULATIONS	What you are permitted to do and what not to do under law. The nature of any contract your customer has with your organisation
METHOD OF COMMUNICATION	When to use the telephone/email or letters and when you need to deal with the customer face-to-face

Figure 1.6 Possible guidelines to follow when responding to a customer

Active knowledge

Find out whether your organisation has guidelines that you need to follow when responding to customers with respect to the following:

♦ time spent on the telephone or in a queue
♦ sending holding letters/emails if you are unable to action a full response on the spot
♦ use of names – your own and what to call the customer
♦ when to use emails or letters
♦ what situations must always be dealt with face-to-face.

Keep a copy of these guidelines handy.

How to select the right method of communicating with customers

Direct communication

With the ever-increasing advance of technology there are now many different ways of communicating with customers. You might be involved in communicating with customers face-to-face, on the telephone, by letter, email or fax. These are direct forms of communication.

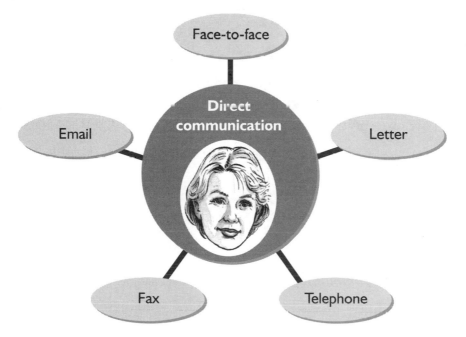

Figure 1.7 Direct forms of communication

Indirect communication

Your organisation may also communicate with its customers through indirect forms of communication such as advertising. Here there is no person-to-person involvement; the communication happens via something else, e.g. posters and leaflets, newspapers, magazines, television and radio adverts. These all need to portray the image the organisation wishes to promote. If you work in an organisation that considers itself very modern, its advertising needs to reflect this. However, if you work in an Olde Worlde Tea Shoppe, an advert in the local press is likely to portray a homely, traditional image, not an ultra-modern one.

The Internet enables organisations to communicate with customers via websites. An intranet may be used to tell employees about in-house developments or changes to products and services and to generally keep people up-to-date with what is happening.

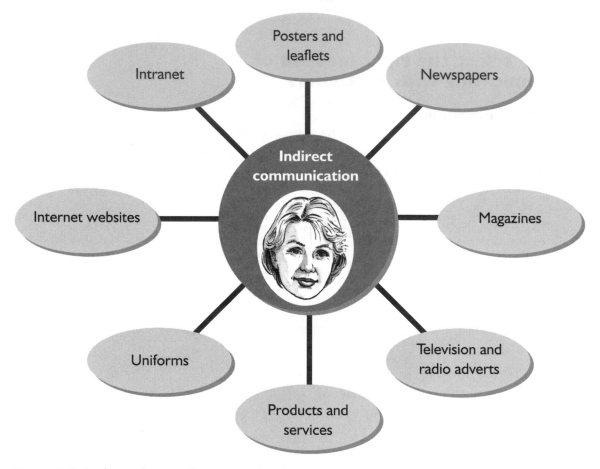

Figure 1.8 Indirect forms of communication

It is unlikely you will have much influence over the indirect forms of communication your organisation uses. However, it is important you recognise how indirect communication plays its part in creating the right image of your organisation to customers.

Selecting the right method

Direct and indirect methods of communication are appropriate in different circumstances. You must know which forms your organisation prefers in order to choose the correct method for each individual situation. For example, you would be seen as very uncaring if you delivered bad news by email.

How was it for you?

Have you ever received a text message or junk mail claiming you have won a fantastic prize but you need to call a number at an expensive rate in order to claim it? Did you think 'I'll telephone right now!'? Did you actually do this? How do you think you would feel (or how did you feel) when you had to wait for a couple of minutes when you knew it was costing you £5 a minute to be kept waiting? Why do you think this company chose to ask you to communicate with them via a telephone call? Why could you just not post back a letter?

Yes, you've got it! This company wanted you to telephone so that they could collect the telephone charges from you. Posting a letter would not enable them to receive any income, so the selected method of communication in this case had to be the telephone.

Your organisation may have set guidelines it wishes you to follow about when to use a letter or when to use email. For example, you should always use the telephone on receipt of a complaint, and the customer must be telephoned within 24 hours. Below are some broad guidelines covering when to use the methods we have mentioned:

Method of communication	When to use
FACE-TO-FACE	When the customer is on your premises. When delivering bad news. When delivering good news, perhaps to support and add weight to a congratulatory letter. When a permanent record is not required.
LETTER	When a permanent record is needed. In formal situations, e.g. where a letterhead showing the company brand/logo adds credibility and confidence in your organisation. When you have the time to allow for a letter to be received.
TELEPHONE	When instant communication is required. When you need to ask questions and get a quick response. When the customer is expecting you to call them back. In situations when personal contact is important.
FAX	When speed is required. When it doesn't matter if someone else reads the contents. When you need to be speedy but are not able to use email. In formal situations, e.g. where a letterhead showing the company brand/logo adds credibility and confidence.
EMAIL	To act as confirmation of what you have said on the telephone. Internally, i.e. to colleagues you work with, but not for bad or sensitive news. When you cannot get hold of someone on the phone. When you are responding to someone who has contacted you.

Figure 1.9 Selecting the right method of communication

You need to ask yourself the following questions in order to select the right communication method:

♦ How did the customer contact me?
♦ Is that his or her preferred way of communicating?
♦ Has the customer told me how he or she wishes me to respond?
♦ How quickly is a response needed?
♦ Do you need to keep a permanent record of what has been said?

You should also consider whether the method you select is cost effective. For instance, if you need to contact someone overseas, emailing may be cheaper than telephoning. However, is an email appropriate for what you need to say?

Active knowledge

♦ Find out if your organisation has any guidelines for selecting the method of communication you should use in your job role.
♦ Are there any other methods available to you that are not mentioned above? If so, in what situations is it appropriate to use them?
♦ What standard letters, if any, are you required to use?

Using the written word

Many organisations will provide you with a pre-prepared format for use when responding to customers in writing. These are known as standard letters. They enable you to start and finish them as appropriate, but the bulk of the contents of the letter will be provided for you.

Before you start to write, you should consider why you are doing so. There are all sorts of reasons for writing to a customer:

♦ to promote products or services
♦ to answer questions
♦ to record what has happened/ will be happening
♦ to thank the customer
♦ to provide information
♦ to seek information
♦ to give advice
♦ to apologise.

Active knowledge

1 For those of you involved in writing to customers, in what other situations do you need to write or email customers?

2 Find some recent letters/emails you have written and make a list of them.

♦ For each one, why did you choose to write rather than telephone or meet the customer?
♦ Discuss with your S/NVQ advisers and your line manager whether it is appropriate to include copies of these within your portfolio. If you do so, ask what you need to do to protect customer confidentiality.

Whatever the circumstances, you should ensure that your written communications achieve their aims. This means you need to be clear about what you are saying as, if you are not, you will confuse the reader and you may find he or she has to return to you and ask you questions. This wastes time and is not good customer service. A well-written letter/email will convey the right image and give a good impression.

Business letters

Case study

Algarve Villas – the best for a rest

Mrs Young
Treetops
Stoneacre Lane
Newport
Oxon
OX15 8TY

15 January

Dear Mrs Young

Villas in Portugal

Thanks for phoning up about our Portuguese villas. They are certainly very popular. Enclosed is a brochure.

The only one we have available on the dates you mention is on page 6 of the enclosed brochure. Sorry about that but they are very popular! It features a private patio area which overlooks a delightful olive grove and the hills in the distance. Inside are two bedrooms, an open plan living area, a kitchen (utensils provided), a TV in the living area, etc. You will have shared use of the swimming pool with the adjoining villa. Prices are as per enclosed tariff. Discount for early booking, i.e. by end of February. Transfers from Faro airport can be arranged if you want. Nearby attractions include a newly opened aqua park, the nature reserve and the beautiful olde worlde town of Tavira. Complimentary wine and flowers will be put in the villa for your arrival.

We really want to welcome you to Algarve Villas – the best for a rest. Let us know as soon as you can. We require a deposit of 10 per cent.

Yours sincerely

F Hopkirk
Sales Manager

Enc brochure: Algarve Villas – the best for a rest

♦ Is the letter polite and courteous?
♦ What do you think of the style; is it too formal or too casual?
♦ Does it start and end correctly?
♦ What about all that information in the middle; how would you improve this bit?
♦ Using all the information that is in the letter, have a go at re-writing it, remembering you are responding to a customer enquiry and you are aiming to promote Algarve Villas in the best possible light.

The case study above shows a letter written by Frank Hopkirk. Frank is a Sales Manager working for Algarve Villas. They specialise in renting villas in the Algarve in Portugal. Mrs Young has called Algarve Villas to enquire about renting a property in August.

As you read through the letter, compare what Frank has written to the following tips for writing business letters.

The start of the letter
♦ You should have a relevant heading, e.g. Algarve Villas.
♦ If you are replying to a letter, you should first acknowledge receipt of it, e.g. 'Thank you for your letter of 6 March enquiring about our villas in the Algarve.'
♦ If you are not replying to a letter from a customer you should introduce the subject of your letter in the first sentence, e.g. 'As you have expressed an interest in our villas in the Algarve in previous years, we are writing to tell you about our new development in the hills around Monchique.'
♦ Remember: always introduce your subject at the beginning of the letter so that the reader knows immediately what you are writing about and why.

The body of the letter
♦ This is where you should write all the information you need to give, or questions you need to ask. Keep one idea or subject to each paragraph. If you were writing about the villas you would mention things such as location, room layout, nearby attractions and price in separate paragraphs.
♦ Keep your sentences short.
♦ Avoid long words.
♦ Avoid jargon.

The final paragraph
♦ The way you finish off a business letter is important. It is where you point the way forward clearly and concisely.
♦ In the last paragraph you need to make sure your reader has fully understood what the letter is all about. You may choose to stress an important point again. You might need to stress the actions you are going to take or, depending on the context, what you need your customer to do, e.g. 'We do hope you have found the Monchique development of interest.'

Opening and closing a letter
Unless your organisation has other guidelines, you should follow the following rules.

♦ Letters starting with the name of the customer, e.g. 'Dear Mrs Young', should finish 'Yours sincerely'.
♦ Letters starting 'Dear Sir' or 'Dear Madam' should finish 'Yours faithfully'.
♦ Include your name and title (if any) underneath your signature.

These guidelines tell you all about how to structure a letter. Following them is just half the story, you will also need to ensure your grammar and spelling is up to scratch. Even the best laid out letter will not be any good if it is riddled with spelling mistakes.

Emails

Think before you write an email; is it really the best method to select? Do not use it to deliberately avoid talking to your customer on the telephone or face-to-face.

♦ Follow any organisational guidelines; find these out now.
♦ Keep your message concise; the same rules apply as when writing a letter.
♦ Give your email an effective title in the subject line that makes the reader want to open it.
♦ Do not type in capitals, the reader will think you are shouting.
♦ Do not type in all lower case, the rules of English grammar apply to emails too.
♦ Always check for spelling mistakes, do not rely on your spell-checker.

Active knowledge

♦ Make sure you know under what circumstances, if any, you are able to change standard letters.
♦ Find out if your organisation has any guidelines that you should follow when writing business letters/emails.

How to communicate with people in a clear, polite and confident way

Selecting the right method of communication will help you to achieve your aim of being clear, polite and courteous. But what exactly does being clear, polite and confident mean? Put simply, it could mean the people you deal with understand exactly what you are saying or writing. They understand you because the language you use is appropriate to their needs. For example, you would not speak to children at a nursery school in the same way that you would speak to their older brothers and sisters at university. It also means avoiding jargon or technical speak. It means using the power of your voice to put across the meaning of your words and it means using the power of the written word to convey your intentions. Its all about speaking or writing in a way that means there is no room for misunderstandings. If you do this you will be communicating clearly.

Being polite is all about having respect for your customers. Being polite often means you need to adapt your behaviour according to the age of your customer. For example, an elderly customer may prefer you to call him or her Mr Smith or Mrs Jones. He or she may not welcome you using his or her first name. A young person may prefer to be called by his or her first name and see this as a more friendly approach. It would be very wrong to stereotype people, so the best thing you can do is ask your customer what he or she would like to be called.

Being confident means speaking or writing in a way that shows the customer you have a strong belief in what you are saying. You will need to have a thorough knowledge of your products or services, or know where to seek help. It will instil confidence in your customers.

Greet customers warmly

You are the human face of your organisation. If you treat customers politely and courteously, you will make your life easier as well as reflecting a positive image of your organisation. You should greet people with a 'Good morning' or 'Good afternoon' or whatever is appropriate for the time of day and the environment you work in. Remember to be sincere and to check that your body language reflects the warmth of your greeting. Smile – even if you are on the telephone.

Always try to make customers feel welcome and that you value them and are pleased to be dealing with them. Treat each customer as an individual; do not make him or her feel like the 101st customer you have dealt with that day. Everyone wants to feel special. Never give the impression that it is an inconvenient time to call, that you are just off to lunch or that you would rather be anywhere else but speaking to your customer.

In face-to-face situations always acknowledge, as soon as possible, that you have noticed the customer is there, even if you cannot immediately speak with them. A quick smile and a nod in their direction will suffice.

Active knowledge

♦ Find out whether your organisation has a standard greeting for customers that you should use.
♦ Check, by asking a colleague to tell you, that you sound sincere when using a standard greeting.
♦ How can you ensure each time you greet customers that you sound genuine?

Choosing the right words to show confidence

We have spoken about the power of being confident with customers and how it will instil confidence and create the right image. If a customer sees or hears that you are confident, he or she will be more likely to trust you.

This trust will only be there if you are genuine and honest in your approach. Emphasising what you can do for customers rather than what you cannot will certainly demonstrate you are confident in what you are saying. If you can back this up by saying what action you will take, then this will continue to instil confidence in your customers.

When talking to customers you will convey messages simply through the words that you use. Your choice of words is therefore very important. Words fall into three main categories:

♦ positive
♦ neutral
♦ negative.

Below is a selection of positive, neutral and negative words and phrases.

Positive	Neutral	Negative
Yes	Perhaps	No
How may I help you?	How can I help?	What do you want?
I	We	They
Definitely	Possibly	Unlikely
I will find out	I'm not sure	I don't know
I will	I'll do my best	I can't do that
Always	Sometimes	Never
I'll be quick	As quickly as I can	I'll do it when I can
I will sort that out	I'll find out who can help	It's not my fault

Figure 1.10 Positive, neutral and negative words

Active knowledge

♦ Find a friend to test out some of the sentences below. Say each sentence but, each time, put an emphasis on any words in bold.

I'll answer the phone **when** I can	I'll answer the phone when I can	I'll answer the phone when I **can**
I'll find out what's happened	I'll find out what's happened	**I'll** find out what's happened
He gave £5 to her	He gave **£5** to her	He gave £5 to **her**
What **I** can do is ...	What I can do is ...	**What** I can do is ...

♦ Ask your friend to tell you the meaning of each sentence.
♦ How did his or her interpretation change when you said the words differently?

Being clear, polite and confident on the telephone

Why is dealing with customers on the telephone different from dealing with them face-to-face? The most obvious answer is you cannot see each other. Because you cannot see each other you are both unable to observe the other person's body language. This lack of a visual dimension means that customers cannot see what is happening, so do not say 'Hold on please' and leave the customer waiting. Say exactly what you are doing and how long you will be. You need to keep the customer informed of the actions you are taking.

Music is often played to customers kept waiting in order to give them something to do, i.e. to listen. This annoys many people intensely. You will need to ensure you do everything you can to make the customer feel valued.

There is such an emphasis in today's world on answering the telephone speedily that when the telephone rings you might feel tempted to grab at it. If you do this you might speak far too quickly and blurt out your greeting. Instead, take a deep breath and answer the telephone calmly. Put a smile in your voice and be polite and courteous.

The telephone also has other effects on a customer. Time spent waiting, e.g. for the telephone to be answered or for you to find out information, is time spent doing nothing. Customers get impatient and frustrated more quickly than they would in a face-to-face situation.

Case study

Colin works in a call centre, taking queries about electricity bills. He deals with customers who want to know what electricity tariff would be best for their level of usage and also deals with customers who query how much they have been charged.

Colin's supervisor has, with his permission, taped him talking to customers on the telephone. (Customers are also aware that their conversations may be monitored for training purposes.) When Colin listened to the tape he found that he tends to say the following phrases frequently.

- 'He's not here right now.'
- 'It's your problem not mine.'
- 'We're here to help.'
- 'Perhaps it might be this.'
- 'That's nothing to do with me.'
- 'I might be able to look at it tomorrow.'
- 'I'm not allowed to do that.'
- 'It's not my fault.'
- 'We look to do things as quickly as we can.'
- 'You should have been told about that.'
- 'Yes, I can do that.'

1 Which of the phrases sound positive and confident?

2 If you were Colin's supervisor, which phrases would you tell him to avoid?

3 Which words are positive?

4 Which words are negative?

5 How might Colin rephrase these?

Being clear, polite and confident when you need to involve colleagues

Sometimes it will not be appropriate for you to deal with a customer. On these occasions you may need to refer him or her to someone else. Perhaps the customer requires specialist attention, or perhaps he or she has simply been put through to the wrong department. When handing over to a colleague always remember the points below.

♦ Explain why you cannot deal with him or her yourself.
♦ Tell the customer you are handing him or her over to a colleague.
♦ Give the name of your colleague if possible and his or her role.
♦ If there will be a wait until the colleague is free to help, tell the customer how long the wait might be and offer a seat if appropriate to your line of work.
♦ Brief your colleague fully with the customer's name and the nature of the help the customer needs or details of their enquiry.

How was it for you?

♦ When were you last passed around from person to person yourself? How did it feel?
♦ What did you think of the organisation at the time?
♦ Did you get what you wanted in the end?

Keys to good practice

Why you need to deal with customers in a clear, polite and confident way

Customers generally need to:

✓ Feel in control.
✓ Deal with people, places and things that make them feel good.
✓ Understand what is happening and why.
✓ Feel valued by you and your organisation.

Customers expect you to:

✓ Be fair.
✓ Be honest.

To understand customer needs and expectations you need to:

✓ Ask questions.
✓ Listen.
✓ Observe.

You and your customers want to have a positive experience

How to deal with customers' questions and comments

If you listen effectively and ask the right questions, misunderstandings are less likely to occur. You need to develop certain skills that will help you to ensure that you have understood the customer and the customer has understood you. Getting it right first time is all part of providing the right level of customer service and helps to establish an effective relationship with customers. The skills you need to develop include the following:

♦ effective listening
♦ asking the right questions
♦ repeating information back
♦ summarising what has been agreed.

Effective listening

As a customer service employee, you should not always be doing the talking. Part of being polite with customers is to show them you are really listening when they are talking. This is called effective listening and it applies both on the telephone and in face-to-face situations.

If you listen well you are going to get things right first time and not have to return to your customer later for clarification. Listening effectively also means you are more likely to be able to meet or exceed your customers' expectations. If you go into a fish and chip shop and order cod and chips, that is what you want, not chicken and chips!

How was it for you?

♦ When was the last time you were talking to someone, either at home or at work when you felt he or she wasn't listening to what you said?
♦ How could you tell?
♦ What did you feel like when you realised?

Effective listening is all about showing your customers that you care. It means that you take notice of the words you hear, the tone in which they are said and the body language of the customer.

Imagine hearing the words 'I am really pleased with the service you have given me'.

These words could be said in different ways:

♦ by someone with a smile on their face who says the words enthusiastically
♦ by someone with a smile on their face who says the words in a sarcastic tone
♦ by someone who is red in the face and shouts out the words.

Here you can see you have a satisfied, a frustrated and an angry customer, but all three said the same words. You will need to listen effectively to determine whether you have Mr Happy or Mr Frustrated or Mr Angry.

Mr Happy   Mr Frustrated   Mr Angry

Tone and facial expression tell you a lot about how your customer is feeling

To show you are listening effectively you need to make sure you:

♦ acknowledge the customer early on in the conversation
♦ are patient
♦ concentrate
♦ pay attention throughout your dealings with the customer.

All you need do to acknowledge the customer is to nod your head gently and/or use those simple sounds that indicate to someone else that you are listening. You can also use words and phrases such as 'Yes', 'I see' and 'OK'. Make sure you say these words at the right time and do not forget to maintain eye contact where appropriate. Do not allow yourself to be distracted by noises or other people and do not make assumptions. You must clarify your understanding of what you have heard.

Case study

Sonia is a cashier in a bank. Just as she returns to her till after lunch, Sonia notices a telephone ringing and takes the call. A Mr Green enquires about changing over his small business account to one where he can pay less in account charges. Although Sonia knows about personal account charges, she is less familiar about what her bank does for small business account holders. The Small Business Advisor, Mr Elliott, is still at lunch.

Here is a transcript of their conversation:

Mr Green: Can I speak to Mr Elliot please?

Sonia: He has gone to lunch. Can you call back after 1pm?

Mr Green: No! Can't you help? All I want to know about is account charges. I have a small business account where I am paying around £10 a month in charges but I only pay in a small number of cheques each month and no cash at all. Why am I being charged so much?

Sonia: You really will have to telephone back, Mr Green. I don't know anything about account charges and there's nobody else available to help. If you give me your telephone number, perhaps I can ask Mr Elliott to ring you when he's finished his lunch.

Mr Green: You weren't listening to me! If I said I can't telephone back it means I'm not available to take calls either. I'm surprised you don't want to help me. So, this is the sort of service I get charged so much money for! I think I'd be better off elsewhere!

Sonia: So, are you going to give me your telephone number?

♦ Why did a simple query go so wrong?
♦ What should Sonia have said, even if she didn't know very much about account charges?
♦ What do you think might happen to Mr Green's account now?

Asking the right questions

In order to check that you have fully understood your customer's needs and expectations you will need to ask questions. This should be done by asking open questions to develop the conversation and establish the customer's needs accurately. Open questions are ones which ask the customer to give you a full response. You would use these when you need to obtain information from the customer. They are used when you want the customer to tell you more. For instance:

♦ When do you want to travel?
♦ How often do you need to have access to your money?
♦ Who is it you want to see?

Repeating information back

Once the customer has answered your questions you still need to be sure that you have understood the situation properly. You can do this by simply repeating back what the customer has said. Sometimes this might mean repeating back words that you have not actually heard, e.g. 'Did you say 5 June?' 'You want four of these and five of the fresh ones?' On other occasions you may need to say more by repeating back chunks of information, e.g. 'So, you need a table for six on 5 June at 7pm and you would like a table with easy access to accommodate your wife who has walking difficulties'.

When repeating back, try to use the words the customer has used. In the last example it would be wrong to say 'So, you need a table for six on 5 June at 7pm and you would like one of the tables that has easy access for your wife's wheelchair'. If the customer has said 'walking difficulties' you should keep to this. Do not make assumptions that a wheelchair is involved. You will need to use some common sense when repeating back. For instance, if your customer's language is unsavoury you would leave certain words out or use alternatives.

It is very important at this stage that you are patient with your customer as he or she may not really know what it is that he or she wants. Give the customer plenty of time to think and explain things to you. Repeating back means saying to your customer everything that is relevant to clarify his or her needs. A waiter might say 'So, your order is for one rare steak, and one well-done, the rare to have no kidneys with it and the well-done steak to come with the pepper sauce instead of the mustard sauce'.

Summarising what has been agreed

This is simply a case of extending the repeating back by adding in what you and your customer have agreed. It enables you to confirm understanding, agreements made and actions to be taken, e.g. 'I have booked you a table for six on 5 June at 7pm. As this is a special birthday celebration, champagne will be available on arrival and there will be red roses on your table which will be situated away from a wall so that your wife has easy access. We look forward to seeing you on 5 June'.

By listening effectively, asking the right questions, repeating information back and summarising, you will ensure you have fully understood your customers' needs and expectations.

Test your knowledge

1   Find a friend who will be able to give you feedback on how you come across when saying the following statements. Do not tell your friend what style you are saying them in. Say them in a negative way, a positive way and a flat or neutral way.

♦   He plays football really well.
♦   I like the taste of this.
♦   When that customer came in I wanted to run away and hide.
♦   I very much enjoyed learning about that new product.
♦   I want to be involved with helping Sarah answer the telephone.

2   Ask for feedback on what you sounded and looked like and how your friend felt at the time.

3   What did you have to do to change from one style to the next?

4   How does this relate to you giving a positive impression to your customers?

- What you need to do to ensure you know all about your organisation's products or services.
- How to use the information your organisation supplies to help you deliver fantastic customer service.
- How to explain to customers the reasons you are unable to meet their needs or expectations.

What you need to do to ensure you know all about your organisation's products or services

We have looked at what you can do to establish an effective relationship with customers and how communicating with customers in a clear, polite and confident way plays such a large part in this. We will now build on this by looking at how you should communicate information to customers.

Customers need to be able to understand what you and your organisation are offering in as clear a way as possible. If there is any confusion, mistakes can happen, customers will be dissatisfied and complaints may be made. There may also be legal reasons why you need to communicate information to customers, such as changes to terms and conditions of a bank account. Again, selecting the right way to communicate this information gives your organisation the best chance of getting its messages across clearly.

You need to know where to find information relating to your organisation's products or services. Finding information quickly and efficiently helps you answer customers' questions and queries promptly. It will also instil confidence in your customers that you know what you are talking about.

You will not need to know in detail about all the products and services your organisation offers, just those that are relevant to you and your role. You will need to know where to go to for help if there are questions and queries about a product or service that is outside your own area of responsibility. Do not feel shy about asking for help, it will help you enjoy your job more and you may even learn something new.

Not all the products and services you deal with will be suitable for every customer.

When finding out about a product or service ask yourself these questions

There are many sources of information where you might find out about products or services, as shown below.

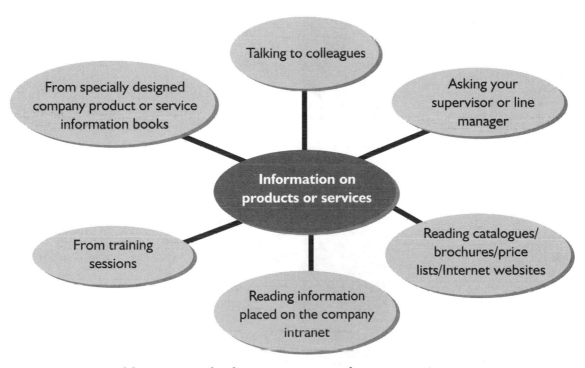

Figure 1.11 Possible sources of information on products or services

Remember

When reading any information make sure you look at the date. Organisations are always looking to improve what they offer, which means that literature goes out of date very quickly.

Active knowledge

- ◆ Find out how many products or services your organisation offers. Which of these are relevant to you and your role?
- ◆ Where will you find the best source of information for products or services?
- ◆ Which products or services are you asked about where you struggle to find out the required details? Sort out now what you need to know and understand about these.

Having found out about the products or services your company offers, you will probably not be able to remember every detail. It is therefore important that you develop your own information bank and store it in a format that enables you to refer to it readily when required. This might mean any of the following:

A company newsletter is a good source of accurate, current information

- ◆ recording details on your computer
- ◆ keeping copies of information leaflets in a special file
- ◆ having any organisational reference book close to your workspace
- ◆ knowing who to ask for help.

If you do create your own information bank, make sure you update it regularly and consider keeping it in your S/NVQ portfolio.

Giving incorrect information to a customer is a serious issue. You will annoy and frustrate a customer by doing so and, in the worst case scenario, giving incorrect information may even be dangerous. For example, if the Foreign and Commonwealth Office issues a warning about a situation that is rapidly deteriorating in a foreign country, a travel agent will be acting irresponsibly if he or she recommends that travel to the country is safe.

How to use the information your organisation supplies to help you deliver fantastic customer service

Having worked through Element 1.2, you are now at the stage where you have identified what products or services you need to know about and you should also have this information somewhere where you can quickly locate it. Using this information effectively is the next step. Customers are individuals and will have different needs. Some may need you to explain things in detail, while others will require an outline or basic information only. You must establish what customers' needs and expectations are. In other words, why do they need to know about the product or service? In order for customers to understand you, you will need to give them the information in a way that suits their individual needs.

Remember

You need to communicate in a polite, clear and confident way. You can do this by:

♦ listening
♦ asking questions
♦ checking understanding
♦ providing information
♦ using language appropriate to the individual customer
♦ using body language appropriate to the individual customer.

Case study

Mrs Jackson goes to her local bank to discuss investing £5000. She is seen by Linda who works on the enquiries counter. Linda knows that there are five different accounts that might be suitable. Linda starts to tell Mrs Jackson about them.

Mrs Jackson is thinking: 'You may not realise this, Linda, but I really don't understand what you are saying to me. I feel a bit intimidated by the jargon you are using and I'm afraid to ask you questions. I don't want to appear thick! I thought I had asked you a simple question: What's the best way for me to invest £5000? But you are confusing me with a range of options. All I wanted was a straightforward answer.'

Linda thinks everything is fine as Mrs Jackson appears to be listening and is willing to take all the literature away with her regarding the five accounts.

- ♦ What has Linda failed to do?
- ♦ Write down the questions Linda should ask Mrs Jackson.
- ♦ Do you think Mrs Jackson followed Linda's suggestions?

Product or service features and benefits

Some product information supplied to you by your organisation will relate to the features and benefits of a particular product or service. A feature describes what a product or service does. A benefit describes how that product or service can help a customer. Knowing all about the features and benefits of a product or service will help you give fantastic customer service.

Take your customers' individual needs into account

If you are in a sales role it is particularly important when passing information on to customers that you describe to them the benefits of the product or service. For example, a good travel agent would not just tell you about the features of a certain resort, he or she would also go on to tell you what it would mean to be on holiday there. He or she might say: 'If you choose this resort, you are going to enjoy the benefit of having reliable sunshine which means no worries over what clothes to take and no heavy baggage. There is a safe beach so you will have peace of mind for the children. The villas have a swimming pool with a lifeguard in attendance at all times; again peace of mind. There is a daily maid service, leaving you free to do what you wish without the need to clean the villa. Nearby there are a variety of local restaurants serving local foods so you can experience the real Portugal'. What the travel agent has done in this example is explain the feature and then link it to the benefit by describing what it means.

Case study

Jo owns three dogs; Bertie, a Red Setter, Ossie, a Golden Retriever, and Henry, a big black Labrador. Winter has set in; it is very wet and both her garden and the park are very muddy. With 12 muddy feet being brought back into her house, Jo needs all the help she can get. She spots a couple of adverts in her monthly doggy magazine:

<table>
<tr><td>

For Sale

Doormat

- 100% cotton
- Rubber backed
- Safety border
- Machine washable
- Five colours

</td><td>

For Sale

Doormat

- 100% cotton: absorbs mud, water and oil.
- Rubbcr backcd: grips floors and carpets.
- Safety border: non-slip.
- Machine washable: no more dirty and heavy hand washing.
- Five colours: black, brown, beige, blue, red (match your interior).

</td></tr>
</table>

◆ Which advert appealed to you most and why?

◆ Which one of these doormats do you think Jo would be tempted to buy?

◆ What two key features are missing from both lists which Jo would probably need to know before making her choice?

Active knowledge

◆ Complete the sentences below to practise thinking about providing the customer with benefits. The first example is completed to get you started:

PRODUCT/SERVICE	FEATURE	BENEFIT
Electrical fan heater	SAFE	Peace of mind
Internet access	CHEAP	
Energy-saving fridge	COST EFFECTIVE	
Airport taxi service	QUICK	
Garden spade	GUARANTEED	
Guest house facilities	EASY ACCESS	
Corner shop	OPEN UNTIL LATE	
Delivered to your door	CONVENIENT	
Pair of jeans	AVAILABLE IN ALL SIZES	
Contact lens cleaner	ALLERGY TESTED	
Locally produced cheese	SUITABLE FOR VEGANS	
Airport waiting lounge	NO-SMOKING AREA	
Office supplies	FREE DELIVERY	
Talcum powder	FRAGRANCE FREE	
Car	THE LATEST MODEL	
Three-piece suite	COMFORTABLE	

◆ Think about the five key products or services that you deal with, For each one, write down how you would best describe them to a customer in terms of their features and benefits.

Identifying the right information

It is very important to understand exactly what your customer needs before you give out any information. In Element 1.2 you learned how to communicate effectively with your customer using the skills of asking questions, confirming your understanding and summarising what you have heard. Never be afraid to go back over areas that are confusing. You need to do this to be able to give accurate information back.

Remember

Helping people is not only about doing or saying the right things. It is also about making sure you do so in a way that best suits the individual customer's needs and expectations.

Before you can answer any of the questions or provide information to customers about products or services your organisation wishes you to promote, you must make some decisions. The figure below shows the key decisions you need to think about before you offer a customer any information. Making these decisions will ensure you are giving information the customer will find useful, in a clear and helpful way.

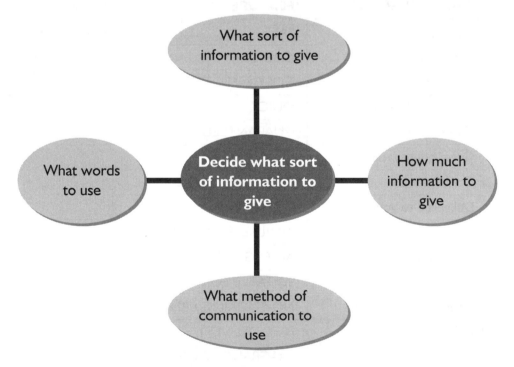

Figure 1.12 Key decisions when offering information

Essentially what you need to do is tell your customer what they need to know, explain the benefits and advise how to take things forward. This might include telling a customer the facts and figures about a product or service that relate specifically to questions put to you. If a customer asks what time a bus leaves, the customer-service practitioner would first need to check the departure point before offering information about bus times. You may be providing facts and figures about a product or service that you feel the customer needs to know in order to get a good understanding. In the above example the customer could be warned of any road works that the bus operator is aware of which might have an effect on the bus driver's ability to keep to the timetable. In this way the customer is forewarned of any possible problems affecting the service he or she expects to receive.

Decide how much information to give

There are some customers who will want to know everything there is to know about a product or service. Others will want only the bare details. For those who seem to want to know everything, do remember that people have their limits as to how much information they can absorb at any one time. Where appropriate, remember to use company leaflets and brochures so that customers can read them in their own time. It does not pay to overload customers with so much information that they become confused.

How was it for you?

What happened when you last requested some information about a product or service? Did you find the explanation clear? Was this because the amount of information was about right? Did you get so much information that you were unable to make your mind up or make a decision?

You can test whether you have given enough information by asking if there is anything else the customer wants to know.

♦ Does that answer your question?
♦ Would you like to know more about the product?
♦ Have I covered everything you need to know?
♦ Are you able to come to a decision now?

If dealing face-to-face with a customer, look for any non-verbal signals the customer may give. If the expression is open and smiling you have probably said enough. If there is a frown present you may have a confused your customer. If this is the case, first check your thoughts are correct:

♦ Am I confusing you? Sorry. Let me try again.
♦ I'm sorry if I am not explaining things clearly. Would you like me to go over that again?
♦ I know this can be very difficult to understand. Let me go over it again.

This will enable your customer to get some breathing space and for you to try once more. Be very careful you do not patronise or insult the customer by making him or her think they are not very clever.

Decide what method of communication to use

There are two key ways of passing information on to customers – the written word and the spoken word.

Deciding which to use may depend on the manner in which the customer has approached you. For instance, if you are in a situation where the customer is speaking with you face-to-face then it makes sense that you talk directly with him or her. If the subject matter is complex then it might mean that you need to follow up the conversation in writing, enclosing some literature to support what you have said.

When writing to a customer, follow their lead. Think about what is important to them. What have they asked you about? What is it they would like to read about first? You can do this by thinking about what has been said or by looking at any letter/email you have received and gauging where the customer's priorities are.

Write about the areas the customer spends most time asking questions about, as this is an important area for him or her to know about. Build in any points you feel are necessary to ensure he or she can make a decision and take any action he or she needs to move forward. Another factor might be time. How urgent is the need to get the information to the customer? Do you need to telephone or will a letter be OK?

Decide what words to use

Remember you are not only answering the needs and expectations of a customer but you are also promoting your organisation's products or services. This means taking the time to choose words that mean you are explaining the benefits of the product or service to the customer.

Remember

♦ Don't confuse the customer.
♦ Avoid jargon.

Make sure you cover all the points the customer has raised with you and respond in a manner that reflects the style in which he or she has contacted you. For instance if he or she has contacted you in a very formal way (perhaps using a formal style of writing) then respond in that way. However, if a customer has adopted a very chatty or friendly style it would be appropriate to respond accordingly, while still being professional.

There is legislation in place which affects the supply of customer service information to people. Principally, this is the Data Protection Act 1998. We deal with what this means to you in Unit 2, page 74.

Keys to good practice

Giving information to customers

✓ Ask questions to find out what the needs and expectations of the customer are.

✓ Check you have fully understood what the customer wants.

✓ Give enough information to enable the customer to make a decision.

✓ Give enough information to answer questions without the need for a customer to continuously have to come back for more.

✓ Choose your method of communication to suit the type of information you are giving.

✓ Consider how fast a response is required.

✓ Make sure the information you give is accurate and up to date.

✓ If appropriate, check you have met the customer's needs and expectations.

✓ If appropriate, advise the customer how he or she can take things forward.

Check your customer has understood the information you have given

Because you work with a product or service on a daily basis you will become very familiar with it over time. This means you may assume that everybody else knows as much as you. What you might say to a colleague may well be understood, but your customer is less likely to be familiar with terms you and your colleague take for granted. Information that customers may find complicated includes the following:

- ♦ technical information
- ♦ mathematical computations, e.g. interest calculations
- ♦ assembly instructions
- ♦ highly detailed explanations that include insignificant information
- ♦ instructions that have been translated from another language.

Customer information can be confusing

Active knowledge

Consider the information that you regularly need to supply to customers.

♦ Are you consistently being asked the same questions by customers who do not appear to understand?

If so, consider whether this is because the manner in which you have given the information is too complicated, or is it because you talk to customers in terms of benefits rather than technical features.

♦ What can you do to improve?

If you are face-to-face or on the telephone with customers, you can ask the following questions to check for understanding:

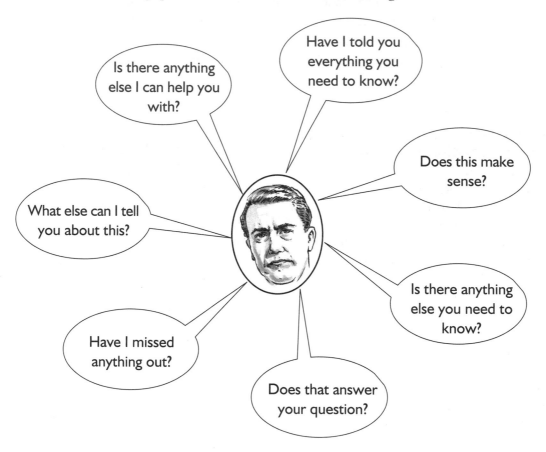

Explaining why you have said something also helps to make sure a customer has understood complicated information. For example, if you were helping a customer understand how to operate a piece of equipment (perhaps explaining how to set up a computer) you could explain that a particular button, **a**, has to be pushed before another button, otherwise it will not start.

You can also use any supporting literature, information leaflets, etc. that your organisation provides to help you explain things to customers. Always make sure you enable customers to leave you with any supporting literature if this is appropriate to your situation.

How was it for you?

Think back to the last time you were confused by a customer service practitioner.

◆ What did it feel like?
◆ What was it that confused you?
◆ What could the person have done differently that would have helped you?
◆ In the end, were you satisfied with the service you received?

Keys to good practice

Giving explanations

✓ Give customers a full and clear explanation.
✓ Act with confidence to inspire your customers.
✓ Talk or write in terms of benefits rather than features.
✓ Avoid jargon and technical terms.
✓ Do not make assumptions that customers will automatically understand.
✓ Ask questions to check for understanding.
✓ Clarify any points where necessary.
✓ Use supporting literature, and information leaflets.
✓ Agree the way forward.

How to explain to customers the reasons you are unable to meet their needs or expectations

We all would like to get what we want, at a price we want to pay, when we want. However, it is not always right or possible to say 'yes' to customers. Sometimes you will not be able to meet needs or expectations and you will then need to say 'no'. From your organisation's perspective, if it said 'yes' to every customer request, it would soon be out of business.

Customers whose needs or expectations are not met are likely to feel disappointed or even angry and frustrated. It is important that you do all that you can to explain why you cannot do what a customer wants.

How was it for you?

Think back to a time when you didn't get what you wanted.

♦ How did the person you dealt with explain to you the reasons why?
♦ What did you feel like?

When you cannot meet customers' needs or expectations

Saying 'no' is not about refusing to help. You should help the customer to understand that on this occasion you are unable to help with X but you can offer Y. You should always offer options and alternatives. You should do this in a way that recognises the first choice may not have been met. This means showing empathy and understanding. Customers need to feel that you appreciate the position they are in and that you have recognised their feelings at not having their needs or expectations met. By offering options and alternatives you will make the customer feel valued because you have not closed the door on him or her.

Active knowledge

♦ With a colleague, list the four main customer needs that you and your organisation are consistently unable to meet.
♦ Discuss why this is.
♦ Discuss the reaction you get from customers when you are unable to meet these needs or expectations.
♦ With any unsatisfactory outcomes, can you do anything to better meet the customers' needs or expectations?

Reasons why you might have to say no

Your organisation's policies and procedures

There will be times when your organisation has a policy which means you have to say no to a customer. For instance, it may not be cost effective for large stocks of bulky items to be kept on the premises, meaning there might be a longer wait for a customer to get what he or she wants. A hairdresser's might have a policy that states that children under ten must be accompanied by a parent or guardian.

Legal reasons

Organisations and their employees must comply with the law. For instance, if you worked in a clothing shop selling fake leather coats and a customer asked to try on your leather coats, it would be wrong of you to help him or her without explaining that the coats you sold were in fact fake leather.

Safety reasons

If an overweight customer requests that you let him or her on to the latest thrill-seeking roller coaster at the adventure park, it would be wrong for you to say yes if you know the safety barrier would not fit properly due to his or her obesity.

Protecting confidentiality

Knowing who your customer is, and protecting information you have about him or her is another reason why you might have to say no. Protecting customers' confidentiality is closely linked to legislation, another key area where you might find yourself unable to meet a customer's needs or expectations.

Out of stock

Sometimes, you may simply not have the product your customer requires in stock.

Staffing problems

If a customer asks to see or talk to a certain person by name, perhaps because he or she always deals with them, this may not always be possible as the person in question might be on holiday or on sick leave.

In all these instances, having to say no does not necessarily mean you will get an unhappy customer at the end. Bear in mind that sometimes you are saying no in sensitive situations and you must be particularly careful in these situations.

If you remember the seven service sins we discussed on page 19 you will recall that customers hate the 'I don't care' attitude of some service providers. Unfortunately, there are a few people who will take the easy way out and say things like:

♦ 'That's not our policy.'
♦ 'I'm not allowed to do that.'
♦ 'I have no idea if we can do that for you.'

Keys to good practice

Saying no the right way

✓ Be friendly.
✓ Show empathy.
✓ Maintain eye contact when face-to-face.
✓ Give a clear explanation that shows the reasons for not meeting a need or expectation.
✓ Discuss options and alternatives.
✓ Explain what you can do.
✓ Agree the way forward.

Case study

1   Jim and Sue are eating out at a restaurant. Jim orders lemon sole. The waiter has just been told all the lemon sole has now gone.

2   Ali receives his credit card bill and notices that interest has been charged to his account. However, he always pays his bills on time and telephones the credit card company to complain.

3   Gina asks for her hair to be coloured deep chestnut at the hairdresser's. However, it turns out orange.

4   George takes his watch to be repaired and is told the cost of the repair will exceed the value of the watch.

5   Clive checks out of a hotel and says to the receptionist 'I could live without my loo roll being turned up at the edge if my room service came when it was promised.'

6   Freda goes to the dentist for a 4.40pm appointment only to find her appointment was at 3.40pm.

7   Ian goes to the gym and finds that three of the six treadmills are not working.

8   The train gets into the station 15 minutes late. Dominic and Zoe go to the ticket counter to ask why.

♦   For each of the scenarios above, write down what the service provider might say to the customer.

Check your knowledge

1   Describe three ways in which you can create a positive impression with customers.

2   Why is eye contact important when dealing with a customer face-to-face?

3   How will you know if a customer is angry or confused?

4   What can you do to adapt your behaviour to respond to

  a   an angry customer?

  b   a confused customer?

5   List four methods of communicating with customers.

6   When would you choose to write to a customer rather than use email?

7   Describe five key points to remember when greeting customers.

8   Where can you find out about the products or services your organisation offers?

9   Name five customer needs or expectations that most customers have.

10 What should you offer customers when you cannot meet their needs or expectations?

11 What sort of information might a customer find difficult to understand?

12 How might working under pressure affect how you behave with customers?

UNIT 2

Deliver reliable customer service

Delivering reliable customer service is rather like making sure you have everything you need to make a long journey a success. First you have to plan the trip: where you want to go, how long you can be away for, how you will get there. This is the same as preparing to deal with customers. Once you are actually on the journey, you need to make sure you are going on the right roads, driving safely and on target to reach your destination on time. Making these checks throughout your journey (perhaps keeping an eye on a map) is just like giving consistent service to customers. Finally, once you arrive at your destination, you want to make sure that you are at the right place, and that everything went smoothly. This helps you to think about what you might do differently next time to make your journey easier or better in some way. This is just like checking your customer service delivery.

What is meant by being reliable?

Different people will want different things and expect different forms of customer service and reliability from different organisations. Below are some examples of what delivering reliable customer service might include:

- ◆ being trustworthy
- ◆ being accurate
- ◆ being efficient
- ◆ being dependable
- ◆ keeping promises
- ◆ doing things on time
- ◆ being professional
- ◆ meeting expectations.

To deliver reliable customer service you will need to show that you can use your organisation's systems and processes to meet and, if possible, exceed customer expectations.

The elements for this unit are:

- ◆ 2.1 Prepare to deal with your customers
- ◆ 2.2 Give consistent service to customers
- ◆ 2.3 Check customer service delivery.

2.1 Prepare to deal with your customers

♦ Ways of keeping your knowledge of products or services up to date.

♦ What preparation you need to do to help you to deal with customers.

♦ How legislation and regulations may affect your customer service role.

Ways of keeping your knowledge of products or services up to date

You will not be expected to know everything there is to know in detail about each and every product or service your organisation offers, after all the number may range from one or two, to many hundreds.

The first thing to do is to sort out the products or services you need to know from those that would be simply nice to know about. There are many ways you can find out about your organisation's products or services:

Figure 2.1 Finding out about your company's products or services

Remember, companies and organisations are constantly changing their products or services. They need to do this to keep ahead of the competition and to provide variety for their customers. Other changes may occur to comply with legislation or for safety reasons. Once you have tracked down the most suitable source of information available to you, it is vital that you regularly keep up to date with changes your organisation might make to the product or service.

Case study

Margaret works as a local authority Environmental Health Officer in health promotions training. There are large Chinese and Turkish populations where she works and there have been many problems with these communities not fully understanding what help they can get from her.

The marketing department at the local authority want to update their leaflets about the services offered by environmental health. They have asked Margaret to let them know what her customers need to know about the services available from environmental health.

To get to grips with this, Margaret sat down and thought about the types of questions she is frequently asked by her customers. She then drew up a table to record them.

Product or service	Frequently asked questions	Feature	Benefit
Training courses	Cost? Duration? On- or off-site? Frequency? Compulsory?	Free. Half a day. Flexible. On request. Ask for more details.	Something for nothing. Quick. We can come to you. Get the training when you want it. Dependent on nature of course.
Chinese community awareness	Interpreter available? Information leaflets in Chinese?	Yes. Yes.	Understanding. No language problems.
Food hygiene information	Where available? Website address? Cost? Translation into Chinese/Turkish?	City Office and library. www.abc.gov.uk Free. Yes.	Pick up a leaflet. Easy access. Something for nothing. No language problems.

Figure 2.2 Product or services table

Active knowledge

- ◆ Using Figure 2.2 as a template, draw up your own list of the ten products or services that customers most frequently ask you about.
- ◆ Now draw up a list of the features and benefits of each one.
- ◆ Ask yourself what the most frequently asked questions you have to answer about these products or services are. Write these and their answers down.
- ◆ Are you able to answer these accurately? If not, find out the answers now.

Keeping a table such as this up to date will ensure you are always ready to respond appropriately to your customers' questions and queries. It will ensure you are also available to offer information by way of promoting the products or services your organisation offers.

Keys to good practice

Keeping your product or service knowledge up to date

- ✓ Make a note to check on the validity of the information you have once a month or more frequently.
- ✓ Make sure you have the most recent information readily available or accessible.
- ✓ Think about things you read in the press or see on TV and how they might affect the products or services your organisation offers.
- ✓ Ask colleagues.
- ✓ Complete a product or services table (see Figure 2.2).
- ✓ Check your organisation's newsletters/website/intranet/updates/in-house magazine.
- ✓ Always look for ways to improve your knowledge of products or services.

Active knowledge

Thinking about your organisation's own products or services, collect copies of adverts and articles from newspapers, in-house magazines, emails and the intranet/Internet. Do this for a month and then read them to see how products or services have changed.

What preparation you need to do to help you to deal with customers

Most people would not dream about going on a long journey without checking their car was roadworthy. Likewise, you cannot even begin to think you will be able to deliver reliable customer service if you have not put in the preparatory work first. This means before you communicate with the customer you must ensure some basic preparations are in place.

If you do all the correct preparations before you deal with customers it will not only help you deliver efficient, reliable consistent service, but also ensure that your experience of your job is enjoyable and rewarding. Relevant preparations include the following:

◆ making sure your product or service knowledge is up to date
◆ making sure any equipment you use is in good and safe working order
◆ making sure your working environment creates the right impression
◆ making sure you have got everything ready before you deal with your customers
◆ making sure you know about legislation and your customers' rights in relation to the work you do.

Create the right impression with an organised and clean workspace

Equipment – making sure it is reliable

Delivering reliable customer service is an impossible task if the equipment you use lets you down. Your equipment must be in good and safe working order. Equipment includes everything you need to deliver customer service as shown in Figure 2.3.

Where does this go?

To ensure that your equipment is in good and safe working order, you must check it regularly and before you deal with a customer. In other words, you must prepare it so that a customer does not see or hear you trying to sort something out while he or she is waiting for you. This is intensely frustrating for a customer and also could cause unnecessary delay or even be dangerous.

You do not necessarily have to perform a detailed check every day. You should check out any essential items of equipment that you could not live without if they did not work. Think about the type of equipment you use and work out a reasonable

Be prepared before your customer arrives

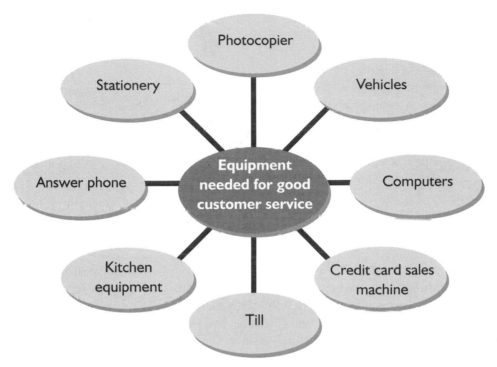

Figure 2.3 Examples of equipment needed for good customer service

timescale to perform a check. You must be alert and aware of your equipment.

If you find an item of equipment is faulty, it does not necessarily mean that you should fix it. Indeed to do so might pose a safety risk. Your organisation has a responsibility to ensure the proper maintenance and upkeep of equipment.

Active knowledge

♦ Make a list of the types of equipment you deal with.
♦ Create a diary note to remind you to check the equipment is in good and safe working order.
♦ Find out your organisation's procedures for repairing and maintaining the equipment you use.

Your work area and its impact

In Unit 1 we looked at how you can give the right impression through the image you create. This image will be dramatically affected for good or for bad by the conditions under which you work, and what your work area looks like. Does being neat matter? Yes, it does, especially if your customers can see your work area. Customers often make decisions about how professional/reliable you are by looking at the conditions under which you work.

Who would you trust to help you?

Neatness is not only about looking neat, but also about being neat and organised. In most cases being messy means you are disorganised. Indeed, even if you are dealing with a customer on the telephone or over the Internet, you will find that you cannot find things easily if your desk or work area is untidy. Being untidy causes delays.

Working surrounded by clutter could add to the amount of time you take to do even routine tasks. Taking the time now to clean out your desk, sort out any paperwork and organise your filing system will help you to deliver reliable customer service and reduce your stress levels.

For those of you who use a desk, you might like to consider operating a clear desk policy. A clear desk policy means just that – keeping your desk clear. You need to store away files, papers and disks when not in use, in order to maintain a clean and tidy working environment. This means putting things away when you are away from your desk for a long period of time and at the end of your working day. Doing this also has the advantage of protecting information and office equipment from unauthorised access, loss or damage. You should also look at other aspects such as cleanliness and the condition of any organisational literature or posters. If leaflets are dog-eared, covered in tea stains and out of date, they are not going to create the right impression.

Active knowledge

Look at your workspace now.

♦ Is it neat?
♦ Are there electrical cables running all over the floor that you or your customers might trip over?
♦ Are there tears in the carpet someone might get their foot caught in?
♦ Have you put chairs or other pieces of equipment in places that make it difficult for customers to get access?
♦ What can you do to improve the safety of your workplace?

Neatness is not just about looking neat and creating the right impression, it is also about making sure that you work in a safe environment. Health and safety are important areas to think about. Figure 2.4 shows a daily checklist that could be used by someone working in any shop or place of work to which a customer has access and that you share with other colleagues. Try to adapt it to your own working environment by thinking about which areas in your workplace you are responsible for and which areas you should report to others.

As you work through this table, remember that your job role may not require you to water the plants, or make sure all the computers in the organisation are working, but it is important to be aware of your whole workspace and make sure that you maintain your personal area, and report problems in general areas.

If you are part of a team, you all need to be proud of your workspace; this is all part of delivering professional and reliable customer service.

Area to be checked	Check	Action needed
Car park	Litter free. No obstacles to easy parking	
Shop front/building frontage	No litter in doorway. Plants in hanging baskets/ window boxes OK. Windows are clean	
Entrance	Steps are clean and clear. No litter. Doormats are clean	
Signage	Signs are in place. Wording is clear and legible	
Customer space	Plants (artificial or real) are clean or healthy. Furniture is in a good state of repair. Leaflet dispensers etc. are well stocked and up to date. Work surfaces, fittings, toilets, bins, all clean. Lighting works. Heating and ventilation works. Cupboard doors/drawers are shut. Equipment is in good and safe working order. Clocks show the right time	
My workspace	Product and service information is well stocked and up to date. Stationery tidy replenished. Work area is clean and tidy. Equipment is in good and safe working order. Internal contact list is up to date	

Figure 2.4 Daily checklist

Remember

When you are personally unable to help, make sure you know who you can go to for advice and guidance.

Your organisation's procedures and systems

You need to know and understand what procedures and systems your organisation has in place to help you deliver reliable customer service. Procedures exist to help you and your customers to know what to expect. They assist everyone by stating what happens, when it happens and how it will happen. Timescales might also be included, e.g. a complaints procedure would set out what a customer might expect to happen after a formal complaint has been made. There are many systems and procedures in place such as those shown below.

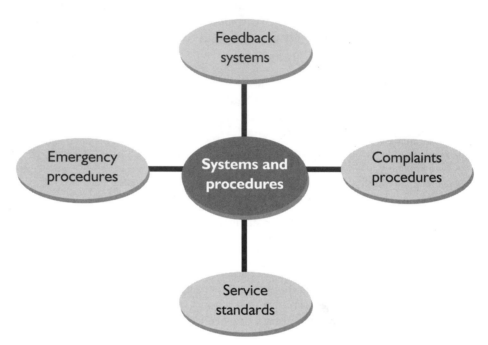

Figure 2.5 Systems and procedures in the workplace

Feedback systems

These are processes that enable your organisation to listen to what the customer has to say. They may be informal processes such as you passing on to an appropriate person comments made to you by customers. Or, they could be formal processes such as writing to customers with questions about the service they receive. At Richer Sounds (the hi-fi retailer) every customer receives a short tear-off questionnaire with their receipt. This questionnaire includes a request for feedback from the customer about the quality of service he or she received.

Feedback is very useful to your organisation. Without it, things will stay the same or be changed as a result of what your organisation wants to impose, regardless of what the customer actually wants or needs. Feedback ensures that a cycle of continuous improvement can occur.

Complaints procedures

Your organisation may have a process in place for dealing with customer complaints, i.e. when to say sorry, when to give refunds, what information to record and how to reach a satisfactory conclusion. Depending on the organisation, you may have full authority to give a refund or a sum of money as a gesture of goodwill, or you may have to refer to someone else for permission to do so.

Case study

Leslie works in an outdoor clothing shop in the Lake District. A tourist comes in to buy a waterproof anorak. Two days later he returns with a complaint: the anorak did not prove to be waterproof. Leslie checked that the label said waterproof – it did. He agreed with the customer that a complaint was justified.

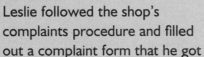

Leslie followed the shop's complaints procedure and filled out a complaint form that he got his supervisor to sign together with the customer. He then helped his customer choose an alternative anorak.

- ◆ Why did Leslie fill out a form?
- ◆ How would this help the shop to improve its service?
- ◆ Write down the procedure Leslie followed.

Service standards

Some organisations will lay down service standards against certain criteria. These standards are simply things an organisation expects of its employees when dealing with customers. They could involve how to answer the telephone and what to say, and timescales involved when replying to a letter. Figure 2.6 shows what some service standards might include.

Area for action	Service standard
Face-to-face initial greeting	Smile at customers as they approach. Say 'Good morning' or 'Good afternoon'. Make eye contact within five seconds. Use customer's name at least twice
Telephone answering	Answer the telephone within three rings
Returning telephone calls	Return all calls within 24 hours
Take responsibility	Give customers your name, telephone number and extension

Figure 2.6 Service standards

Emergency procedures

When preparing to deal with customers it is important that you know what to do in the event of an emergency. Do you know what to do if a routine fire drill happens while customers are with you? What contingency plans are in place to deal with industrial action that might affect your job, e.g. tube strikes? Do you know about health and safety issues if your customer has an accident whilst with you? Something as simple as someone spilling a cup of hot tea can escalate into a full-blown emergency if you do not know what emergency procedures are in place to help you.

Active knowledge

Find out the procedures and systems your organisation has in place in relation to the following:

♦ customer feedback
♦ complaints handling
♦ service standards
♦ emergency procedures:
  ♦ Who are your company's first aiders?
  ♦ Who is the fire warden?
  ♦ Where are the fire drill assembly points?

How legislation and regulations may affect your customer service role

There are three legal systems in the UK:

♦ English law (which also covers Wales)
♦ Northern Ireland law
♦ Scottish law.

There is little difference between English and Northern Ireland law, but Scottish law is different. The courts have different names and follow different procedures. Some English laws do not apply to Scotland and vice versa.

There are several significant Acts and many more regulations that affect the workplace. They may not all be applicable to you and your role. Read through the regulations that follow and decide which are relevant to you and your role. Make a note of these for your portfolio.

Significant Acts that may affect your work

In terms of products and services, Acts that may affect a customer service professional include the following:

♦ Sale of Goods Act 1979 (as amended)
♦ Supply of Goods and Services Act 1982
♦ Unsolicited Goods and Services Act 1971

- Trade Descriptions Act 1968
- Consumer Protection Act 1987
- Consumer Credit Act 1974
- Consumer Protection (Distance Selling) Regulations 2000.

Sale of Goods Act 1979 (as amended)

This law is very important if you are involved with selling goods. (There is a separate law covering services which we will deal with on page 67.) All goods bought or hired from shops, street markets, by mail order or from door-to-door sellers are covered by these rights. They include goods bought in sales. These laws also apply to online sites, i.e. goods and services purchased on the Internet, providing the trader is based in the UK.

In the 1990s two further Acts extended the basic 1979 Act: the Sale and Supply of Goods Act 1994 and the Sale of Goods (Amendment) Act 1995. That is why the words 'as amended' are in the title of the Act. The Sale of Goods Acts lay down several conditions that all goods sold by a trader must meet. The goods must be of:

- merchantable (satisfactory) quality
- as described
- fit for purpose.

'Satisfactory quality' includes all the minor and cosmetic defects that a product may have, as well as substantial problems, and it also means that product must last a reasonable time. It includes the appearance and finish of the goods, their safety and their durability. The Act does not give a customer any rights if a fault was obvious or pointed out when the customer bought the product.

'As described' refers to any advertisement or verbal description made by the trader. If a yoghurt is described as '100 per cent fat free' then it must be.

'Fit for purpose' covers not only the obvious use or purpose of an item, but also anything you say the item will do when you are trying to sell the product. If you tell a customer that the overcoat you are selling is 'waterproof even under extreme conditions' then it must not leak water in a shower.

If a product bought by a customer does not meet any of the conditions set out in the Sale of Goods Act 1979 they are entitled to their money back. The customer is not entitled to a repair or replacement or credit note.

Customers are only entitled to their money back from the trader they originally bought the item from, not from the manufacturer. Technically it is up to the trader to collect the faulty item, although customers usually find it easier to return the faulty goods themselves.

If customers wish to accept a repair, and many people do, they would be wise to put in writing that they 'reserve the right to reject the item if the repair is not satisfactory'. If there is a dispute, the customer has to prove their case, not the trader.

Under the Sale of Goods Act 1979 the customer does not have any rights to a refund if he or she has:

♦ changed their mind about buying the product or service
♦ made a mistake and bought the wrong product
♦ been told about the fault before a purchase was made.

If a customer wishes to return a kettle because 'the colour doesn't match the work surfaces in the kitchen' then the trader does not have to give a refund. However, many shops may exchange or give the customer a refund as a gesture of goodwill.

Keys to good practice

Customers' rights to a refund

If the goods are of satisfactory quality, as described and are fit for purpose:

✓ The customer has no automatic right to a refund if he or she has a change of mind, made a mistake or where a fault was pointed out prior to purchase.

If the goods are not of satisfactory quality, as described or not fit for purpose:

✓ Your customer does not have to produce a receipt.
✓ You may ask for proof of purchase, perhaps a cheque book stub or credit card sales voucher.
✓ Your customer does not have to accept a credit note.
✓ You are obliged to offer a cash refund.
✓ If the customer prefers, he or she may accept a replacement or an offer to repair the original product.
✓ If the goods were bought in a sale, the customer has the same rights to a refund.
✓ Notices saying 'no refunds on sale items' are illegal.
✓ If an item is in a sale because it is a 'second' and is described as such, then a customer cannot bring it back and ask for a refund because of that particular fault.

You may work in an organisation that also has goodwill policies that go beyond a customer's statutory rights. For example, some shops will allow you to exchange goods that are not faulty, such as clothes that are the wrong size, or a book that you have received as a present but have already read. A hairdressing salon might agree to do a customer's highlights again free of charge if a complaint is made that the effect was not what he or she wanted.

Supply of Goods and Services Act 1982

This law will affect you if you are involved with supplying goods or services to customers. It covers the work done and products supplied by tradesmen and professionals. This will include people such as builders, plumbers, landscape gardeners, dressmakers, dentists and hairdressers, i.e. anybody who is supplying goods or services that a customer has to pay for.

The Act states the following:

♦ A tradesman or professional has a 'duty of care' towards the customer and his or her property. ('Duty of care' means the tradesman or professional must act with reasonable care and skill when dealing with customers.)
♦ Any price or standard agreed with the customer must be honoured. Where you and your customer have not agreed a price, the customer does not have to accept an outrageous bill. All the customer has to do is pay what he or she considers is reasonable. (A reasonable charge will be the charge that other similar tradesmen would make in the same geographical area for the same job.)
♦ The work must be done to a reasonable standard and at a reasonable cost (if not otherwise agreed in advance). A reasonable charge will be the charge that other similar tradesmen would make in the same geographical area for the same job.

Remember

The Supply of Goods and Services Act 1982 extends the protection of customers provided by the Sale of Goods Act 1979 to include goods supplied as part of a service.

Unsolicited Goods and Services Act 1971

Have you ever had a book or a CD land on your doormat that you have not ordered? If you work for an organisation that sends items out to customers to promote them or with an introductory offer attached, then this law might affect you. The Unsolicited Goods and Services Act 1971 is designed to prevent traders charging for goods customers have not ordered. This law states that a customer is under no obligation to return items he or she has not requested.

I don't even have a CD player!

Receiving unsolicited goods can be very annoying

If a customer receives something unsolicited, he or she should keep it for six months (or just one month if the customer contacts the supplier to say he or she has not ordered it and does not want it). After that it can be thrown away. If a trader demands payment for unsolicited goods, he or she is guilty of a criminal offence.

Trade Descriptions Act 1968

This Act states that:

♦ traders must not falsely describe something on sale
♦ traders must not make false claims for services, accommodation or facilities.

It is a criminal offence to falsely describe something on sale.

This applies to any description a trader might make; it could be an advertisement, a sign or label in a shop window or a verbal description from a sales assistant.

For example, a silk shirt bearing a label saying 'machine washable' would be falsely described if it really needed specialist cleaning at a dry cleaner's. A sales assistant keen to reach his or her monthly sales target might say to a customer 'this is the DVD player you need; it is state of the art, simple to use and comes with really straightforward operating instructions'. But, what does 'state of the art' mean? Will the instructions be simple to follow for that particular customer? The Act also applies to services, but only if a description is reckless as well as false.

A customer has three years in which to take any legal action. Every year many traders are prosecuted under this Act. Most are fined and a few are sent to prison. It is the most important criminal consumer law.

Consumer Protection Act 1987

This Act states that:

♦ Customers can claim compensation for death, injury or damage to property over £275 (apart from damage to the product itself) if a product they use turns out to be faulty. Action is usually against the manufacturer or producer, but a customer can sue the retailer if the retailer will not say who the manufacturer is.
♦ Producers and distributors of goods are required to ensure their products are safe.
♦ It is an offence to display a misleading price. For example, it is an

offence if you gave a customer misleading information relating to the price at which goods, services, accommodation or facilities are available. It is an offence if you say something is '£50 less than the manufacturer's recommended price' if no such recommended price exists.

Consumer Credit Act 1974

This Act describes the rights customers have when they are dealing with credit companies (organisations who provide credit to customers). This Act gives consumers a wide range of rights, for example:

♦ to look at a credit file: an individual's personal records
♦ a 'cooling-off period' of five days when customers can cancel any credit agreement signed at home
♦ the right to pay off credit early
♦ liability limited to £50 when a credit card is stolen or lost.

The Act also lays down conditions and procedures that credit companies have to follow when they advertise or sell credit. These are backed up by criminal sanctions. If a customer uses their card to buy a product that turns out to be faulty, Section 75 of the Act gives them the right to their money back from the credit card company. It applies only to goods worth more than £100 and less than £30,000, and it does not apply to debit, charge cards, bank loans or certain shop cards.

However, if a customer uses a credit card to purchase something that breaches laws like the Sale of Goods Acts, he or she can get their money back from the credit company as well as from the trader.

Case study

Darren bought a mobile telephone costing £325 from his local mobile telephone dealer. He used his credit card to make the purchase. When trying to use it, he found the buttons kept sticking. Darren felt the telephone was faulty and wanted his money back.

♦ Which Act(s) cover the right for Darren to get his money back?
♦ Should he approach the shop?
♦ Should he approach the manufacturer?
♦ Should he approach the credit card company?

Consumer Protection (Distance Selling) Regulations 2000

These regulations give new protection to customers who shop by telephone, mail order via the Internet or digital TV. Customers have the right to:

♦ receive clear information about goods and services before deciding to buy
♦ receive confirmation of this information in writing

- a cooling-off period of seven working days in which the customer can withdraw from the contract
- protection from credit card fraud.

Remember

Existing laws that govern the sale of products and services apply equally to online trading.

It is important that you keep yourself up to date with changes to legislation. Both the Trade Descriptions Act 1968 and the Consumer Credit Act 1974 are currently under review. Go to www.consumer.gov.uk for information on how the Government is intending to change UK consumer law.

Working in the NHS – a special note

For those readers working in the National Health Service, from 1 April 2001, the customer information contained in *Your Guide to the* NHS has replaced *The Patient's Charter* in England. It sets out what customers can expect from the NHS today and what they can expect in the future as improvements to health services are made. *The Patient's Charter* still applies in Wales, Scotland and Northern Ireland.

Other forms of legislation

Apart from consumer law, i.e. legislation that relates to customers' rights in connection with goods and services, there is other legislation that may affect you in the work place in the areas of:

- health and safety
- equal opportunities
- copyright
- data protection.

Health and safety

The basis of British health and safety law is the Health and Safety at Work Act 1974. It covers the responsibilities employers have to employees and also to customers who are on their premises.

- The Workplace (Health, Safety and Welfare) Regulations 1992 state that non-smokers should be allocated separate rest areas from smokers.
- The Manual Handling Operations Regulations 1992 deal with the manual handling of equipment, stocks and materials. Where reasonably practicable, an employer should avoid the need for his or her employees to undertake manual handling involving risk of injury.
- The Personal Protective Equipment Work Regulations 1992 deal with protective clothing or equipment that must be worn or held by an employee to protect against health and safety risks.

Figure 2.7 Responsibilities employers have to employees

◆ The Health and Safety (Display Screen Equipment) Regulations 1992 introduced measures to prevent repetitive strain injury, fatigue and eye problems in the use of technological equipment. This includes eyesight tests on request, breaks from using the equipment and provision of health and safety information about the equipment to the employee.

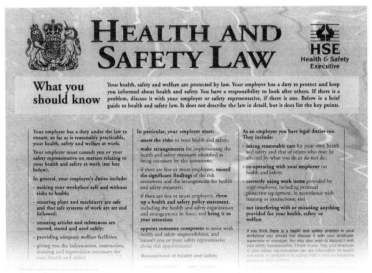

The Health and Safety Law poster

If you work for an organisation that employs five or more people, your organisation must provide a written health and safety policy that should be made available to all employees. It is often to be found on notice boards

Case study

Grant was waiting at his local garage for his car exhaust to be fitted. He had been sitting in the waiting area for a while and decided to go to the vending machine to get a cup of tea. The machine only filled the cup up halfway so Grant pushed the water button again to fill the cup. He took his finger off the button and reached to get the cup with his other hand. To his horror and immense pain, the boiling water was still coming through.

Ray, who worked behind the counter, rushed out to help but said there was nothing he could do except to take Grant to a wash-basin where he could keep his hand under cold water. Grant wanted some cream to put on it. Ray refused 'in case he developed an allergic reaction to the burn cream'. Ray also refused to give Grant a pain-killing pill.

Annoyed at not getting any help except for cold water, Grant demanded the incident be put into the accident book. 'That's only for people who work here', said Ray. 'In any case, the machine does say push button once'.

♦ Discuss with a colleague how Ray handled this situation.
♦ Do you think Grant felt he was getting good service?
♦ What would Ray need to do to ensure Grant understood what was happening?
♦ What skills would you expect Ray to use?
♦ Which Act covers this situation?

Equal opportunities

It is important to treat people fairly and equally, regardless of who they are, or how much you like or dislike them or where they live. In other words, while you should treat people as individuals, what makes one person different from another does not mean he or she should have any advantage or disadvantage over anybody else in relation to customer service delivery.

Equal opportunities legislation aims to prevent people being discriminated against on the grounds of their:

♦ race, ethnic origin, nationality and skin colour (e.g. people with white skin, brown skin, black skin, people from different countries, different backgrounds, etc.)
♦ gender or sexual orientation (e.g. men, women, homosexuals, lesbians, bisexuals, etc.)
♦ disability, sensory impairment or learning difficulty (e.g. people with hearing aids or people who are visually impaired, wheelchair users or those with Down's syndrome)
♦ physical characteristics (e.g. people who somehow look different due to birthmarks or skin diseases)
♦ age (e.g. children, young adults, adults, senior citizens, etc.)

♦ personal beliefs (e.g. people who hold different opinions, thoughts and beliefs).

Disability discrimination

The Disability Discrimination Act 1995 is one of the most important pieces of legislation you are likely to need to know about regarding disability discrimination and equal rights. Under this Act a customer is defined as disabled if he or she has 'a physical or mental impairment which has a substantial and long term adverse effect upon his or her ability to carry out normal day to day activities'.

The Act makes it unlawful for service providers to refuse to offer a service they offer other people to anyone with a disability and also makes it unlawful to offer disabled people a lower standard of service than anyone else.

There are more than 6.2 million disabled adults in the UK. This means that it is highly likely that in some stage of your career in customer service you will deal with customers who have a disability. By 2004, all service providers will need to ensure that people with disabilities can use or access services. This is why many service providers are currently installing ramps in their premises, building toilets suitable for wheelchair users, adding Braille to menus and signs, etc. Do you know of any shops, theatres, sports grounds or village halls that are undergoing premises alterations?

These signs indicate that there are facilities to accommodate wheelchairs and guide dogs

Examples of disabilities covered under the Act are:

♦ physical disabilities that affect movement and the senses such as sight and hearing
♦ medically recognised mental illnesses and mental impairments such as learning difficulties
♦ severe disfigurements such as scars, birthmarks and skin diseases (the degree of severity is important, as is the location the disfigurement)
♦ progressive diseases, in which the degree of disability worsens over time, e.g. multiple sclerosis, cancer, HIV, muscular dystrophy.

Remember

Disability discrimination is not only about dealing with people who use a wheelchair. In fact, 95 per cent of disabled people are not wheelchair users. It is all about customer service practitioners and employers having the right attitude: give people with disabilities the same level of service as you would give to non-disabled customers.

Sex discrimination

Sex discrimination means being treated unfairly because of your sex or marital status or because you are pregnant. The main law covering this type of discrimination is the Sex Discrimination Act 1975. It does not cover discrimination on the grounds of sexual orientation.

Racial discrimination

Racial discrimination occurs when an individual is treated less favourably than someone else in a similar situation because of his or her race, skin colour, nationality or ethnic or racial origin. The Race Relations Act 1976 covers this area.

Copyright

If you are in a role that involves you in providing information to customers (perhaps a photocopy of something) or in a role where you may wish to use information or pictures that have been produced by someone else (e.g. including a photograph in a poster you are designing) then you must make sure you obtain the permission of the owner first. This is because the law treats the work as the owner's property: he or she has copyright.

The copyright owner has the exclusive right to:

♦ copy the work
♦ issue copies to the public
♦ adapt the original work.

Data protection

You may be in a role where you ask for, receive and have access to lots of personal information about your customers, such as information about account details, addresses, shareholdings, doctors' notes on patients, etc. It is important that you understand you absolutely cannot disclose this information to anyone who might want to see it.

If you deal with the processing of customer service information, you and your organisation need to make sure that the information is being used

Make sure the information you request from a customer is needed for a genuine reason

for a valid purpose. The Data Protection Act 1998 gives customers certain rights which include the right to:

♦ be informed where the data is being processed
♦ a description of the details being held
♦ the reason why the data is being processed
♦ know to whom the data may be disclosed.

As a general rule, sensitive information such as details on race or ethnic origin, health or medical conditions and sexual orientation may not be collected and processed unless your customer has given his or her consent. It is your organisation's responsibility to obtain this consent.

Active knowledge

Find out what your organisation expects you to do in connection with:

♦ copyright law, e.g. if asked to photocopy an item, what should you do?
♦ data protection: what information (if any) can you provide about customers to a third party?
♦ health and safety law: if a customer asked you for a headache pill, what would you do?

Test your knowledge

With a friend, try role-playing a situation where you start to deal with a customer and find you have nothing ready. Wear clothes that are unsuitable for the occasion and have lots of clutter around you. Behave in a way that indicates you want to help but cannot find the information your customer has asked for.

1   Notice the impact on your 'customer' when you simply cannot help.

2   Think about how *you* feel when your 'customer' notices you are in a muddle. How do these feelings make you react?

3   Are there any changes to your behaviour, i.e. do you become more flustered/get annoyed with yourself/start making excuses?

4   What does your 'customer' end up doing?

5   Ask your 'customer' what he or she would like you to do differently and why.

6   What could you have done to ensure you were able to help your 'customer'?

2.2 Give consistent service to customers

- What you need to do to ensure you keep your promises to customers.
- How to manage situations where your customers' needs or expectations change.
- How to help customers that you are personally unable to deal with.

What you need to do to ensure you keep your promises to customers

Think back to our long car journey where the driver kept checking the map to make sure he or she was on the right road. Making these checks throughout the journey meant he or she was consistently making sure the destination would be reached on time. Similarly, delivering reliable customer service means not just doing so every now and then, but doing so on a consistent basis, no matter what is happening around you. This will include giving excellent service during the following situations:

- when you need to make extra effort to keep your promises
- when the unexpected happens
- when customers change their minds
- when you are personally unable to help
- when you are in a quiet period (or a busy period)
- when people, systems or resources let you down.

In the 2001 Service Excellence Research Report commissioned by the Institute of Customer Service, it was found that service excellence could be talked about in one key phrase: 'Excellent service organisations are those that are easy to do business with'. You have your part to play in making it easy for the customer by keeping your promises. Take a look at the table overleaf, which shows some of the comments made by members of the public for the Service Excellence Report.

A genuine smile is one aspect of excellent service

Excellent service	Poor service
They deliver the promise	**They don't do what they said**
They do what they said	They didn't have it/do it; it was wrong
They don't let you down	You can't get through
If you ask them to do it, it just happens	They let me down
They make it personal	**They are so impersonal**
They give you the time	There was no eye contact
They make eye contact and smile and they mean it	They didn't even acknowledge me
They treat me like an individual	It was plastic service
They go the extra mile	**They don't make any effort**
It's the little touches	They ignored us
They went out of their way	They didn't listen
They explain things	They don't care
They call you back, I didn't have to chase them	The customer is just a problem to them
They deal well with problems	**They don't deal with the problem**
It was quick and easy	They denied responsibility
They took responsibility	They gave me the run-around
They believed me	I ring them every month and each time I have to tell them the whole story

Figure 2.8 Comments about service excellence extracted from the Service Excellence Report, 2001

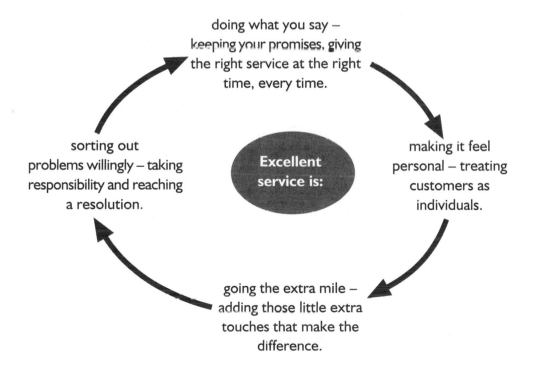

Figure 2.9 The service excellence cycle

Active knowledge

In the context of your own role, write down how you might fulfil each of the stages of excellent service.

Doing what you say

Sin 3 of the seven sins of customer service (see page 19) is the sin of bouncing people around organisations. One reason this can happen is because someone somewhere has not kept a promise to call a customer back. The customer has to call the organisation him- or herself and then ends up getting bounced around various departments trying to be connected to the original person who failed to keep a promise.

To ensure you keep your promises you need to be realistic about what you are saying you will do. Being realistic means not promising you will do something if you know it will never happen. For instance, you may know your customer is excited about obtaining the latest video of his or her favourite pop star, but if you also know you are out of stock of this particular video, there is little point in saying you will have the video by tomorrow if new stocks are not due in until the following week. In this instance you can give the customer a number to call to check if the stock has come in. Asking the customer to call and check is more realistic than offering to call yourself, as you may end up having to call 20 people and not have the opportunity to do so.

Active knowledge

If appropriate to your role, check what your organisation's policy is in connection with customer orders.

♦ Are you expected to keep the customer informed?
♦ Are you expected to give the customer information on how he or she might track progress of an order?

If you promise to pass information on to someone else, make sure you do. Have a notepad handy to write reminders to yourself.

Remember

Only make promises you can keep.

Under-promising and over-delivering

You under-promise when you advise a customer you will do something, knowing you should be able to improve on what you promise. For instance, if you know you can get a customer a product within a week, you might tell him or her it will be delivered in two weeks. That way, if something goes wrong you are covered and the customer is not disappointed. If it turns up within a week, then the customer will be delighted about the early delivery.

By under-promising you are creating an opportunity to over-deliver. For instance, if you promise to telephone a customer within the next three days, he or she may be pleasantly surprised if you are able to get back to them tomorrow. Be realistic about what you say you will do.

You should never promise or raise a strong expectation for anything unless you are virtually certain you can meet the expectation. By keeping your promises and your commitments to customers you will be helping to build trust and loyalty between the customer and your organisation. Customer loyalty means customers will come back for more.

Keys to good practice

Keeping your commitments

✓ Make realistic promises.
✓ Offer timescales you know are achievable.
✓ Only say someone else (e.g. in another department) will do something if you are sure they will be able to carry out your promise.
✓ Accept responsibility: do not blame the policy, other people or equipment.
✓ Return all telephone calls when you say you will.
✓ Be organised.
✓ Do not over-promise.
✓ Do what you say you will do.
✓ Keep your product or services knowledge up to date.

Making customer service feel personal

In Unit 1 we looked at why it is important to communicate in a clear, polite and confident way. We looked at body language, greeting and acknowledging the customer and creating a good impression. Making it feel personal is about using excellent communication skills and little touches to make a customer feel as if you are treating him or her as an individual.

Figure 2.10 How to make a customer feel you are treating him or her as an individual

Going the extra mile

When you do more than you need to for a customer, this is called going the extra mile. It need not mean making huge efforts over and above what you are expected to do. Sometimes the little personal touches you and your organisation can bring to customer service mean the most. Going the extra mile will help to surprise and delight your customers and will probably give you more job satisfaction too. Your customers will come back for more. Here are some examples of how organisations go the extra mile:

♦ the unexpected bowl of fruit or box of chocolates in a hotel room
♦ the toothbrush, socks and hygiene bag provided by an airline
♦ the ferry operator who cleans car windscreens while en route
♦ the mortgage company that sends flowers to a new home owner.

These are all tangible examples of how an organisation might set up a system that provides both a personal touch and goes the extra mile. There are also things that you can do to go the extra mile:

♦ do something different and special, be creative
♦ surprise the customer (e.g. telephone to ask whether he or she is satisfied with a product or service you have given)

- send thank-you notes (e.g. a note to say thanks for doing business with you)
- do something that is not expected (invite a customer to a wine and cheese evening)
- always give more than expected (be flexible)
- use your initiative
- always check that what you do has the approval of your organisation.

Sorting out problems caused by unforeseen circumstances

Sometimes, despite all your best intentions and all your planning, things can go wrong. In these situations it is very important that you use your initiative. You will often need to use your initiative to make extra efforts to keep your commitments to your customers. For example, when the unexpected happens, and a commitment you made in good faith can no longer be fulfilled, use your initiative: tell the customer about the unexpected change and offer an alternative or options to do something different.

Active knowledge

Put yourself in the shoes of the customers in the following examples. How would you feel in each situation if nobody had bothered to update you on what was happening?

- It is 10.00am and you are sitting in the doctor's surgery for a 9.30am appointment.
- You were promised information about a holiday: a coach tour around Scotland. It was meant to be sent to you in the post that same day. A week later it still has not arrived.
- The answer phone system tells you 'Your call is of value to us. Please hold the line. We will get to you shortly'. You have been holding for ten minutes.
- The dry cleaning is not ready when you go to pick it up.
- You have arranged to meet your solicitor Mr X to discuss making a will. You are seen by his assistant, Mr Y.
- The supermarket promises there will only ever be one person queuing at each till. There are three people in the queue in front of you.

Figure 2.11 shows you what you should be considering when dealing with customers in situations where you are unable to keep your commitments due to unforeseen circumstances. It will depend on the individual situation you are in as to whether all the steps are relevant at any one time.

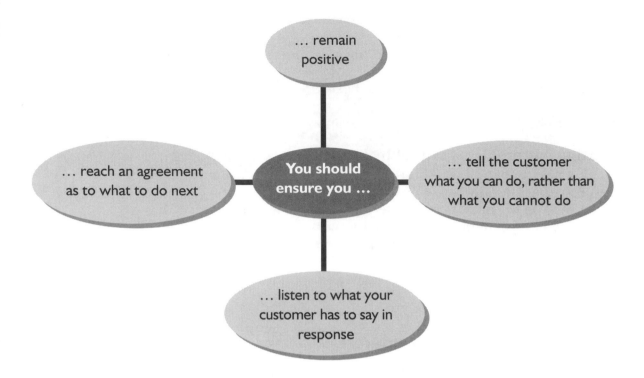

Figure 2.11 What to do when you cannot keep your commitment to a customer

We can now use Figure 2.11 to try and solve the problems on page 81.

The doctor's surgery. You are the receptionist

Here we have a situation where a customer has arrived expecting to see his or her doctor at a specified time. The appointment time has not been met; perhaps because the doctor has been called out or simply because other people have taken a long time with the doctor. The appointments system that states each customer gets five minutes has let you down. It is not your fault. However, keeping the customer advised of progress rather than just letting him or her sit there wondering what is happening will show you care.

The travel agency. You are the customer service assistant

In response to a telephone request, you have promised to send out information in the post. Later that day you realise this particular tour has been very popular; there are no more catalogues and new ones will not arrive until after the weekend. A quick telephone call to the customer will keep him or her interested and possibly keep the business within your travel agency. Here resources have let you down. You might think about telling an appropriate person the Scottish tour is proving very popular so that it does not happen again.

The call centre. You are the call centre customer service agent

There is little you can do here to help customers who have been kept waiting in a telephone queue. If you and your colleagues are answering calls efficiently, that is probably the best you can do. This type of answer phone system is often very annoying to customers, so when they do get to talk to you they might not be in the best of moods. Here systems have let you down.

The dry cleaner's. You are the shop assistant

Before the customer called to collect their dry cleaning (due to be ready at a certain time) you may not have been in a position to telephone the customer to advise of a delay, simply because you only had the customer name and no contact details. Here, again, the system has let you down.

The solicitor's. You are Mr Y

In this scenario, Mr X would have been wise to advise his customer he could no longer keep the appointment due to unforeseen circumstances. He could then check to see if the customer was happy to see Mr Y or whether an alternative date and time should be arranged.

If Mr Y stepped in without the customer being aware of the situation there is potential for a great deal of dissatisfaction. Mr Y (not to mention the customer) has been let down by Mr X – a clear example of not working well with colleagues. Here people have let you down.

The supermarket. You are the checkout assistant

In this scenario, the supermarket has promoted itself as being quick to deal with customers, i.e. it has promised only one person will need to queue. This type of very broad promise may in practice be hard to deliver consistently. If a number of assistants are off sick it may not be possible. At peak times such as the run-up to Christmas there may simply not be enough checkouts to cope even if they are fully staffed. As one of many checkout assistants, you need to be aware of the impact of this promise on your customers' expectations and deal with this appropriately. Systems and resources have let you down.

Remember that solving problems does not mean laying blame; it is about finding the best possible solution that ensures that the customer is happy.

Active knowledge

♦ Think of ways where you can personally go the extra mile on behalf of customers. Include ways of putting yourself out to make sure you keep commitments to customers.
♦ What can you do to add the personal touch to your dealings with customers?

The final stage of the cycle of excellent service involves dealing with and solving customers' problems willingly. We look at this in Unit 4.

How to manage situations where your customers' needs or expectations change

It is not only you or your organisation that may initiate a change in circumstances; sometimes a customer's needs or expectations may change for a number of reasons. Figure 2.12 shows some reasons why a customer's needs or expectations change.

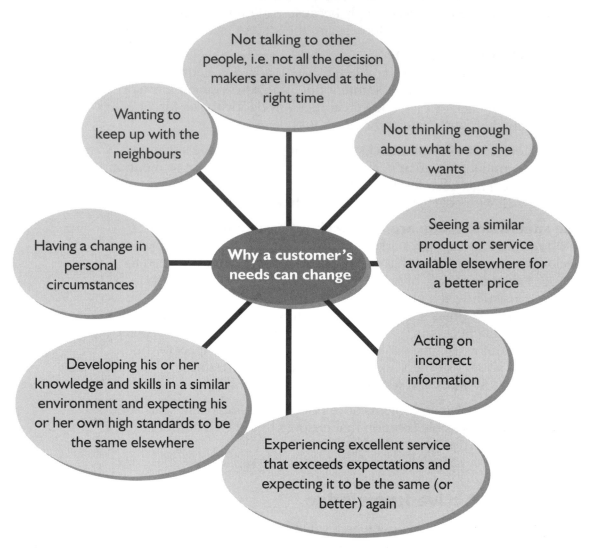

Figure 2.12 Reasons why a customer's needs or expectations change

Figure 2.13 shows the reasons why a customer, Bill (and his wife Lesley's), needs and expectations changed and how these changes may affect you, the customer service practitioner.

Reason for change in a customer's needs or expectations	Possible impact on you
Bill hasn't given enough thought to what he wants	You think you are meeting his needs but you are not
Bill has not included Lesley in the decision to buy the product or service	Bill may return to you with a request that you give him a refund
The shop down the road sells the same product more cheaply	Bill expects your shop to reduce the prices in line and tells you so
Bill can no longer go on the holiday he has booked with you due to illness	Bill wants to use his holiday insurance to get a refund
Bill and Lesley have a weekend away and are upgraded to an executive-class room	Bill complains to you on his next short break that you have not upgraded him
Bill and Lesley receive out-of-date information in the post	You cannot give them what they want
Lesley changes jobs and now works in a call centre where she always answers calls within the laid-down timescales	Lesley expects you to deliver the same high level of service
Bill and Lesley's neighbours have had their garden professionally landscaped	They want you to make their own garden (which is much smaller) look the same

Figure 2.13 Possible reasons why a customer's needs or expectations change

The impact on you as a customer service practitioner can be varied. It is very important that you remain calm when a change of mind occurs. It would be very easy to lose patience, having spent some time with a customer who seems to have made a decision and then suddenly starts all over again. Think about shoe shop assistants and the amount of patience needed to help customers get exactly the right pair of shoes in the right colour and size. You need to be very patient. Take a deep breath and tell yourself that while this customer may be taking a long time to make his or her mind up, the next one will not.

In situations where a decision seems to be a long time coming, just tell yourself it is very important your customer makes the right decision. If he or she does not, there is an increased chance of a dissatisfied customer and possibly even a complaint.

It is easy to adjust your service if a customer tells you of a change of mind. In these situations you would need to check your understanding of what was happening and

Customers often change their minds

seek clarification as to what is required. On other occasions you may see from a customer's body language that all is not well. Do not be afraid to ask questions to clarify what a customer wants.

♦ Is that OK?
♦ You don't seem very sure about that one? Can I get you something else?
♦ What about me looking elsewhere for you?
♦ Have you changed your mind about that?
♦ How else might I help you come to a decision?

Case study

Natasha works in a shoe shop on a busy main road. A customer, Mr Connor, asks for a pair of real leather moccasins, size 7 in black. On trying them on, he tells Natasha he likes the style and they fit well. However, he did not say he wanted to buy them and Natasha noticed him rubbing his hands over the leather and frowning.

Natasha asked him if there was a problem with the moccasins. Mr Connor said he expected the leather to feel softer. Natasha asked him if he would like to try a similar pair of moccasins in a softer leather. He did and Mr Connor liked the new pair. When Natasha told him the price (£60 dearer) he said he would have expected an even softer leather for the high price of the moccasins.

♦ What could Natasha have done to avoid this change in expectations?
♦ How should Natasha deal with Mr Connor's feelings?
♦ What should Natasha do to keep her patience?

How was it for you?

Think about a time when you last changed your mind about something that involved customer service.

♦ How did the service provider know your needs or expectations had changed?
♦ How did the service provider react?
♦ What did you do to get what you wanted?
♦ How satisfied were you with the service you received following a change of mind?

How to help customers that you are personally unable to deal with

You cannot know everything there is to know about everything all the time. Customers know that too, and they will not expect you to be able to help on every occasion. However, in cases where you are not the right person for the job, customers will expect you to know who can help. They will also expect you to hand them over in a professional way. This may be to another person or perhaps to another organisation. Below are some suggestions as to why you might be unable to help.

Reasons you may not be able to help

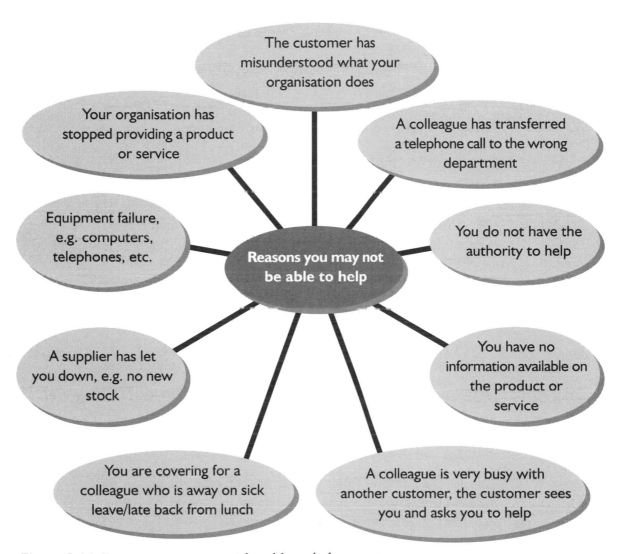

Figure 2.14 Reasons you may not be able to help a customer

Steps to take to ensure that you can help

We all know that the unexpected can happen at any time. Just when you thought everything was safe, something happens to make you jump. So that you can help the customer in the most effective way possible, you need to be prepared for all eventualities.

♦ Make sure you understand the roles and responsibilities of other people in your organisation. You do not need to know what everyone does – just those who deal with issues, products or services that are associated with your own line of work. This means you can pass customers on to the right person and you will not be committing customer service sin 3 – bouncing people around your organisation.

♦ Know where to get easy access to information that may provide you with the right answers in order to help customers.

♦ Use your listening and questioning skills to find out what it is the customer wants.

Keys to good practice

Helping customers you personally cannot deal with

✓ Tell the customer what you can do, not what you cannot do.
✓ Tell the customer what you are doing.
✓ Keep the customer informed of progress.
✓ Know who to go to for help.
✓ Know how to operate the telephone system to transfer a call.
✓ Keep up-to-date telephone contact lists.
✓ Remain positive and confident.
✓ Where necessary, apologise for any delay.
✓ Record the customer's details/needs/expectations.

Referring customers to other organisations

If your organisation is unable to help a customer, you can often help by pointing the customer in the direction of an organisation that can. This may be a case of saying 'We don't stock that, however the corner shop will have it', or referring a customer to a more specialist organisation who deal uniquely with what is required. For example, you may be a landscape gardener specialising in cottage gardens. However, if a customer is expecting a Japanese themed garden you might think you are not the best person for the job. So you might recommend another gardener who you know specialises in this type of garden. In this instance, you would be referring a customer to a competitor.

In both of the above cases, while you are not obtaining the business yourself, you are showing that you want to help and in recommending another organisation you are maintaining an element of goodwill. In the future, the customer may remember this and come back to you. (Likewise, other companies may recommend you to one of their clients.)

Remember

In some organisations it may not be felt appropriate to recommend other organisations. Find out now what the policy is where you work.

Test your knowledge

If you were asked to help a colleague new to customer service understand what it means to deliver reliable customer service, how would you complete the following statements?

- I keep my promises to customers by ...
- On the telephone, I can tell when a customer has a change of mind because he or she ...
- If I cannot personally help a customer I ...
- Sometimes a customer wants me to do something I need to seek permission for. On these occasions I tell the customer ...
- Excellent service is ...

2.3 Check customer service delivery

♦ What your organisation does to check the effectiveness of its customer service.

♦ How to find out if you have met your customers' needs and expectations.

♦ How to identify if you could improve your customer service.

♦ Ways of sharing customer service information with others.

Elements 2.1 and 2.2 looked at the planning and delivery of reliable customer service. We talked about how this was similar to the start and duration of a long car journey. The final stage of this journey involved the driver thinking back to what happened during it in order to see if something could be improved upon. The driver was checking out the success of the trip, just like checking customer service delivery.

What your organisation does to check the effectiveness of its customer service

In order to find out if the service you and your organisation give meets your customers' needs and expectations, you will have to use some of your organisation's systems to measure the effectiveness of its customer service. There are various systems or procedures that your organisation may use, but they will all involve obtaining, analysing and using feedback.

What is feedback?

Feedback is information given to you or your organisation on what both you and your organisation do. Sometimes customers will give feedback without prompting, e.g. a thank-you or complaint letter. On other occasions feedback may be given as a direct result of you or your organisation requesting it. You may also receive feedback from colleagues who have observed what you are doing, or from a line manager or supervisor as part of your organisation's performance and appraisal system.

Every organisation will differ as to how it obtains feedback. This may depend on the following:

♦ the size of the organisation
♦ how sophisticated the organisation's systems and processes are
♦ whether funds are available to undertake research
♦ whether it has the will to listen to customers
♦ its ability to put any changes (as a result of its research) into effect.

Obtaining feedback: what your organisation can do

There are many ways you and your organisation can set about obtaining feedback from customers. Figure 2.15 illustrates some of the methods

Figure 2.15 What your organisation might do to obtain feedback from customers

organisations can implement to capture valuable information from customers.

While more and more people complain or mention they would like something to be different, there is still a huge silent majority that do not give any feedback, whether pleased or displeased with the customer service received. It is very easy to assume everything is fine if customers do not complain. It would be very easy to believe you are doing everything right. Similarly, your organisation might believe its products or services are exactly what customers want. However, they might not be.

If your organisation does not actively seek feedback, it runs the risk of making assumptions on behalf of its customers. The customer might find it very easy to walk away and find what he or she wants elsewhere.

Remember

If you or your organisation does not deliver the right customer service at the right time and at the right price, someone else is waiting to do just that.

Questionnaires

These are a series of questions put to customers (usually on a form or in a letter) that ask about the quality of the service received. The first step in devising a questionnaire is to identify why feedback is required, i.e. which specific area(s) of customer service does your organisation need to know about? With this information, questions can be devised to create a questionnaire that gives valuable feedback on an organisation's customer service.

Questionnaires may have a single focus, or research question, or they may include many issues. For example, an airline might want to know about helpfulness of crew, quality of in-flight meals, cleanliness of aircraft and range of products offered during duty-free service. Alternatively, the airline might want to find out about only the quality of the in-flight meal. It could base its questions on this alone. A customer might be asked to answer questions such as those shown below.

How was your meal?

1 Was the food served at an appropriate temperature?   Yes ☐   No ☐

2 Would you like to have had a vegetarian option?   Yes ☐   No ☐

3 Was your meal served at the appropriate time, bearing in mind the duration of the flight?   Yes ☐   No ☐

4 What else would you like to see in the hygiene bag?

_____

5 Was there anything you would add to the meal?

_____

6 Was there anything you received with your meal you did not require? If so, what and why?

_____

7 Were you provided with enough tea/coffee/fruit juice throughout the flight?   Yes ☐   No ☐

This type of questionnaire would enable the airline to obtain specific feedback. It would then need to analyse the responses and use this information to improve or make changes to how it meets customers' needs and expectations.

Questionnaires can be distributed in various ways, some questionnaires can be handed directly to a customer at the point of service. For example, as in this airline example, a flight crew attendant could hand one out with a meal. Others are left in shops, in hotel rooms or on reception desks – anywhere where they might be picked up by a customer, completed and returned.

Direct mailings

When a questionnaire is posted direct to customers; this is called direct mailing. The number of customers who complete questionnaires that land on the doorstep is usually very small – this is known as a low response rate. To overcome this problem some organisations offer gifts or incentives to people who complete the questionnaires. For example, BT promised to donate money to charity for each returned and completed questionnaire. As a result of the high response rate they received, BT was able to raise more than £1 million for ChildLine.

Answering a recent questionnaire helped BT raise money for ChildLine.

Telephone surveys

These are much the same as a questionnaire approach, except the questions are asked over the telephone. They are not always popular with customers, who may feel they do not have the time or inclination to respond. Such telephone calls tend to be made when the caller knows people are at home, e.g. mealtimes. These are found to be intrusive and time-consuming and often result in telephones being slammed down on the caller.

Focus groups

These are meetings run by an organisation with a specially selected group of customers, often fairly small in numbers. Organisations who choose this method usually have specific questions on an important issue that they want feedback on. For example, if an insurance company is changing its range of pensions, it may run a focus group for a selected section of its customers to seek reactions and feedback. The advantage of a focus group is that an organisation has the opportunity to discuss points raised by customers, which is not possible when using a questionnaire-type approach. Focus groups normally include refreshments and many customers often feel valued or special when invited to attend a focus group.

Street surveys

When you see someone standing on a street with a clipboard under their arm, the chances are they are being employed to obtain feedback from

Can I ask you a few questions?

Street surveys can be an effective way of collecting information

people who might be interested in a range of products or services. This is known as a street survey. Such surveys are often used to seek information about customers' buying habits, rather than to seek feedback on the quality of a service provided.

Mystery shoppers

These are people employed by an organisation to undertake anonymously the role of a customer, i.e. they will pretend to be a real customer. This may be face-to-face or on the telephone. The organisation will tell the mystery shopper exactly what areas to look at and give feedback on. The mystery shopper method is very useful to obtain feedback on customer service practitioners. He or she will be well placed to say exactly what it felt like to be dealt with. They will experience first hand the attitude and behaviour of customer service practitioners. Did they make a good first impression? Did they make the customer feel welcome? Were they able to answer any queries? Did they give a good explanation?

A mystery shopper will also be able to comment on what the working environment was like, e.g. how neat the shop floor was, or whether there were enough clean leaflets on display.

Comments/suggestion boxes

Customers are often invited to give feedback by way of writing their thoughts down on a form and dropping it into a comments or suggestion box. You will see these boxes or collection points in some customer service environments accompanied by a leaflet dispenser

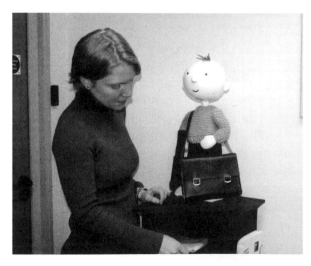

A novelty suggestion box can encourage staff to use it

holding a questionnaire or by posters simply inviting people to put suggestions into the box. Boxes can range from a shoe box placed in a noticeable area, to custom-made collection boxes, or even a response page on your company intranet.

Comments and suggestion boxes are sometimes abused by customers, but sometimes an organisation might receive an exciting suggestion for a new product or service using this method.

Asking you

You, as the customer service practitioner, have a wealth of information about your organisation's customers. After all, you are at the front line dealing with them every day. It would therefore make sense for your organisation to ask you what you think and how you might improve the service given. Any suggestions you make should be based on feedback you have received from customers, not on any assumptions on what you think your customers feel.

Active knowledge

♦ Find out which of the methods outlined above your organisation uses to obtain customer feedback.
♦ What does your organisation expect you to do in relation to using this feedback?
♦ Find out what procedures your company has set in place for you to tell them about customer feedback.

How to find out if you have met your customers' needs and expectations

Having looked at some methods your organisation might use to measure its effectiveness in delivering customer service, we will now turn to look at what you can do to check if the service you give meets your customers' needs and expectations.

Obtaining feedback: what you can do

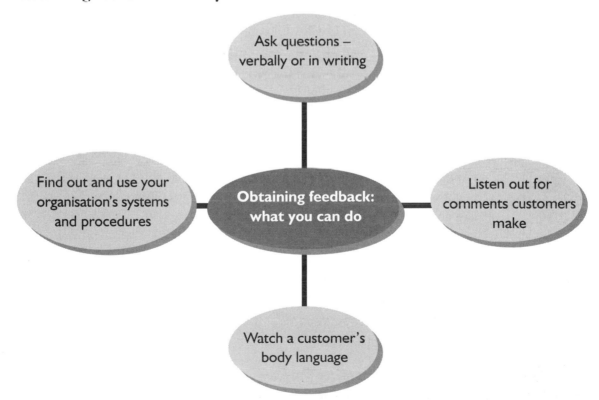

Figure 2.16 Methods you can use to obtain customer feedback

Ask questions

Asking your customers questions is the most direct and effective way of getting feedback on your service. However, you need to be tactful. We are not suggesting you deliberately set out to ask customers blunt questions such as 'Have I done that right?' or 'Did I get the right answers for you?' and most customers would not like to be continually bombarded with questions. Nor should you ask a customer if they like you.

The following are appropriate questions to ask a customer:

♦ Is that OK?
♦ Are you happy with that?
♦ Have I been able to sort this out for you?
♦ Would you like me to change anything?
♦ Is there anything else I can do to help you?
♦ Have I understood you correctly? What you wanted is ...

This last question is more about checking your understanding of what the customer wants or simply clarifying the situation.

Listen

Sometimes you might get to the end of dealing with a customer when you notice he or she is talking to another customer or even to him- or herself. These mumbles might well be a sign that all is not well, especially if you notice a frown too. You should check this out before the customer leaves you by simply asking 'Is everything OK?' If you get the response 'Well actually no it isn't', you can then try to get to the bottom of the problem and sort it out quickly.

This applies just as well on the telephone. You may not be able to see the customer, but you should still be listening carefully for feedback. Things like groans and a change of voice, i.e. a rising voice, will tell you you need to enquire more.

Remember

Feedback should be about listening for the positive news as well as the negative. Be alert to happy customers who want to share what they really like about you and your organisation too.

Check body language

In face-to-face situations you can use your observational skills to give you an indication of whether or not you have met customers' needs or expectations. Watch the customer's body language.

Remember

It is important to consider body language together with what the customer is actually saying.

Find out and use your organisation's systems and procedures

The main system an organisation will have for giving you feedback is an appraisal system or a performance-related reward system. These systems are very important as they will determine how well you are doing against set objectives. This may affect any promotion prospects, your career and your pay.

An appraisal usually covers a 12-month period. During those 12 months you should meet with whoever is your designated line manager on a regular basis in order to obtain feedback on your work. Your line manager is responsible (with you) for agreeing what you are expected to do and what standards you should reach. For instance, achieving your S/NVQ in Customer Service might be a target to reach by the end of an appraisal year.

Other more informal ways of receiving feedback would be from colleagues. A colleague might say to you 'I really like the way you handled that situation'. Follow this through and ask your colleague what exactly it was that he or she liked. You will then be receiving feedback on something that will help you to understand what you do well.

Remember

The feedback you seek should link into your organisation's systems and procedures for obtaining feedback from customers. It is important that you seek guidance as to what is acceptable in your own organisation.

Case study

Nadine is using her questioning technique to try to meet the needs and expectations of Ivan, who is badly in need of some help with his computer. Nadine works on an IT help desk dealing with queries from people who have problems operating their computers. Here is an extract from a telephone conversation between Nadine and Ivan. Ivan has called to seek help in sorting out a problem. He has been told the help desk will deal with any problem, and that the people there are very friendly.

Nadine: IT customer support, how may I help you?
Ivan: Yes, thanks. I'm having trouble with my system.
Nadine: What sort of trouble?
Ivan: Well, I was busy typing and all of a sudden the words vanished.
Nadine: Vanished?
Ivan: Yes, they disappeared from in front of me.
Nadine: Tell me what your screen looks like now.
Ivan: Nothing.
Nadine: Nothing there?
Ivan: Yes. It's blank.

Nadine: Can you see the C:\ prompt on the screen?

Ivan: What's a cprompt?

Nadine: OK. It doesn't matter about that. Try moving the cursor around the screen.

Ivan: I have no cursor. It won't let me type in anything.

Nadine: Is the light on for the power monitor?

Ivan: What's a power monitor?

Nadine: It's the thing with the screen on it. It looks like a TV.

Ivan: Yes. I can see the monitor.

Nadine: Is there a light on it? Possibly a little green one?

Ivan: No. No light.

Nadine: Go to the back of the monitor and check to see if the power cord is firmly in place.

Ivan: There are lots of cables there. Which one is it?

Nadine: Go to the plug in the wall and follow the cables back to the monitor.

Ivan: I can't see where it's plugged in.

Nadine: Why not?

Ivan: It's a bit dark.

Nadine: Pardon? Turn the light on.

Ivan: I can't. We've got a power cut.

Nadine: How come you can talk to me?

Ivan: I'm using my mobile.

Nadine: There's only one solution to this.

Ivan: Good – glad you can help.

Nadine: Go and find the box the computer came in. Put it back in the box and take it back to where you bought it from.

Ivan: Really. Is it that bad?

Nadine: Yes. The problem is terminal. Tell the shop you are too stupid to own a computer and ask for your money back!

In terms of meeting Ivan's expectation that Nadine would get his computer to work again, Nadine used lots of questions to try to get to the heart of the problem.

♦ How good do you think Nadine was at clarifying the situation?
♦ At what stage did she lose patience?
♦ Did she meet Ivan's needs and expectations?
♦ Do you think Ivan laughed at the end?
♦ How would you handle a situation where a customer does not appear to know what he or she wants?

How to identify if you could improve your customer service

The pace of change in business can be very fast, so if you don't watch out, you and your organisation will be left behind and your customers will find new places to go. In order for this not to happen, everyone needs to be alert to the need to continuously improve what they need to do. You can play your part in this, by looking at your own performance and asking yourself 'Is what I do meeting or exceeding the needs of my customers, my organisation and my colleagues? Am I satisfied with my own performance?'

The obvious way of finding out if you need to improve the service you give is to listen to what your customers, colleagues and managers say about your service. You then need to deal with the feedback you receive about your own performance in an appropriate way. This feedback may come to you in a variety of ways. You may receive feedback because you have personally asked for it, or it can sometimes be given to you without a request being made.

To improve the service you give, you must have a clear idea of what skills and knowledge you need in order to do your job effectively. Once you have identified these, you need to decide in which of these areas your strengths and development needs are, i.e. you need to know what you are good at (your strengths) and also where you need to improve (your development needs).

Active knowledge

Before you can act on feedback you need to know what your organisation expects from you in your role.

♦ Find out what skills and knowledge you need to do your job effectively.
♦ Copy the table on page 100. Are any of the skills listed important for your particular job? Add any other skills you need and decide where your strengths and development needs are.

Skills	Yes	No	Strengths	Development needs
Telephone handling				
Communication				
Decision-making				
Flexibility				
Time management				
IT				
Asking for help				
Product knowledge				
Systems knowledge				

Sources of feedback

There are many different ways in which you can receive feedback. Some will be linked into your organisation's systems and procedures. Others will be more informal.

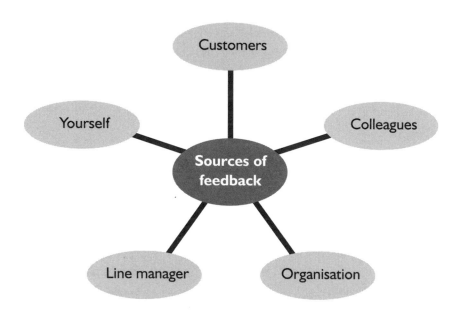

Figure 2.17 Possible sources of feedback

Informal feedback

This occurs when you observe a customer's body language and their behaviour. It also happens when you talk to customers. In other words, it is unplanned and spontaneous. It includes feedback obtained in the following ways:

- from customers or colleagues observing what you do and how you do it
- from colleagues saying things to you in passing (e.g. over lunch)
- from having a chat or a gossip with colleagues
- from yourself thinking back on experiences you have had.

Formal feedback

This type of feedback is much more structured. Everything is planned in advance by you, your organisation or your customer. Formal feedback includes comments received in the following ways:

- verbally, i.e. over the telephone or face-to-face
- in writing, e.g. thank-you letters/emails or letters of complaint
- customer-completed questionnaires/comment forms
- mystery shopper reports
- appraisals/performance reviews.

Remember

You may receive positive and negative feedback. Do not panic if you receive negative feedback, it is still constructive, and you should not be offended – take it as a learning opportunity. It is your chance to improve what you do.

Feedback from customers

This feedback can come in the form of letters of thanks or complaint, or verbally while you interact or over the telephone. Customer feedback will tell you about areas where you might need to improve. You are, after all, in a role where your interaction with customers is one of the most important aspects of your job. This can be difficult, especially if a customer tells you you are not doing well enough and you do not understand why. All feedback is valuable, and you should use it to improve what you do. Equally, positive feedback will tell you what you are doing well and then you can pat yourself on the back.

Feedback from colleagues

Colleague feedback can occur both informally and formally. Formal feedback from colleagues could occur when you attend a training event, e.g. a telephone handling skills course. Alternatively, a colleague might be asked to spend some time with you to observe you at work. On these occasions you could get some valuable feedback on your knowledge, skills and behaviour. Ask your colleagues questions when receiving the feedback. If you are being told you do not have much patience with customers, make sure the person who is giving you feedback tells you about a specific time when this happened. Ask for a description of what you did that showed you were not patient. That way, you will be able to use the feedback more effectively and work on improving what you do.

Informal feedback can take the form of comments made to you over lunch or even overhearing your colleagues gossiping. You might overhear someone talking about you in a negative way to someone else. This may not be very pleasant, but it may tell you a lot about your behaviour or that of your colleague.

Feedback from your organisation

This form of feedback will only be relevant to you as an individual if the systems and procedures in use in your organisation are specific enough to name you as the person the customer dealt with. Often, this is not the case. Organisational feedback will come in the form of customer-completed questionnaires, comment forms or mystery shoppers' reports and tend to be a general view of the overall customer service. Here you would need to review the feedback and accept that all employees had some part to play in that overall view. You need to remember that you are part of a wider team of people to which the feedback relates. It is up to you to take responsibility as a team member for improving the overall performance of the team in which you work.

Case study

Morwenna works shifts in a coffee shop inside a smart department store. Every two months a mystery shopper exercise is carried out and it includes the coffee shop. When the latest report was pinned up on the staff notice board she was delighted to see top marks had again been awarded to the coffee shop for cleanliness and presentation.

Over lunch her best friend Sophie had a little moan about the mystery shopper exercise, saying it was unfair to include the coffee shop as it was bound to get top marks as it was required to be clean under health and safety rules. Morwenna asked her why she was moaning and Sophie told her the cleanliness of the ladies' changing rooms (which she was responsible for) had received poor feedback on the last three reports.

♦ What could Morwenna do to encourage Sophie?
♦ If a customer had a coffee and then used the ladies' changing rooms to try on a new outfit, how might her impression of the department store change?
♦ Why is teamwork important to create the right impression?

Feedback from your line manager, boss or supervisor

Many companies have formal feedback systems in place that are directed at you as an individual. These will form part of your performance and appraisal reviews. Feedback from your line manager can also be less formal, in fact it can even be an off-the-cuff comment made as a result of walking past you in the office and seeing something happen. For example a line manager might see you calming down an angry customer and praise you for the way in which you dealt with the situation.

Active knowledge

Find out if and when your company conducts its performance appraisals.

Feedback from you

One of the most valuable tools you have for improving what you do is the process of being disciplined enough to reflect on what you have done. This is simply a case of thinking about the customer service skills you need to do your job effectively and asking yourself some questions. In other words, you are giving yourself some feedback.

Dealing with feedback

If you are alert and aware you will pick up feedback constantly. Once you have collected all this feedback, what do you do with it? You can reject it, accept it, or reflect on it.

Rejecting feedback

You could reject the feedback. Perhaps you strongly disagree about someone else's version of events or what he or she heard or saw. If you feel a colleague has given you feedback that simply did not recognise the situation you were in, e.g. you were dealing with an angry customer or someone behaving irrationally, you might think the feedback is not based on facts because your colleague wasn't actually experiencing what it was like to be on the receiving end of unpleasant behaviour. So you reject the feedback, but at the same time you should view it as constructive even if you do not agree with it.

When rejecting feedback you do not agree with, never get angry and try not to get too defensive. Stay in control of your emotions.

Accepting feedback

You can accept the feedback. Accepting feedback involves taking the feedback you have been given and using it to establish where you have a need to improve what you do. This means working out ways of developing yourself and improving the service you give. You may need to ask for help or advice on this in order to find out what is available to you. Figure 2.18 shows some possible options you might be able to use.

Figure 2.18 Ways of improving the customer service you give

You should talk through your plans for improving the service you give with an appropriate person. That way you can both reach an agreement as to what you will achieve. This is also known as a personal development programme, which is covered in detail in Unit 6. This concentrates the mind and makes your personal development more structured as you have something to aim for.

Reflecting on feedback

We all need time to think sometimes. When you receive feedback, do not jump to conclusions or make assumptions about what has been said. Try to absorb the comments and think carefully about them later in the day. This is especially important if you have been in a fraught or upsetting situation. Below is a checklist of things you might ask yourself. Imagine you have got to the end of the day. Think back and reflect on the day's events.

For the good times	For the bad times
What happened today that was great?	What went wrong?
Why was it so good?	What have I learned?
How do I know that?	What was the impact on my customer?
How can I make it happen again?	What do I need to do to improve?

Figure 2.19 Reflecting on the day's events

Case study

Here is an example of what Nadine (from the case study on page 97) might have said to herself:

'Today I had a man ring up who wanted some advice on getting his monitor to work. He didn't seem to know anything about computers. I asked lots of questions. I was really patient but he was so thick! In the end, I realised there were lots of other people in the queuing system so I made a joke of it and told him to take it back to the shop. Unfortunately, he didn't like my sense of humour and got through to my boss to complain that I was rude and unhelpful. I have learned to always remain patient and to be very careful with my **sense** of humour. I will only make a joke if I know the other person very well.'

By reflecting back on the days events, Nadine has learned from her mistakes and is more likely to improve her service by doing so.

Active knowledge

Using the template below as a basis, keep a diary for a month where you write up all the feedback you receive and how you dealt with it.

Date	Feedback	Source	How I dealt with it
13 March	Email praising my contribution at team meeting on the new product launch	My line manager	I won't be afraid to speak up during team meetings and will encourage others to do the same. It helped me to research the new product before the meeting so that I knew what I was talking about

Keys to good practice

Improving your own customer service

✓ Find out the specific skills needed to do your job.
✓ Find out what your own strengths and development needs are.
✓ Find ways of obtaining feedback from customers and colleagues.
✓ Use the feedback you are given to improve your service.
✓ Give yourself some feedback by reflecting on your day-to-day work.
✓ Ask questions on how you could improve your service.
✓ Learn from your mistakes.
✓ Seek feedback again on changes you make to what you do.

Remember

Getting and using feedback to improve your customer service is a continual process.

Ways of sharing customer service information with others

As well as obtaining feedback from others about your own personal performance, you are also in a position where you will receive all sorts of comments and information about your organisation as a whole. This could come from customers or suppliers or from colleagues. In the same way that feedback about yourself can be used to improve your job, feedback about your organisation can be used to maintain its standards for service delivery.

It is very important that you are alert to warning signs that may indicate standards are slipping and report them to the appropriate person. This could be anything from extra long queues developing on a certain day of the week, to equipment breakdowns, to information leaflets being in short supply, to dirty premises. In other words, if you spot anything that has the potential to cause standards to slip then you have a responsibility to let an appropriate person know. Remember to make a note of the issue if you are not able to deal with it on the spot. That way you will not forget. Be as specific as you can so that the person who has responsibility for dealing with the issue is armed with the best information.

How to share the information you have

Always remember to be tactful, especially if what you have to say is sensitive. Perhaps you have frequently had customers tell you a colleague seems reluctant to be of assistance. It would not be appropriate to mention this at a team meeting. When should you mention it? You should be very sure of your facts and be able to state why you are saying what you are saying, giving real examples of instances when this has occurred. You can share feedback with others using a number of methods including those shown in Figure 2.20.

Figure 2.20 Methods of sharing feedback with others

Case study

Vikki works for a small mail-order company specialising in clothes for tall women. Being tall herself, she often bought clothes from the catalogue and bought a T-shirt costing £15. The catalogue stated it was washable.

Vikki noticed her T- shirt was losing its shape after a few washes. She had also taken a number of telephone calls from customers complaining of the same thing. She told her supervisor and brought in her own T-shirt to explain. As a result of sharing this information, her supervisor became concerned and realised something had to be done quickly.

Every customer who had ordered the same T-shirt received a letter from the company. It stated a number of customers had complained about the deterioration in the quality of the garment after a few washes. The letter went on to state that the company were dissatisfied with a batch of material used by their suppliers to make the garment. Customers who had received a

T-shirt which was not washing well, were invited to contact the company stating the size and number of T-shirts ordered. A replacement T-shirt would be sent as soon as a new batch was available. Customers were not asked to supply a receipt or proof of purchase, nor were they asked to send the original garment back.

Some customers phoned Vikki, saying they had no problems with the T-shirt but that they were impressed with the offer being made. Vikki was often told 'It only cost £15', i.e. her customers' expectations of the garment lasting a long time were not high. She advised these customers that the offer would remain open in case of problems in the future and made a note of who they were.

A month later, after several more washes, several of these customers said the T-shirts were indeed going out of shape and the material seemed thinner. Vikki confirmed that a replacement would be sent out. She did this and enclosed a personalised letter apologising again for the inconvenience. Washing instructions were included and the letter stated that no further problems had been encountered with the new batch. The company also sent their Spring catalogue and details of their Winter Sale. Vikki was pleased to see several new orders coming through.

♦ Describe how the company used customer feedback to exceed expectations.
♦ Do you think the company went the extra mile? If so, what did they do?
♦ Would you have thought about including a new catalogue with the replacement garment?
♦ How confident should the company be in expecting repeat business? What are the reasons for your answer?

This case study illustrates how one individual working for a mail-order firm had received a number of customer complaints regarding the quality of a T-shirt. She shared this information with her boss, who was then able to rectify the situation to the benefit, not only of those customers who complained, but of others too. Customer expectations were exceeded, standards for service delivery were maintained and there was the bonus of new business too. All in all, a very satisfactory outcome was achieved, and all because one customer service representative had taken the time to notify her boss of a problem.

Test your knowledge

1   Think of five things that you believe would improve the service you give to customers. Include the following in your list:

♦   something to do with your personal skills
♦   something to do with your product or service knowledge
♦   something to do with your working environment
♦   something to do with feedback received directly from customers
♦   something to do with your organisation's systems and procedures.

2   What do you need to do to take action on each of your points?

Check your knowledge

1   Name the three steps associated with customer service delivery.

2   Name the three most important pieces of legislation which impact upon your role.

3   How do they affect what you do?

4   From where might you be able to obtain feedback about your own customer service performance?

5   How can you tell if you have met a customer's needs or expectations?

6   What should you do if a customer's needs or expectations change?

7   What methods does your organisation use to obtain feedback from customers?

8   What should you do to ensure you are ready to deal with customers at the start of each working day?

9   How can you ensure you keep your commitments to customers?

10 List five reasons why customers might change their minds.

11 What do you need to do when you are personally unable to help a customer?

12 How does your organisation set about checking its service delivery?

13 What can you do to keep your product or service knowledge up to date?

14 What areas might you include in a checklist which helps you to maintain a tidy and safe working area?

15 Define reliable customer service.

UNIT 3

Develop customer relationships

As we have seen from Units 1 and 2, creating a positive impression is the first vital step in building customer relationships, and delivering consistent, reliable customer service is the second vital step. Developing your customer relationships ensures your customers want to continue to do business with you and your organisation. You will need to build their confidence, making them aware of the nature of the products or services you deal with and finding out about their expectations of you and your organisation.

Developing customer relationships is also known as building customer loyalty. This means building a lasting business relationship between the customer and your organisation. Customer loyalty means having customers who **want** to do business with you and your organisation because they trust you to deliver a reliable and appropriate service in a manner that suits individual needs and expectations. Having loyal customers is very important; not only for repeat business but also because if things do go wrong, a loyal customer is likely to trust you to put it right.

There is also a feel-good factor in having loyal customers. It is fantastic for any customer service practitioner to have customers who ask for him or her by name because of the service provided. Sometimes this is not possible, people working in call centres are unlikely to be asked for by name as they are one of many people in a team.

For your S/NVQ level 2 you will need to show that you can build customer relationships on your own as well as with the help of others, e.g. in your team or with other colleagues.

The elements for this unit are:

♦ 3.1 Build customer confidence in the level of service provided
♦ 3.2 Meet the ongoing needs and expectations of your customers
♦ 3.3 Develop the relationship between your customers and your organisation.

3.1 Build customer confidence in the level of service provided

- ◆ What helps your customers have confidence in you and your organisation.
- ◆ How your behaviour affects the behaviour of your customer.
- ◆ What you can do to maintain the commitments made by your organisation.

What helps your customers have confidence in you and your organisation

We have already discussed the various ways you can deal with customers, and the values that you and your organisation should uphold in Units 1 and 2. To recap, these include the following:

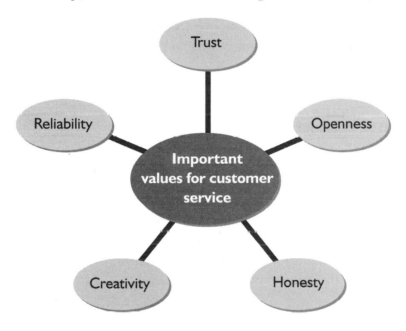

Figure 3.1 Important values for customer service

Practising these values throughout your dealings with customers, from the first meeting to the time you have solved any queries, will help instil confidence in your customers. This will in turn ensure that they become repeat customers of your organisation.

Remember

Customers are more sophisticated today than they have ever been. They want value for money and need to be reassured that their decision to deal with you and your organisation is the right one. They also know that it is relatively easy to find what they want from another organisation.

Customers will be confident in you when:

♦ you show you are trustworthy
♦ you make life easier for them
♦ you deal with them in an appropriate manner
♦ you get it right first time.

Customers will be confident in your organisation when:

♦ products or services meet or exceed needs and expectations
♦ systems and processes help, not hinder
♦ your organisation listens.

All this does not happen overnight. Confidence is built by a gradual process of customers seeing that service is consistently given to the level (or greater) that they expect.

Remember

Without customer confidence, customer loyalty will not be built. Without customer loyalty, there will eventually be no customers.

How to instil confidence

Instilling confidence is easy, it includes the following:

♦ keep up to date with what is new, regarding your organisation and its products or services
♦ keep any promises you make

Repeat service users are a sure sign that you are doing a good job

- keep your customers informed
- watch your body language: eye contact is important in making a customer feel valued
- watch what you say and how you say it
- look for opportunities to seek feedback.

Rapport

All the steps above are known as developing a rapport with your customer. Establishing a rapport starts when you simply 'get off on the right foot' with a customer. Sometimes there is a mutual respect for one another (the customer likes you/you like him or her). This might occur instantly without either of you having to do anything in particular to make it happen. For some reason your customer senses you can be trusted to deliver great customer service. This might be because you display the same values he or she holds, and your customer knows this from your behaviour and from your actions.

On other occasions you will need to work hard at building rapport. The obvious occasion when you need to do this is when a customer has a complaint. In order for customers to maintain confidence in you and your organisation, you must ensure the rapport you work hard to build is sustained every time you deal with the customer.

Bad habits to avoid

As you can see it is very easy to build rapport and instil confidence in your customers. It is also just as easy to lose customers.

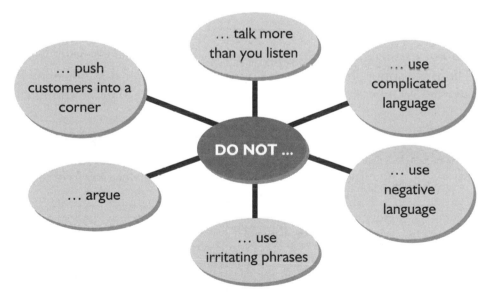

Figure 3.2 Bad habits to avoid in order to build rapport

Do not talk more than you listen

You may feel very confident that you know exactly what a customer needs and what you can do for that particular customer. This might lead to you doing the talking instead of the customer. The customer could feel that you are not listening to what they want. Here rapport is not sustained because assumptions have been made without effective questioning having taken place to ascertain the customer's needs and expectations.

Do not use complicated language

Jargon is guaranteed to confuse a customer who will go elsewhere if you confuse him or her with technical language. For example 'What you need is our latest edition. The 2WD version has a powerful 2.0 litre VVT-I engine, ABS, EBD, and a brilliant power-to-weight ratio. All guaranteed to give you a smooth drive'.

Do not use negative language

You will build confidence in the service you provide if you point out the things that you can do rather that those that you cannot. Think back to the seven service sins (on page 19); sin 6 talked about lack of knowledge. You might fall into the trap of saying you cannot do something simply because your product or service knowledge is not up to date. For example, the nurse who tells a mother she cannot stay with her young child because there is no family room available but does not offer to help with alternative accommodation nearby; or the refuse carrier who says he cannot take garden refuse but does not explain what the householder needs to do in order to get it taken away.

Remember

You need to be realistic about what you can do. There is no point in telling a customer that you can cut their hair to look just like Jennifer Aniston if they have the wrong type of hair.

Do not use irritating phrases

There are some phrases that annoy people no matter how sincerely they are said. Often irritating phrases can be interpreted to mean the exact opposite of what you have said.

Customer service practitioner says	Customer thinks	What you could say instead ...
I hear what you say	You haven't been listening to a word I have said	I understand what you have said
With respect, I think you mean ...	How dare you assume what I mean! I've just said ...	May I just check my understanding?
I really am doing everything I can	You're not trying hard enough	Everything is being done to help you; let me tell you what I have done
Let's be realistic, you are never going to find that	I will find it, but elsewhere as you don't want to help	Let's just check out whether this will be possible
I might be able to get that for you	You are fobbing me off	I wouldn't want to promise I can get that for you without checking first. Won't be a minute
What you really mean is ...	I know what I want!	Let me make sure I understand what you want

Customer service practitioner says	Customer thinks	What you could say instead ...
What you haven't taken into account is ...	You are making excuses	May I just explain what else ...
You don't need that! What you want is ...	Don't you tell me what I need!	Before you decide, let me tell you about ...

Figure 3.3 How phrases can be misinterpreted

Do not argue

No matter what the circumstances, if you get into an argument with a customer you are in a no-win situation and confidence in you and your organisation will be lost immediately. In Element 3.2 we look at how behaving assertively is the correct approach to take at times when there are disagreements.

Do not push customers into a corner

If you are so sure of your approach and what the customer needs, you might be tempted to push a customer into a situation that does not really meet his or her needs. Sometimes the harder you push, the harder a customer will resist. Your efforts to make sure the customer gets the most suitable product or service are lost because the customer may feel you are trying too hard. In the end, the customer walks away not at all confident about you or your organisation.

On other occasions, a customer may end up buying a product or service he or she later finds out is unsuitable. This is not a good way to build confidence.

Be careful not to 'bully' a customer into buying your product

Keys to good practice

Helping customers have confidence in you and your organisation

✓ Acknowledge customers as soon as possible.
✓ Be friendly and welcoming.
✓ Show the customer you are really listening.
✓ Create a good first impression and sustain it.
✓ Keep your promises.
✓ Do things on time.
✓ Give accurate information.
✓ Know about your organisation's products and/or services.
✓ Know where to seek assistance if you are unable to help.

Active knowledge

1 Review the keys to good practice above and add any points you feel will also help build confidence.

2 Now pick a colleague whom you respect in terms of their ability to instil confidence in you, your colleagues and customers.

  ◆ Think about how he or she behaves in order to meet the keys to good practice.
  ◆ What can you learn from the behaviour of your colleague?

3 Now think about a retail outlet or any other customer service operation where you have no hesitation in going in order to make a purchase or take up a service.

  ◆ What are your reasons for selecting this organisation?
  ◆ How will you use your findings to develop your own performance?

How your behaviour affects the behaviour of your customer

It is important that as you progress through your Level 2 S/NVQ you develop an awareness of how what you do and the way that you do it have an impact on your ability to perform effectively. In other words your behaviour is directly related to your effectiveness.

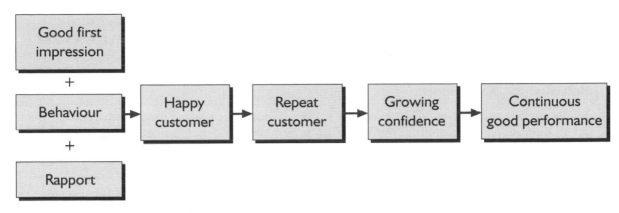

Figure 3.4 *Maintaining a happy customer*

Your behaviour

Your behaviour towards a customer is about sustaining and building confidence. You may not have realised it but behaviour is a choice. Even if something has happened to make you feel sad or angry, you do have the choice to approach a customer with either a negative style or a positive style. This might mean making an extra special effort on your part to smile and be friendly. It will pay off as smiling is contagious; it will help to instil confidence in your customer (and probably help lighten your mood too). If you choose to be a little down in the mouth you will get the same back from your customers.

How was it for you?

Think about the last time you dealt with an unhappy customer. How did you react? What happened to your behaviour when you dealt with your next customers?

When dealing with your customers your behaviour should be:

♦ **Professional:** do not allow any negative personal feelings to affect your performance.
♦ **Understanding:** your customers need you to help them. They will return to you and your organisation if you show them you fully understand their needs and expectations.
♦ **Patient:** you may have already been asked the same question over and over again. However, it is the first time for your customer. Treat him or her as an individual and give the respect he or she deserves.

Whatever happens today I need to look like this

Being professional, understanding and patient takes practice

Your behaviour will have a direct impact upon the behaviour of your customers. The table below suggests some behaviours you need to be aware of and how they might affect your customer.

Behaviour	Impact
Bodily contact and physical position	Notice the effects of: shaking hands v not shaking hands with your customer; moving closer to someone to discuss something; standing up while your customer is sitting down; facing the customer v sitting next to your customer
Facial expressions	Notice the effect of: eye contact v no eye contact; movements of eyes, eyebrows, mouth; frowning v smiling
Gestures	Notice the effects of: head nod/shakes; wagging foot/fidgety legs; crossed arms v open arms; hand movements such as pointing, clenching, holding
Voice	Notice the effects of: loudness v softness; pitch – high v low; speed – fast v slow; silences; interruptions; hesitations
Clothes and physical appearance	Notice the effects of: smartness v untidiness; attracting attention through what you wear v blending into the background; smartness v casual; cleanliness v scruffy

Figure 3.5 Significant behaviours that impact upon customer service

Your attitude

Choosing the right behaviour also involves choosing the right attitude. The right attitude shows you are a customer service professional.

♦ Having the right attitude will enable you to to choose the right behaviour in the first place. Having the wrong attitude might lead you to pass a customer on to somebody else because you do not want to help.

♦ Having the right attitude will mean you want to help whatever the situation. Having the wrong attitude will mean you want to help only if you like the customer.

♦ Having the right attitude will mean you want to help however close it might be to the end of your working day. Having the wrong attitude will mean you hurry a customer up or avoid them completely.

♦ Having the right attitude will mean you leaving your personal problems at home (however difficult that might be).

You should take responsibility for helping the customer even when he or she is annoying you or is proving difficult in some way. Only pass the customer on if you are genuinely unable to help, or if the scope of what he or she needs is outside your responsibility. If a customer is a little awkward to deal with, you might decide to push him or her onto a colleague. With the right attitude, instead of seeing this customer as irritating, you will listen to what they have to say. They could bring your attention to something amiss in the organisation. Be grateful that this customer has taken the time to complain; most don't. Often customers will say everything is fine (when it is not) and take their business somewhere else.

Remember

Customers may not always be right but every customer deserves to be treated fairly and with respect.

Courtesy and its impact in relationship building

Using courtesy is a key factor in building confidence in the level of service you and your organisation provide.

Figure 3.6 Using courtesy in building confidence

Being courteous is about combining the right attitude, behaviour and words. Courtesy is a means of showing you care, that you recognise customers' needs and expectations and that you appreciate them doing business with you and your organisation.

Often the only difference between your organisation and its competitors is the people it employs. Do not look on being courteous as something extra you need to do. It is the hallmark of a customer service professional and as such an essential part of your job. You provide the distinctive edge that might make the difference between customers using your organisation or going elsewhere. For example, at one market stall a customer might be met with a long queue only to find a hostile assistant who is interested only in getting off to lunch. At the stall across the road,

In the long-term, courtesy could equal more sales

the same customer could easily find a customer service professional who acknowledges the wait the customer has had, by saying 'I'm very sorry about the wait you have had. Now, what can I do for you?' before going on to explore the customer's needs and expectations. This makes all the difference and makes the wait worthwhile.

Courteous behaviour is contagious. When you are treating a customer in a friendly and polite manner they will behave similarly. Even when a customer appears to be ready for a fight, if you show sincere courtesy and a desire to help then the customer will respond to you and become more reasonable to deal with.

How was it for you?

What happened when you last kept your cool when dealing with a customer who was about to rage at you?

Did the customer calm down? If so, what were you doing that helped your customer become less agitated?

A word of warning!

False courtesy is easily spotted and will make for poor customer service. When you say 'Thank you' you really do need to mean it. If you use the right words with the wrong attitude the customer will not trust you. For instance, saying 'It's nice talking to you' without giving eye contact will not have the right impact. Similarly, saying 'Thanks for calling' and very quickly cutting the customer off will not make him or her feel very welcome.

Keys to good practice

Courteous behaviour

✓ Show you want to help and that the customer is not interrupting you.
✓ Keep your workspace clean, tidy and prepared for your role.
✓ Show you remember regular customers.
✓ Acknowledge customers immediately.

✓ Say please and thank you appropriately.
✓ Volunteer to help others when you can.
✓ Give eye contact.
✓ Do not shout or talk to customers from too far away.
✓ Keep customers informed.

Case study

Ellen works in the customer service quality control department of a chain of hotels. They have recently taken over a smaller group of hotels that Ellen is reviewing. She has been visiting the hotels and has written a report about the standard of service she witnessed. Here is an extract taken from her report of unacceptable phrases she heard that she thought were rude and discourteous.

To a conference organiser complaining a room was not ready: 'You can't see the Duty Manager right now. Come back in half an hour'.

To a customer trying to check in: 'You booked over the Internet and got it wrong. The dates I have down are 25 June not 25 July'.

To a customer checking in with heavy baggage: 'Would you like some help taking your baggage to your room?'

To a customer trying to check out: 'Can you wait please? I am just serving this gentleman'.

To a vegan customer: 'The chef is unable to change the menu'.

To a customer checking in very late at night: 'It's really late. The restaurant is shut. Can I order you something now from room service?'

To a customer asking for a taxi: 'You can use the telephone over there to call a taxi'.

To a customer requesting a feedback form: 'We don't have any customer service feedback forms left'.

Look at each of the scenarios in turn, and answer the following questions:

♦ How helpful was the hotel employee?
♦ In terms of courtesy, how would you improve what the employee said?
♦ How likely is it that a lasting rapport has been built between the customer service practitioner and the customer?

What you can do to maintain the commitments made by your organisation

How much do you know about your organisation? Do you know its history and reputation? Do you know the part you and your colleagues play in the wider organisation? What are its aims and objectives? Policy makers within organisations make commitments to customers based on what they see as their vision for the future success of their organisation. At a high level, these commitments might be about reaching out to a larger section of the community. For example, a television company might commit to produce more TV programmes for ethnic minorities, or a hotel might commit to upgrade its leisure facilities.

At an operational level, commitments tend to concentrate more on what the customer can expect by way of standards of service. This type of commitment tends to relate to things such as delivery times, product quality, standards of cleanliness or simply just promises made in the process of delivering customer service.

There are many ways in which an organisation creates and distributes information on its commitments, as shown in the figure below.

Figure 3.7 Ways in which an organisation creates and distributes information on its commitments

Active knowledge

Knowing about the commitments your organisation makes to customers will mean you know what you need to do to help it maintain them. If you have this understanding, you will be more fully prepared to carry out your roles and responsibilities more effectively.

♦ Find out about your own organisation's commitments in areas that are relevant to your role.

Annual Reports

These describe the progress an organisation has made and the key activities it has undertaken over the past year. Included within an Annual Report will be details of the organisation's financial position and also details of its directors.

Customer charters

These documents set out to explain to customers what an organisation aims to do in order to meet customer expectations, how it will meet or beat targets, how it will provide information to customers, how it will give equal access to services and how customers can complain.

Mission statements

These are statements put together by an organisation to demonstrate what it stands for. A mission statement should set out the importance of quality service and the organisation's basic commitments. You will find

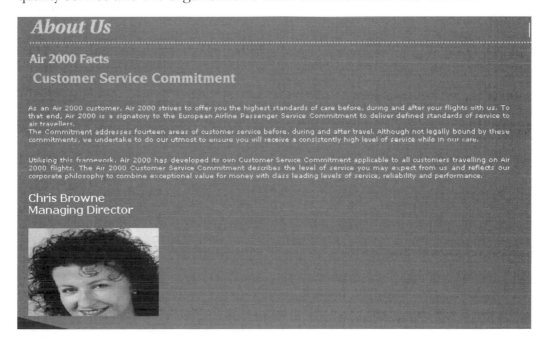

Air 2000's mission statement focuses on customer care

mission statements in all sorts of places, from promotional literature to framed notices on the walls of offices and shops.

Typically a mission statement will include the following:

♦ the purpose of the organisation
♦ the mission of the organisation
♦ a statement outlining its commitment to its customers
♦ what the organisation's values are (often in relation to both customers and employees).

Not all organisations will have a mission statement. Indeed, many people look on them as hollow words written by individuals far removed from dealing personally with customers, i.e. people who do not see what life is like in reality. Whatever your view of mission statements, do remember they are in the public eye and therefore customers will hold *you* accountable for fulfilling them.

Did you know?

Part of The Walt Disney Company's mission statement is: 'To make people happy'.

Active knowledge

1 Seek out information on your organisation's mission statement (if appropriate to your organisation).

♦ What commitments is your organisation making to its customers?
♦ Does what it sets out to do match what you believe is happening?

2 Find out if any specific commitments to customers have been made by your team and/or the department in which you work.

Advertisements

A further example of where commitments are made is through the written word on promotional literature or other advertisements. If a leaflet says you will deliver a product within seven days, then your customers will expect just that. The promises made by your organisation are only going to be met if you and your colleagues play your part in fulfilling them.

Test your knowledge

Your organisation is likely to make some form of commitment to customers through the media and advertising, by way of a mission statement or simply through posting a notice in a shop window.

Similarly, commitments might be made at department or team level.

♦ When you read (or hear about) these commitments, what does it make you feel about your organisation's/team's ability to fulfil them?

♦ What part do you play in fulfilling these commitments?

3.2 Meet the ongoing needs and expectations of your customers

WHAT YOU NEED TO KNOW OR LEARN

♦ What the limits of your authority are within your organisation and how they influence your ability to meet your customers' needs and expectations.

♦ How to recognise when there may be a conflict between the needs of your customers and what you can provide.

♦ How to behave assertively.

♦ How to work with others to resolve difficulties in balancing the needs of your customers and your organisation.

What the limits of your authority are within your organisation and how they influence your ability to meet your customers' needs and expectations

You will need to be skilled at performing a balancing act between the needs of customers and the needs of your organisation. We will look at how you can do this and also why it might not always be possible, or appropriate, to do everything the customer wants you to do.

Working in a service organisation means you and your colleagues will have responsibility for ensuring customer service is delivered to a high standard. The standard is determined by your organisation and is often set out in the mission statement or customer charter.

Directors

↓

Executives

↓

Managers/Line managers

↓

Supervisors

↓

Team leaders

↓

Team members

Figure 3.8 Levels of authority in most organisations

There will probably be various levels of authority within your organisation, depending on a person's position within the organisation. All these individuals are likely to have different amounts of power in terms of what they are able to do and what decisions they can take without referring to others. Alternatively, you may work for an organisation where there are no formal job titles but where named individuals have different levels of authority.

It is important for you to know the following:

♦ the scope of your personal authority, that is how much you can do or what you are able to decide on your own
♦ who you need to speak to when you need to get a decision from someone in higher authority
♦ your organisation's policies and procedures.

Active knowledge

Copy the table below and ask yourself the various questions. If you have answered 'No' to any of the questions, find out who does have the authority and fill their names in.

Do I have the authority to ...	YES	NO	WHO
give refunds?			
send goodwill gifts?			
change my working hours?			
take longer for lunch?			
carry out repairs to equipment?			
give discounts?			
switch voicemail/answer phone on?			
shut down early to do other work?			
write to customers?			
telephone customers?			
email customers?			
discuss products or services I am not responsible for?			

Why is it important to know the scope of your authority?

There are many implications associated with ensuring you act within the limits of your own authority. There are cost and legal implications for your organisation, but there are also implications for you. If you do things you are not authorised to do, you will have to constantly explain your actions and your performance will be called into question.

Read the following scenarios that describe various situations a customer service practitioner might need to deal with. Some thoughts he or she should consider before acting, together with some suggestions as to what he or she could find out about are provided. Relate each of the scenarios to your own role – would you have known what to do?

Mrs Baldock asks for a discount on a new TV. She says she is going to buy one off the Internet if the price is not matched or bettered to the price she has seen on the Internet.

'The business might go elsewhere. I don't want to lose the business. If I give a discount am I setting a precedent? I don't know the prices on the Internet – they may not be cheaper. What exactly is my organisation's discount policy?'

Finding out about your organisation's policy on giving discounts will enable you to be prepared for this sort of question. There might also be some literature/research available to you on your competitors' prices.

Mrs Fairley enquires about a coach trip around Scotland. The call centre agent tries to help, although she specialises in cruises.

'There's no-one else to take this call so I'll find the information on the screen and talk to her. I would rather do that than get someone else to call her back.'

Sometimes it might be better to take the details of the query and forward it on to a more appropriate person. If you get involved in a conversation that does not relate to your role you may be tempted to help so much that you end up unwittingly giving out inaccurate information. Knowing what your organisation expects of you when dealing with queries that concern issues outside of your role and responsibilities is vital. This includes knowing where to seek help when you cannot deal with the customer.

A credit control officer has an internal customer who is visiting from the human resources department. The officer puts voicemail on to stop the telephone ringing.

'Using voicemail enables me to devote all my time to my colleague from human resources. However, other customers might complain they cannot get through to me.'

Overuse of voicemail is unpopular with many people, who complain that they can never get through to speak to a real person. Knowing your organisation's policy will enable you to use voicemail or any other similar system appropriately.

An estate agent sends a bunch of flowers to a couple who have just bought their first house. The purchase has been long-winded.

'This is the first house for this couple. I am sending a bunch of flowers to the house on the day after they move in to thank them for their business. I have the authority to spend up to £25 on gifts to customers where our level of service has fallen down.'

Knowing your organisation's policy on goodwill gifts will help you to build relationships. These customers might spread the word among friends and family.

Mrs Jones doesn't like the colour of the sweater she has been given as a present and takes it back to the shop assistant and asks for it to be exchanged.

'I will swap the sweater for another colour. It is still labelled, the customer has a receipt (although I don't need it) and I know about our exchange and refund policy for garments that are returned unworn.'

You must know about the relevant legislation that affects your role as well as any organisational policies. In this scenario, under the Sale of Goods Act 1979, Mrs Jones had no automatic right to exchange the sweater as it was fit for purpose. However, this organisation had a goodwill policy and so made the exchange.

How to recognise when there may be a conflict between the needs of your customers and what you can provide

We all have expectations of what particular service providers can do for us. These can be either positive or negative expectations based upon a perception of what an individual service provider is like. A perception is having a picture in your mind of what to expect from individuals that work for the organisation and the organisation itself.

Figure 3.9 How perceptions of what service providers can do are formed

Case study

Catherine has been troubled by the fact that her front garden is looking shabby and uncared for. Not having the time to tend to it herself, she spots an advert in the local paper saying 'No job too big, or too small. Qualified gardeners with over 25 years' experience'. Alongside the advert are photographs of gardens the firm have transformed.

Discussing it with her mother, she realises the same firm have been working for her mum over the years. Pleased with what her mum's garden looks like, she telephones them and asks for a quote.

♦ What helped Catherine decide this was the firm to use?
♦ What influence did her mum have?
♦ At what stage do you think Catherine would be influenced by cost?

How was it for you?

Pick a couple of organisations you do business with.

♦ Think about why you do business with them.
♦ What (if any) advertising do they do?
♦ How does this advertising affect what you expect from the organisation and its employees?
♦ What do you think about the service you receive from the organisation when your expectations are not met?

Positive expectations

Organisations that are known for the quality of their service generate a perception that is positive. Customers expect things will be done right first time and they will get value for money simply because of that particular organisation's reputation. The organisation is easy to do business with. Part of this positive perception may be built on an organisation's advertising. Is it portraying a young, fresh image or a traditional image? Does it promise to do things through its advertising and do customers trust these promises?

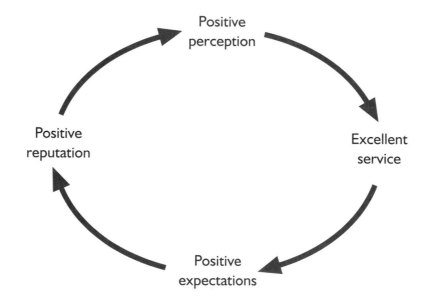

Figure 3.10 The cycle of positive expectations

It is important that a company maintains positive customer expectations. One small blip in service and the reputation will be damaged. If the expectation is not met, disappointment, anger and frustration might set in.

Working for an organisation that has a positive reputation is immensely satisfying as well as challenging. Customers have high expectations of

Figure 3 11 Examples of positive expectations

you and your organisation and you should feel proud to be part of that and proud that customers come back to you with their business time and time again.

Negative expectations

Unfortunately, some organisations will be in situations where their reputation over the years had been so poor that customers expect virtually nothing from them by way of good service. This can mean that, even when there are signs of improvement, these go unnoticed because customers' minds are always fixed on the fact that certain organisations are simply a pain to deal with.

However, people can make a difference. You can show, by your behaviour and your actions, that things can change for the better. If every customer service practitioner had this attitude, the pace of change would accelerate and you could help make customers sit up and notice the difference. Imagine someone standing on a railway platform or waiting for a bus. Although many people expect trains or buses to be late, they may still be disappointed, and probably a little angry too, if they hear the announcement: 'May I have your attention please. The 7.53 to Victoria is running 30 minutes late due to a trackside fire in the Haywards Heath area'. The customer will understandably be disappointed and possibly angry. The customer set his or her expectations to the timetable information. Now expectations have changed, the customer will now expect the train to arrive at 8.23. If it does not, he or she will feel even worse about the train service.

Sometimes a change of plan will occur for reasons outside your control, as in the case of the trackside fire. At these times, remember to keep customers informed of progress and of the reasons why expectations have not been met. For example, in the railway situation, if the announcer gave constant updates on the fire, perhaps saying that no one is hurt and where the train is, this would help to encourage people on the platform that all is being done to keep them in the picture about when they might be able to board the train. If a delay becomes extended, some train operators might offer free drinks/snacks from the buffet as a gesture of goodwill in recognition of the inconvenience caused.

Active knowledge

Think back to a time when a customer expressed dissatisfaction to you that his or her expectations had not been met.

♦ Why did this happen?
♦ What could you have done differently to ensure the customer received a full explanation?
♦ What (if anything) could your organisation do differently to ensure customer expectations are met?

Did you know?

Researchers at Walt Disney World and Disneyland found out how long on average it took to wait for a ride, and then added 10–15 minutes to the expected waiting time shown as customers wait in a queue. This way, customers expecting to wait for an hour will be pleasantly surprised when they get to the front of the queue 15 minutes early.

Potential conflict and expectations

A conflict might occur when a customer's expectations are not met. Positive expectations born out of an excellent reputation mean that high service standards must consistently be met. Negative expectations are simply confirmed when poor service is received. Both positive and negative expectations are therefore sources of potential conflict.

There are many reasons why expectations may not be met, such as the following:

♦ a commitment not being kept, e.g. a cancelled appointment or broken delivery times
♦ cost implications, e.g. insufficient staff to handle the volume of calls in a call centre, shabby premises not refurbished, unwillingness to travel a long distance to meet a customer
♦ advertising not matching reality, e.g. expensive products not being of high quality

- a genuine misunderstanding, e.g. human error, lack of information
- expectations not being fully explored, e.g. customer needs not clarified, assumptions made by customer service practitioner
- inaccurate information, e.g. out-of-date literature, lack of product or service knowledge
- legal implications, e.g. lack of awareness on the part of the customer and/or the organisation of how legislation affects what can and cannot be done, e.g. the need to respect confidentiality under the Data Protection Act 1998
- poor communication between customers, you, and your colleagues/suppliers.

Not all customers will react in the same way, and not all will get angry. However you need to recognise a potential conflict and deal with it effectively as it arises.

Active knowledge

- What other reasons can you think about for expectations not being met?
- Make a list of the situations where customer expectations are not met that occur regularly in your line of work. Discuss with an appropriate person what can be done.
- Are there any situations where you can make an exception to the service you would normally offer?

Case study

Michael, a salesman, booked himself into a hotel for a three-night stay to enable him to visit prospective new customers. Wanting a good night's sleep and some superior service, he paid extra money for what he thought was a five-star room.

To his horror, he found on arrival that he had lost the key to his suitcase. This was not the first time he had done this, and his business partner was always telling him he would land himself in deep trouble one day. However, he expected to get some help from the hotel staff; after all, wasn't that why he had paid for a five-star room?

Somewhat embarrassed by his predicament, Michael went to reception and asked the receptionist, Hugh, for help.

Michael: Can you help me, please? I seem to have lost the key to my case.
Hugh: Can't help you there, sir. You'll have to slit the case open and buy another.
Michael: Surely not. Don't you have any spare keys? It's only a standard padlock.
Hugh: No we don't, sir. I can give you a knife from the kitchen.

Michael: I won't be needing a knife. Don't you have any imagination? Can't you even tell me where there's a locksmith?

Hugh: I haven't a clue. I don't live here.

Michael: Well really! You're not exactly putting yourself out to help me. I've paid £165 a night for that room. As far as I'm concerned that entitles me to you going the extra mile to help me.

Michael stormed off, leaving Hugh to wonder why his customer felt that paying for an expensive hotel room entitled him to ask the hotel for help with a lost suitcase key.

Why did Michael expect this kind of help?

Was this an opportunity for Hugh to show how good the hotel was at providing good customer service?

If so, what might Hugh have done to meet or exceed Michael's expectations?

Does the amount of money a customer spends make any difference to the level of service he or she might expect?

Remember

Knowing what you have authority to do to help a customer is the first step in resolving any potential conflict.

Gone are the days when a customer got absolutely everything he or she demanded. If this happened, organisations would soon go out of business. This does not mean that you and your organisation should not respond to a customer's needs and wants. You should listen carefully to customers' needs and demands, however unrealistic they might be. Feedback these needs to an appropriate person in order for any trends in customer wants to be dealt with. Remember, your competitors are waiting to take your customers from you.

There is potential for conflict when customer expectations and an organisation's products and services are not balanced. For instance, a customer might expect a shop selling fruit and vegetables to stock organic fruit and vegetables. If the shopkeeper is unable to attract enough customers to buy organic, then he or she will not stock an organic range. Similarly, a customer entering a hospital for day surgery might not expect to be put into a mixed ward. However, the hospital might only be able to offer screens to separate men from women on a day ward.

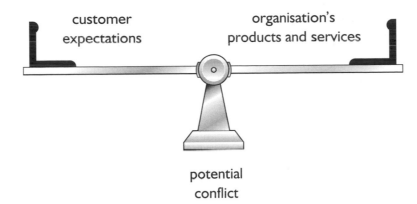

To avoid conflict you must balance customer expectations against what you can offer

How to behave assertively

Keeping the balance between expectations and what organisations can offer is very difficult, particularly as different customers have different expectations and different ways of reacting. However, there are ways of minimising the disappointment and dissatisfaction some customers might feel when their needs or expectations are not met. These involve you behaving assertively and professionally in order to deal with a difficult situation and to stop the situation from getting worse.

I can see how this situation may be upsetting, sir. If you could take a seat and fill in our complaints form we will help you as soon as we can!

Assertive behaviour will help calm an irate customer

When under pressure, humans will literally heat up: faces will turn red, collars will feel tight, the temperature rises until boiling point is reached and an explosion occurs. Being assertive means turning the heat down; not just your temperature but your customer's temperature too. You can do this by learning how to be assertive.

Assertive behaviour

Some people confuse assertiveness with aggression. Behaving assertively is not about being forceful, shouting at customers or doing absolutely anything to get your way. To behave in an assertive way you need to do the following:

◆ remain calm
◆ listen
◆ demonstrate that you understand
◆ consider the consequences for all parties of getting what you want/need
◆ ask for what you want/need without offending others.

How do you react in difficult situations?

Do you fight back by attacking?	Do you give in and submit to demands?	Do you stand up for yourself and your rights without giving offence?
AGGRESSIVE behaviour	SUBMISSIVE behaviour	ASSERTIVE behaviour

Assertive behaviour is about standing up for your rights without violating the rights of your customer. The table below illustrates how assertive behaviour differs from aggressive or submissive behaviour.

Assertive behaviour	Aggressive behaviour	Submissive behaviour
Discuss calmly	Use threats	Be humble and apologetic
Listen	Interrupt	Say nothing
Make brief statements	Use 'I' a lot	Ramble and waffle
Ask open questions to seek information	Ignore what the customer wants	Simply accept what the customer wants
Stand up for your rights while respecting the customer's rights	Stand up for your rights but violate the customer's rights	Give in and don't stand up for your rights
State your views	Demand acceptance of your views	Fail to state your views
Show you understand the customer's views	Show you are not interested in the customer's views	Show an interest in your customer's views but hide your own
No blame; seek right solution	Blame others	Blame yourself

Figure 3.12 How assertive behaviour differs from aggressive or submissive behaviour

As we have seen, behaviour is expressed in various ways through your voice, body language, use of eye contact and the way that you express yourself. The table below shows how an individual might change their expressions when they are being assertive, aggressive or submissive.

	Assertive behaviour	Aggressive behaviour	Submissive behaviour
VOICE	Sincere, steady pace, calm	Harsh, loud, shouting	Quiet, flat, dull,
SPEECH	Fluent, emphasise key words or points	Fluent, abrupt, interrupting, emphasises blame, sarcasm	Hesitant, struggles to find right words
EYE CONTACT	Steady	Stares	Shifting or little direct contact
FACIAL EXPRESSION	Open, steady, genuine smile	Rigid, chin out, scowling, eyebrows raised in disbelief, frowning, no smiles or false smile	False smile
OTHER BODY LANGUAGE	Head up, hands open	Moving around unnecessarily, thumping fists, pointing fingers	Head down, hands fiddling with things

Figure 3.13 Using voice and body language in an assertive, aggressive or submissive manner

Case study

Paul works for a posh hotel in the heart of London. He parks cars in the hotel's underground car park, saving customers the trouble of doing so. He then arranges for any luggage to be taken straight to the customers' rooms. One night a customer drove up at speed, got out of his car clearly agitated and said he was very late for an appointment. Taking one look at Paul the customer said he couldn't possibly allow Paul to park the car; he felt Paul looked far too young to drive and could not be trusted with his valued and very expensive car. The customer asked for a security supervisor to do it. When Paul said he was fully competent to drive, the customer exploded and demanded to see the Duty Manager.

♦ What do you think Paul felt like to be told he wasn't trustworthy?
♦ What was it important for Paul not to do?
♦ Write down what Paul could say to his customer and how he should say it.

The advantages of adopting assertive behaviour

Figure 3.14 Advantages of assertive behaviour

If for some reason you are not able to meet the ongoing needs and expectations of your customers, you should expect that some customers will react badly.

Remember that aggressive and submissive behaviours are both automatic. In other words, you are most likely to react to a difficult situation by being aggressive or submissive. This is because our bodies naturally react to a stressful situation by wanting to fight back (aggressive behaviour) or run away (submissive behaviour).

You need to learn how to be assertive and make a conscious effort to adopt this style of behaviour if you are to make the most of the advantages of dealing with people in an assertive way. The 'Keys to good practice' below show what you can do to become more assertive.

The advantages are clear: you will be dealing with people in an open and honest way whilst at the same time showing them that you understand.

By adopting an assertive and professional approach you will help to calm the situation down. This will help you deal with customers who are frustrated, disappointed or angry.

If you can develop the skill of being assertive without being aggressive, you will be able to turn a negative experience into a win-win situation. In other words, you and your organisation win as well as the customer. (See page 140 for more information.)

Adopting assertive behaviour will make your job much easier during times of conflict. This is because you will not be using behaviours which only serve to make a bad situation worse, e.g. when you hear someone shout at you, your natural inclination might be to raise your voice in reply. This will mean that the shouting continues and everyone comes out of the situation feeling unhappy.

Your own confidence will increase because you will be able to control a difficult situation to ensure that both your customer and yourself come out feeling understood and with a solution that both parties find acceptable.

Keys to good practice

Assertive behaviour

- ✓ Remain calm.
- ✓ Always listen and acknowledge that you have heard the customer.
- ✓ Demonstrate that you understand.
- ✓ Consider the consequences for all parties of getting what you want/need.
- ✓ Ask for what you want/need without offending others.
- ✓ Find solutions without heated arguments.
- ✓ Do not blame others.
- ✓ Avoid overuse of the word 'sorry'.
- ✓ Take responsibility for your own success.
- ✓ Take control by focussing on assertive behaviours.
- ✓ Treat others as equals; recognise other people's abilities and limitations.
- ✓ Work towards a win-win situation.

Test your knowledge

♦ Take a look at the following situations and think about whether the responses are assertive, aggressive or submissive.

SITUATION	RESPONSE	TYPE OF BEHAVIOUR
A customer is annoyed because the delivery time you promised has not been met.	'Sorry, it's no good getting angry with me; our delivery van has broken down and won't be fixed for a while. Ring back at the end of the week.'	

SITUATION	RESPONSE	TYPE OF BEHAVIOUR
A colleague asks you to take over his telephone.	'You must be joking! I've got enough work of my own.'	
A customer queries the price of a product.	'That's the right price. I checked it yesterday. What do you want me to do about it?'	
A colleague interrupts you when you are dealing with a customer.	'I'm not able to deal with you right now, as you can see I'm with Mrs. Jones. I'll be with you just as soon as we've finished.'	
A customer wants an appointment next Tuesday. The date clashes with other customer commitments.	'I'm sorry I cannot make that day. I have appointments already booked with other customers. However, I can make Wednesday.'	
A team meeting is called. The date is OK for others but not for you.	'Oh well. I guess I can make it. I'll be there.'	
A customer praises you for your excellent service.	'Thank you but I didn't do very much.'	
A customer phones to check opening times and gets annoyed with the information you provide.	'I'm sorry to hear the opening times don't suit you. Let's see how I can get you what you need in another way.'	
A customer writes to say she was sent out-of-date information by colleagues working in another department.	'They're always getting things wrong. It wasn't my fault but I'll see if I can send you out something more appropriate.'	

- ◆ Now look back at each scenario and decide if you react in similar ways.
- ◆ Consider how you might make your own behaviour and the things you say or write more assertive in their nature.

How to work with others to resolve difficulties in balancing the needs of your customers and your organisation

In looking for a win-win situation between the needs and expectations of customers and the products or services offered by your organisation, you will need to seek the assistance of others in the following circumstances:

- ◆ when you need permission
- ◆ when a decision is not yours to make
- ◆ when you need to commit resources that are not your responsibility
- ◆ when you are unsure of what alternatives are available

♦ when you are sure of the alternatives that are available but need to seek permission to act
♦ when you want to make an exception to the service you would normally offer.

Active knowledge

Reflecting on situations relevant to your own role, use the list above to identify situations when you have worked with other people to resolve difficulties.

♦ What did you do that helped the customer?
♦ What did you do that helped your organisation?
♦ Why did you need to seek the support of other individuals?
♦ What, if anything, would you do differently?

In working with others to resolve difficulties in balancing the needs of your customer and your organisation you may need to use your negotiation skills. Unit 4 deals with developing your negotiation skills in detail. Here we will concentrate on identifying who you need to negotiate with. It is important to remember that your customer is waiting for an answer. Knowing who to go to quickly will assist you greatly in maintaining the level of service required. Having identified who you need to communicate with, you should do the following:

♦ gather all the information you can about the customer's needs
♦ work out why these cannot be met
♦ be clear about any alternatives
♦ present to him or her the facts
♦ suggest a solution
♦ reach a joint decision
♦ keep your customer informed.

Always respect the needs of your colleagues. Sometimes picking the right moment to approach someone might make the difference between a successful conclusion or not.

Keys to good practice

Working with others to help customers

✓ Develop a basic understanding of the roles and responsibilities of other departments.
✓ Form positive working relationships with colleagues working elsewhere.
✓ Keep address/telephone/email contact lists up to date.
✓ Know the limits of your own authority.
✓ Develop a good working knowledge of key products or services.
✓ Develop a good working knowledge of alternative products or services.
✓ Keep the customer informed.

Test your knowledge

Try practising your assertiveness skills with a friend or colleague.

♦ Using the following scenario ask your friend/colleague to play the part of Cathy while you are the nurse.

You work in a hospital as a nurse. While admitting your patient Billy Mackay and taking his history, you find that his wife (Cathy) is constantly answering the questions you are asking him. You know you must obtain the answers from him and so need to take control of what is happening.

 ## Develop the relationship between your customers and your organisation

♦ What you need to do to go further than just answering questions about your organisation's products or services.

♦ How to discuss with your customers the way in which their expectations compare to what you and your organisation offer.

♦ How customers' needs and expectations may change over time.

♦ How to identify new ways of helping customers based on feedback they have given you.

What you need to do to go further than just answering questions about your organisation's products or services

Not all questions can be answered with a straightforward answer. You need to be open-minded about the nature of the questions a customer asks you. For example, a customer may ask what the quickest way to get from Manchester to Liverpool is. There are many possible answers to this question, depending on the customer's specific needs. Are they travelling by train, bus or car? How much money do they want to spend on transport? When answering questions you, the customer service practitioner, have a choice: you can give one solution or you can ask more questions to get a better understanding of what the customer really needs and expects. Asking more detailed questions will help to give the best solution to your customer's question and therefore the best service.

Open questions

Open questions are questions that require the customer to give you a full response. They cannot be answered with a one-word answer. Asking open questions will enable you to give additional help to customers.

Figure 3.15 Open questions

For example: Who do you want it for? What type do you need? Why do you need one that colour? Where do you want to go to? When do you need it by? How much is your budget?

Active knowledge

Write down five more open questions that you could use in your particular customer service role.

Asking open questions will help you to develop the relationship between your customer and the organisation because they help you to find out exactly what the customer wants and needs. Using the information you gain will enable you to be better able to match what the customer wants to the products or services of your organisation. You can also use any additional information you get from the responses to think about ways you can give customers added value. Giving added value is all about going the extra mile. It's about remembering customer names, bringing in the personal touch, surprising the customer and showing you care.

Reasons for asking open questions:

♦ to find out what the customer really needs
♦ to develop a dialogue between you and the customer
♦ to show an interest
♦ to find out how the customer feels
♦ to understand the customer
♦ to show that you are listening.

Case study

Neil is a father of three teenagers and is very aware of their desire to have the latest mobile telephones. Neil has resisted having his own mobile, believing that if he really needed one he could borrow one from his family.

Now, after many years without a mobile, he has finally succumbed to the fact that all his friends and family have mobiles and he really needs to buy one. Having shown no interest whatsoever in mobile telephone technology, Neil knows very little about what is available. He walks into a shop in his local shopping mall and is surprised at the range available.

Damian (who works in the shop) spots Neil looking at the banks of telephones on the wall. He sees that Neil looks a little confused and that he is about to walk out.

♦ Should Damian wait for Neil to ask for what he wants?
♦ What might Neil be doing or look like to make Damian think he is confused?
♦ How could Damian prevent Neil from walking away?
♦ What would be the first thing Damian could ask Neil?
♦ Write down some open questions for Damian to ask Neil.

Adding value – the personal touch

Goodwill is that feel-good feeling people have about one another or about an organisation they are dealing with. Often goodwill stems out of the personal touch you can bring to your work; the little things that mean so much to people are often the biggest way of building customer loyalty and developing lasting relationships. This is so important for repeat business and also when facing a problem solving situation with a customer.

Did you know?

♦ A well-handled problem breeds more loyalty than no problem at all.
♦ It costs five times more to get a new customer than keep an existing one.
♦ A dissatisfied customer will tell ten others.

Things such as providing comfortable seating, offering to carry baggage or acknowledging customers who are queuing mean the difference between a dissatisfied customer and one who is prepared to stay and will come again. You might think this is no more than being courteous. That may be so, however, it is all too often lacking from the service customers receive. Below are some examples of how a car dealership might add the personal touch and therefore add value.

♦ The salesperson who notices a family with three dogs looking at estate cars on the forecourt and then invites them into the showroom with the dogs.
♦ The salesperson who arranges for a bouquet of flowers to be on the passenger seat for the purchaser to have when the car is delivered or collected.
♦ The salesperson who telephones after a month to check the customer is happy.
♦ The garage mechanic who, after completing a car service, leaves on the passenger seat the car's service history manual duly completed and open at the right page.

There are also lots of things organisations do to try to build loyalty:

♦ loyalty cards, e.g. Nectar
♦ subscriber discounts, especially when a customer first signs up, e.g. satellite TV
♦ invitations to previews, e.g. an evening event in a department store to see the new season's fashions
♦ invitations to special sales days (a sale might start a day early for selected customers)
♦ special loyal customer promotions (discounts for regular users)
♦ BOGOFs (buy one get one free). Initially an enticement to use a product or service
♦ buy three from a selected range and get the cheapest free (again, an enticement, but once using the product or service, a customer might repeat buy).

When you combine what you can do personally to go the extra mile for customers, together with the initiatives your organisation takes to build loyalty, you are well on the way to doing all that you can to develop the relationship between your customers and your organisation.

Customers look to organisations to have a reputation that inspires them to continue to do business with them. Having a good reputation increases customer tolerance. If something does go wrong, a customer is more likely to keep doing business there if the reputation is strong and the problem is handled well. Loyalty inspires trust in you and your organisation.

How to discuss with your customers the way in which their expectations compare to what you and your organisation offer

Often without realising it, we jump to conclusions about what people need and want. We imagine what we would want and assume the customer wants the same. It is important to apply your listening skills carefully. Make sure you know what the customer needs and that you do not make assumptions.

Customers make assumptions about what an organisation can do in terms of its products or services. These assumptions (or misunderstandings) often link back to an organisation's image or brand. For instance, an elderly woman who wants to have a shampoo and set might think, on looking at a modern hair salon, that this would not be done there. Similarly, if a customer wanders around a town looking for somewhere to eat for a modest price, he or she may assume a restaurant is too expensive simply because it looks posh. What if this restaurant has a variety of menu options available? The customer might not even get as far as looking at the menu.

If you are not able to provide the product or service the customer wants, this does not necessarily mean you have lost the customer altogether. If you try to offer an alternative from another source, your customer is likely to be more tolerant of the situation than if you had not made the effort to try. Being helpful in this way is part of developing a good and lasting customer relationship as the customer knows how helpful your organisation is.

How to discuss expectations with a customer

The following points will help reassure the customer that the service you provide is the correct one for them. Remember not to push a customer into a corner. You do not want to force him or her to make a decision quickly.

- Always remain positive and discuss with the customer what you or your organisation can do, not what you cannot do.
- Get the information you require by listening and asking appropriate questions. This is especially important when dealing with customers over the telephone.
- Discuss the product or service with the customer in terms of benefits rather than technical features.
- Give the customer a full and clear explanation of how a particular product or service compares with what he or she needs.
- Do not use jargon or confuse the customer with long-winded explanations.
- Repeat back key points you are making and check the customer has understood by seeking his or her agreement
- Avoid using the word 'but'. Instead, use the word 'however' to explain what you can do, rather than what you are unable to do. For example, instead of saying 'I can get you this in the size you have requested but not in the colour you want' say 'I have it in the size you want. However, the colour I can deliver it in by tomorrow is red not blue. Will that be OK?'

 Keys to good practice

Discussing expectations with a customer

- ✓ Create a friendly and courteous environment.
- ✓ Listen to the customer's needs.
- ✓ Ask open questions to seek information.
- ✓ Check back your understanding of the customer's needs.
- ✓ Say what you can do not what you cannot do.
- ✓ Avoid jargon and technical terms.
- ✓ Offer alternatives where needs or expectations cannot be met.
- ✓ Seek agreement to what you are proposing.

How customers' needs and expectations may change over time

There are many influences that will affect your customers' needs and expectations. It is important you recognise that these needs and expectations will change, in the same way your own preferences alter over a period of time.

Figure 3.16 Influences affecting customers' future needs and expectations

Did you know?

The following changes will occur in the UK over the next ten years:

♦ there will be fewer young customers in the 15–25 age band
♦ there will be more customers in the middle-age and over-65 customer groups
♦ there will be 40 per cent more customers in single households
♦ customer lifestyles will change because of the 24 hours a day/7 days a week/365 days a year mentality
♦ web-based information and communications technology will spread their influence.

Source: Emerging Skills for a Changing Economy – Evolution of the Customer Service Professional, May 2001

This means organisations will need to look at areas such as the following if they are to keep up with changing needs:

♦ the range of products or services the organisation offers (to see if these are age-specific)
♦ opening hours
♦ how customers can communicate with the organisation
♦ who the decision-maker is in a household

♦ how the organisation can help its employees to engage with customers in new and effective ways.

What customers will want in the future

Unless an organisation keeps itself alert to changing customer expectations it will not succeed. It will continue to live in the past and will rapidly be seen as being out-of-date or out of touch. As a result, customers will go elsewhere to find what they want.

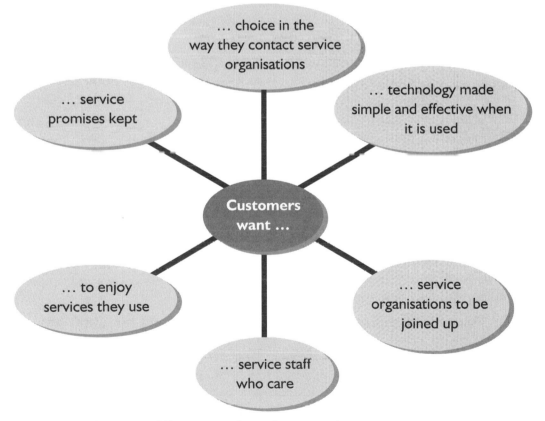

Figure 3.17 Customers' future needs and expectations

Active knowledge

♦ Does the information in Figure 3.17 reflect your own needs and expectations?

♦ How do you think the above needs could impact on you and your customer service role?

♦ What does this mean you need to do to ensure the relationship between your customers and your organisation continues to develop positively?

Now, and in the future, customers want to have a choice in the way they contact an organisation. It is no longer acceptable for the only choice to be using the telephone or writing. Customers may still choose to telephone or write, but they also want the freedom to be able to use email, fax, or the Internet. This has an impact on customer service delivery. Using email is an immediate form of communication. The expectation is that an immediate response will follow. Similarly, customers using the Internet to make an online booking for a hotel or theatre ticket will also want fast responses. Your organisation may already have changed the way in which it allows customers to communicate with it. There may be more people contacting you by telephone than writing, or by email rather than face-to-face.

Instead of customers calling an individual department, an organisation may have set up a call centre to deal with customers covering a geographical area.

When they need to use it, customers want technology made simple and effective. They do not want to experience difficulties. It is also a huge waste of resources if customer service practitioners need to spend vast amounts of time explaining technology to customers. Customers also want service organisations to be joined up. This is like having a one-stop service; if you cannot help, you know someone who can. To do this, organisations need to make it easy for employees to communicate with one another. Employees need to know who can help if they are personally unable to do so, and where to access information or people quickly. Having a joined-up service means customers do not get bounced around an organisation.

Now, and in the future, customers want service staff who care. They want good memories of dealing with an organisation. They want to feel employees identify and understand what they expect and what they are feeling. They want reliability and reassurance, and they want to be shown courtesy. Customers want to enjoy the services they use. They would like to be surprised from time to time and to see that the personal touch has not been lost. They need products or services to change to reflect changing needs and aspirations in order for this to happen. Finally, customers want service promises to be kept. This all comes down to trust and inspiring loyalty in customers. A promise broken may be a customer lost.

Case study

Jacqui works in a local advice centre providing information and guidance on a wide range of issues including giving help and advice on careers. She has worked there for five years. Over those five years Jacqui has noticed a significant change in what her customers need from her. For example, she no longer gets lots of queries from school leavers about jobs in the nursing profession or in the airline industry. Instead she seems to get a great deal of queries from people who have been in employment but who are now facing redundancy.

She has got into the habit of recording comments received from customers in a feedback diary. Here is a note of some of her entries:

Since the local printing firm shut down, more and more people have requested help with retraining opportunities.

Help with CV writing is requested more and more frequently.

Older customers do not seem to like talking to me about redundancy.

A customer complained we were not open in the evening.

Three customers wanted to be able to email me this week.

I was told my list of Independent Financial Advisers is out of date.

♦ What should Jacqui do with the information she has recorded?
♦ What would happen if Jacqui had not taken the time to record this information?

How to identify new ways of helping customers based on feedback they have given you

Asking open questions and finding out about your customers' expectations are all methods of getting feedback from your customers. However, it is no use listening and collecting feedback if you do not do something with it. You need to be responsive to the feedback you receive from customers. If you work in a very busy environment it is often easy to forget the comments customers make; this means nothing will change or improve in your organisation. Using customer feedback is a four-step process:

♦ identify customer service issues/feedback and record them
♦ discuss feedback with others (when necessary)
♦ plan and carry out action to be taken
♦ monitor the results.

Following these steps will enable you to react to comments made by customers so that you can do something to help improve the service you and your organisation give to customers.

Case study (continued from page 151)

As well as writing down the comments Jacqui received from her customers, she decided to write down the actions she took as well.

FEEDBACK	ACTION
Help with CV writing is requested more and more frequently.	Produce guidance notes. Refer people to online help.
Older customers do not seem to like talking to me about redundancy.	Ask for feedback from colleagues as to why this is. What am I doing differently with mature clients?
A customer complained we were not open in the evening.	Speak with my manager about this trend.
Three customers wanted to be able to email me this week.	We have no facilities to offer email as a method of communication. I think we are behind the times. Speak to my manager.
I was told my list of Independent Financial Advisers is out of date.	Update list and circulate around office.

We will now look at the process Jacqui worked through in order to use customer feedback effectively. We'll take one example – the increase in the number of enquiries received on CV writing.

The first step Jacqui took was to identify that there was an increasing trend. She was able to do this because she completed her feedback diary on a regular basis. When reviewing the diary she was able to prove the trend was significant and this enabled her to give the advice centre manager some real facts and figures.

Having discussed it with her manager (it was important to seek approval as any changes would have cost implications) a joint decision was made to offer some formal help on CV writing. Jacqui's manager asked her to find out what the options were. Jacqui did this by thinking about the different methods of learning how to write a CV. These included reading information leaflets, accessing websites, using a CD-Rom, and attending a workshop.

With her manager's agreement, Jacqui took action to update the centre's information leaflet to include useful website addresses and also to schedule half-day workshops where groups of people could come to the centre to learn how to write a CV. Jacqui then made a note to monitor the success of her initiatives. This included seeing how popular the new information leaflet was and also the take-up of places for the workshop. Where possible, she also asked her customers how helpful the advice had been.

Advising others of customer feedback

It would be very easy to make assumptions on behalf of customers and set out to take action on feedback received, just because the customer wants you to. This is unwise and should not be done unless it is within the scope of your authority.

It would be far better to discuss feedback with the appropriate people in your organisation. That way, you will be doing your part to contribute to the overall perception of the standard of customer service. The appropriate people might be your line manager, your supervisor or whoever has the responsibility for dealing with feedback or making change happen.

This is just what Jacqui has done. She identified customer service issues, made a note of them, and only took action after she had discussed the feedback with her centre manager. Finally, Jacqui monitored the results. This way she can see if her actions have been worthwhile and whether she has correctly responded to the customers' needs.

Active knowledge

◆ Write down five comments you have received from customers recently. Now think about the action you took.
◆ For those comments received where you took no action, identify what you might have done to find new ways of helping customers. Consider who else should be involved with your plans.

Remember

Your organisation may have a formal process in place to capture customer feedback, such as one or more of the following:

◆ customer satisfaction questionnaires
◆ mystery shopper
◆ monitoring complaints and compliments
◆ focus groups
◆ telephone surveys
◆ comments/suggestion boxes
◆ street surveys.

Case study

Formuz and Stefan work as car park stewards at a stately home during the summer break from University. Neither has much experience at dealing with

people from a customer service perspective. However, Formuz has become increasingly embarrassed by his colleague's actions. One night, while on duty for a Proms in the Park concert, a hired minibus drew up which was full of young people. The driver requested access to a disabled parking bay but did not have the necessary badge with him. Stefan peered into the van and said 'Which one of you is disabled then?' Somewhat shocked by this,

one of the occupants identified himself as being a wheelchair user. Stefan advised the driver that the wheelchair user could get out together with a helper, but that everyone else would need to go to the main car park with the minibus. Stefan also asked them to hurry up as the minibus was in danger of blocking the entrance. Formuz watched while all the occupants got out of the minibus to get the wheelchair out together. Two of the young people proceeded into the park while the rest went off to park the minibus, wondering how they would find each other again.

♦ What was wrong with the way Stefan handled the situation?
♦ How might he be more flexible in future?
♦ What should Formuz do about what he saw happen?

Test your knowledge

Think about a product or service you have used regularly in the last five years, e.g. buying a newspaper, using public transport or filling up the car with petrol.

♦ What do you expect now from your service provider that you did not expect or need five years ago?
♦ Have you ever given feedback to an organisation on the service provided? If so, what was the reaction?

Check your knowledge

1   When should you seek permission from an appropriate person to change the products or services you offer your customers?

2   How does behaving assertively help you to deal with difficult situations?

3   List four things that help your customers have confidence in you and your organisation.

4   List five ways you can demonstrate courteous behaviour.

5   Name three commitments your organisation makes to its customers.

6   List five expectations your customers have about your organisation's products or services.

7   Assertive behaviour means always getting my way. True or false?

8   What can you do to ensure the way in which you work with others helps to develop the customer relationship?

9   You should always do what the customer wants. True or false?

10 Open questions begin with the words ...?

11 Why do open questions help to develop the relationship between the customer and the organisation?

12 What should you do if you are unable to provide the product or service the customer wants?

13 What can you do to stop a potential conflict occurring when what you can offer differs from what your customer wants?

14 How can keeping a feedback diary help you to develop the relationship between your customers and your organisation?

15 How should you go about exploring your customers' expectations?

UNIT 4

Resolve customer service problems

As a customer service practitioner, you are always striving to get things right first time. If you are able to achieve this, then most of the time problems will not occur. Getting it right first time means you will be meeting and exceeding customer expectations.

However, there are a number of factors that may be outside your control that will impact upon the quality of service you deliver. Problems may occur as a result. These factors include problems that occur for the following reasons:

♦ customers' expectations differ from what you and your organisation offer
♦ there is a system or procedure failure
♦ there is a lack of resources (e.g. time, money, people, technology)
♦ human error.

It is important to try to avoid problems, but if they do occur, solving them is as important as making sure they never happen in the first place. Many customers who feel they have been treated badly can actually feel better about an organisation by the manner in which a problem is sorted out. These customers will judge the customer service of your organisation by the way in which their problems are resolved.

The elements for this unit are:

♦ 4.1 Identify customer service problems
♦ 4.2 Select the best solution to resolve customer service problems
♦ 4.3 Implement the solution to customer service problems.

The following statistics were obtained through research undertaken by The Institute of Customer Service in its National Complaints Culture Survey, 2001:

♦ The trend for complaining is steadily increasing: 50 per cent of customers complain most or all of the time.
♦ Customers want a fast response: over 50 per cent of people who complain in person or by telephone expect a resolution on the same day.
♦ Nearly 80 per cent of those who complain in writing expect a resolution within two weeks.
♦ Over 35 per cent of customers believe that organisations never encourage complaints, with only 10 per cent believing complaints are welcome.

This means you have to be able to respond professionally and efficiently to every complaint. Just as customers want you to get things right first time, they also give you just one chance to put things right when problems do occur.

The National Complaints Culture Survey also found that if a complaint is handled well, over 90 per cent of customers are likely to continue to do business with the organisation concerned. Ninety-seven per cent of customers are then likely to tell other people if they have had a good experience following making a complaint.

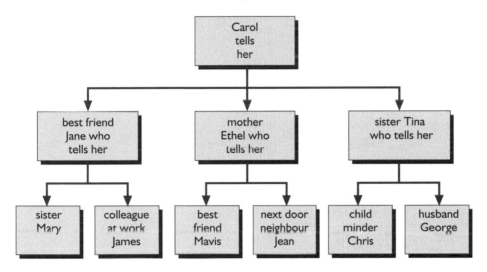

Figure 4.1 News travels fast

Problem-solving can be viewed as a sequence of events: you start with identifying the problem, you work out a solution, and then implement that solution.

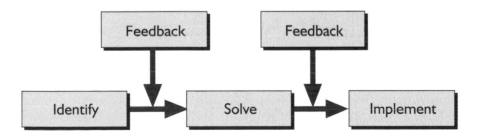

Figure 4.2 The problem-solving sequence

At all stages of the cycle you will receive feedback from various people. For instance, your customer may be the one who first brings a problem to your attention: the identification stage. Then they might tell you what they think and feel as you seek to solve the problem. Finally, your customer may let you know how they feel about the outcome after you have taken action: the implementation of your solution. Other people who might be involved with giving feedback are your colleagues and suppliers.

Remember

You are not alone. You will need to call on the support of your colleagues at times to help sort things out and/or use your organisation's systems and procedures.

- ♦ What factors might lead to customer service problems occurring.
- ♦ How to check you have understood customers' problems.
- ♦ How to help prevent problems occurring.
- ♦ How to deal with potentially stressful situations.

What factors might lead to customer service problems occurring

The reasons why problems occur in the first place might include some of the following factors.

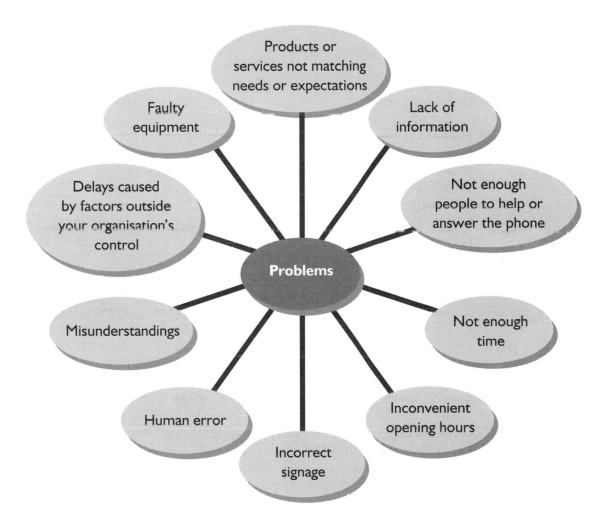

Figure 4.3 Reasons why problems can occur

The factors shown in Figure 4.3 might lead to problems in the following ways:

♦ **Faulty equipment:** mechanical breakdowns leaving you unable to work, e.g. a car that will not start, computer failure, tools that have not been looked after. Machinery that is too complicated for customers to operate, e.g. computers, videos, etc.

♦ **Lack of information:** insufficient information about products or services. Lack of communication keeping customers informed about changes to products and services. No updates on how problems are being resolved. Your customer is kept in the dark leading to misunderstandings and a lack of trust.

♦ **Not enough people to help or answer the telephone:** this is a resource issue leading to dissatisfied customers who are not prepared to wait, e.g. a call centre where customers put the telephone down rather than be kept in a queue while their telephone bill is rising.

♦ **Not enough time:** this is also a resource issue. Do you have to rush serving a customer because there are so many others waiting for you to help? If so, will customers feel valued?

♦ **Inconvenient opening hours:** customers increasingly expect access to products or services when they want it. For instance, some hairdressers now offer a service late into the evening. If customers cannot get what they want from your organisation they will look elsewhere.

♦ **Incorrect signage:** this means customers literally get lost. They are unable to find where they want to go because there are not enough (or incorrect) signs (e.g. in a hospital or airport).

♦ **Human error:** mistakes made because nobody's perfect.

♦ **Misunderstandings:** these occur frequently where people say something that is interpreted as meaning something completely different. If someone is not listening properly it is all too easy to get things wrong.

♦ **Delays caused by factors outside your organisation's control:** industrial action may have a snowball effect on many different organisations, e.g. a tube driver's strike will affect all people (including customers) who need to use the tube to get to work. The weather can also have a huge impact on your ability to deliver customer service; strong winds may bring down power lines, rain may force the cancellation of an outdoor event.

♦ **Products or services not matching needs or expectations:** customers will have expectations about a product or service. Customers get this from advertising, from your organisation's reputation and from what you might say. If these expectations are not met, problems may occur. For instance, a customer expects fresh flowers to last seven days because that is what it says on the wrapper, yet they die within three days.

How was it for you?

Think about the worst customer service experience you have encountered as a customer in the last six months

♦ What were you trying to do?
♦ Was it people that upset you or got things wrong?
♦ Was it the organisation's processes that let you down?
♦ Could you (as the customer) have done things differently to get what you wanted? If so, what?
♦ What did you think and feel about the organisation?
♦ What did you think and feel about the people who dealt with you?

Active knowledge

Thinking about your own organisation, make a list of the types of problems that consistently occur. Do this by thinking about the following:

♦ problems brought to your attention by customers
♦ problems with systems and procedures
♦ problems with colleagues and/or suppliers misunderstanding one another.

What part do you play in ensuring these problems are solved?

How to check you have understood customers' problems

You may become aware of customers' problems in many different ways. Some problems might be brought directly to your attention by the customer: he or she may tell you of his or her concerns face-to-face, over the telephone or in writing. Feedback can reach you via a number of different ways as shown in the table below.

VERBALLY	Face-to-face. By telephone
IN WRITING	Letters of complaint. Letters of praise. Emails
OBSERVATION	What you see the customer do and how you interpret this behaviour
COLLEAGUES	What your colleagues tell you
ORGANISATIONAL PROCESSES	Customer comment cards. Questionnaires. Customer suggestion boxes. Surveys

Figure 4.4 Methods of obtaining feedback

Probably the most valuable source of feedback stems from what you see your customers doing and what they tell you. If you combine this important information with the other forms of feedback and use it effectively you will be well on the way to helping to understand and resolve customer service problems. In order to check you have understood the customer's problem you need to do the following:

♦ get all the facts
♦ listen non-defensively
♦ repeat the problem back to the customer as you understand it.

Getting all the facts

This means making sure you have every bit of information you need to start helping the customer. This might include dates, times and who else was involved. Importantly, it also includes finding out what the customer needed or expected, but did not get. This might mean finding out what was previously promised.

It is easy to jump to conclusions when you are trying to solve customers' queries quickly, especially when a customer might be confused or distressed. You may jump to the wrong conclusion if you do not gather all the facts about the nature of the problem properly.

Listening non-defensively

This means listening without interrupting, and listening without showing you are out to pass blame on to someone or something else. You can do this by nodding at appropriate moments and by not showing any expressions of annoyance, dismay or frustration in your face or in the tone of your voice.

Repeating the problem back to the customer

It is important that you say in your own words what you think the customer's problem is all about. This gives the customer the chance to say 'Yes that's right' or 'No, my problem is more to do with ...'.

Active knowledge

Think back to the last three occasions when a customer gave you feedback.

♦ What was the problem?
♦ What did you do?
♦ How did you check you had fully understood your customer's concerns?

Gathering additional information

One way in which you can make sure you get all the facts and that you do not jump to conclusions is to gather additional information. Customers sometimes leave out important information. They might simply forget to tell you, or are unable to recognise the significance of what turns out to be a crucial piece of information. This might involve you finding out the answers to questions such as the following:

♦ What happened?   ♦ When did it happen?
♦ What were the circumstances?   ♦ Have other people been involved?

♦ Has anything been done to try to sort out the problem before?
♦ What does the customer want?

Case study

Elliott works for a telecommunications company and is responsible for building relationships with a key corporate customer, following the departure of the customer's previous accounts manager. In his new role, Elliott was keen to make a good first impression and so invited his contacts to visit him on site. Much to his dismay the customer declined his invitation. Elliott felt put out and offered an alternative date. This was again declined in a short email message which read: 'Operational constraints mean we are unable to visit you on site. We would however appreciate a quick response to the outstanding queries we have with your engineers.'

After reading this message Elliott realised that he needed to do some research into the problems. He spoke to his predecessor, Trudi, and to other colleagues in the engineering department. He found a list of unanswered queries relating to this customer. Trudi told him that she had not had a very productive relationship with the customer and indeed had never met anyone face-to-face in the last 12 months. He also talked to his Team Leader who told Elliott that there had been a number of short-term staffing difficulties in the engineering department which had caused a backlog. In addition, the customer was not using the correct process to log a query or complaint with the engineering department, and so they were not being dealt with efficiently. From this information Elliott realised the following:

♦ he needed to apologise to the customer for the backlog
♦ he needed to develop a rapport with the customer
♦ he needed to visit the customer on site rather than them visit him
♦ he needed to set out objectives for this meeting
♦ he needed to advise his customer of the internal procedures to be followed
♦ he needed to tell the customer what he was going to do to deal with the backlogged queries
♦ he needed to identify which of the queries needed to be dealt with first.

1 What else would you add to this list?
2 What questions should Elliott ask the customer to make sure he had fully understood what the customer wanted?
3 What would be the best method of communication for Elliott to use with his customer?
4 Should anyone else visit the customer as well as Elliott?
5 How might Elliott stop this happening again?

Being aware of problems can be the result of two things: being reactive or being proactive. Being reactive means that you react to a complaint made directly to you by a customer. For example, a customer telephones to complain about non-receipt of an item, a customer writes to let you know goods are damaged or a customer shouts from the back of a queue. On other occasions, you may spot the problem first and be able to sort it out before the customers realise. This is called being proactive. In this situation, you have managed to prevent a potential complaint occurring. Although Elliot needed to act reactively in order to help his customer (solve problems rather than prevent them) he focused on collecting information on the customer first.

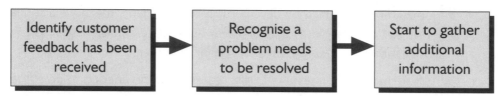

Figure 4.5 Active steps taken to understand queries

In the case study above, Elliott needed to understand what the underlying problems were, so he sought up-to-date information on the current situation using internal resources and then asked his customer questions. Providing a customer feels you have bothered to show an interest in any information he or she has already advised you or your company about, questions which seek to clarify the situation will be well received.

Checking your facts

Making sure you fully understand what a customer needs is especially important when you are dealing with an upset or distressed customer. He or she is unlikely to present information to you in a tidy, coherent package. Double-checking your facts becomes very important if your customer is difficult to understand. For instance, an accent might mean you are struggling with hearing the words themselves, or some people might talk very quickly, again this can make it quite difficult to listen effectively.

Repeating or summarising

By repeating or summarising what your customer has said, you are double-checking your understanding of what the customer has told you. For example, a customer might telephone to enquire about an order: 'Last week I told you I needed to change my order so that it is delivered between 10.00 and 11.30am and not after 4.00pm as I am going out. It is now after midday and I am still waiting'. To make sure you have understood what the customer has said, you might summarise what you have heard by saying: 'What you have said is that your order was originally planned for delivery after 4.00pm today and that you changed this to a delivery between 10.30 and 11.30am this morning, but it hasn't arrived yet, is that correct?'

In this example, the customer service provider has used the customer's own words to check the information given. It is very useful to do this when numbers, times and dates are involved, to make sure that you do not get confused. It also shows the customer that you are really listening to what they are saying. If the customer's story is long and complicated, you might need to repeat it back in the form of a summary of what has been said. Make sure you include in your summary the most important facts.

Expressing empathy

When listening to a customer and checking your facts it is important to also express empathy. This means showing you understand the customers' feelings. You can do this by saying one of the following:

♦ 'That must have been really frustrating for you.'
♦ 'I can understand you are feeling really upset about this.'
♦ 'I understand things have not been going right for you.'

Keys to good practice

Checking you have understood the customer

✓ Listen without interrupting.
✓ Do not get defensive.
✓ Express empathy.
✓ Ask questions to understand the problem.
✓ Repeat back or summarise what you have heard.
✓ Use the customer's own language.

How to help prevent problems occurring

If you become aware that things are going wrong (or might go wrong), then it would be sensible to make sure (or at least try to make sure) it will not happen again.

Identify repeated problems

Identifying repeated problems means recognising similar errors and feedback. It is about spotting trends, realising something needs to be done and then taking action. The action you take will depend on the amount of authority you have to act on your own. If you do not have the necessary authority, you still have a major role to play in highlighting to others the nature of the problems you have encountered.

You should make a note of problems because:

♦ it helps your colleagues to sort things out if you are not around and a customer returns with the same problem

♦ it helps your organisation to save money and time as repeated problems can be prevented

♦ it helps you to give great customer service.

The best way to do this is to keep accurate records of the feedback you receive. This will help you to spot trends in service breakdowns and the more routine problems that might develop into bigger service issues. For instance, an administrative assistant in a bank might notice she receives several telephone calls enquiring about missing bank statement pages and that these calls usually occur around the turn of the month.

Active knowledge

Look back to page 157 where we discussed feedback.

♦ Find out if your organisation has a process for dealing with customer feedback.
♦ What records should you keep?
♦ How does your organisation analyse these records?

If your organisation does not have a system, you could develop your own feedback diary. This might look something like this:

FEEDBACK DIARY		
DATE	PROBLEM	ACTION TAKEN
5 May	Unable to open window in consulting room	Advised premises 6 May
12 May	Customer complained the cool water machine was empty	?
15 May	I lost a customer's business because we make a charge for using credit cards	Advised my supervisor
18 May	Another complaint regarding the water machine	Spoke with Terry. He has back problem; helped him to rearrange this duty
28 May	Customer late for appointment due to no parking space in our car park	Keep an eye on misuse of car park to ensure only our customers use it
30 May	Could not find package due for collection	Did not know about this; Terry hadn't told me. Not the first time this has happened. Will speak with Terry

Figure 4.6 Extract from feedback diary

As you can see, over time, this would develop into a diary that you could review periodically to spot repeated problems. This diary is just as useful for dealing with one-off problems and for trying to identify potential problems before they occur. On 5 May, our customer service practitioner noticed a problem with a window in a consulting room. By advising the people who could sort it out, he or she took steps to prevent a problem occurring, i.e. the room getting too hot/stuffy. On 28 May, a problem with car parking was identified. Here the customer service practitioner decided to periodically review the car park as he or she felt it was being used by people who were not customers.

Once you get into the habit of recording problems you then need to take action. This might involve the following:

♦ telling someone else who has the authority to act
♦ identifying your own solution (within your authority)
♦ using your colleagues to help you identify a solution.

Working with others to identify problems with systems and procedures

You may be involved in working with others to spot a potential problem before it occurs. This may be something that has been brought to your attention by a colleague or supplier. For instance, a colleague might tell you that because an individual is on long term sick leave, telephone calls are not being responded to as quickly as they should be.

Work closely with your colleagues to ensure problems are dealt with

You will need to be tactful as to how you deal with the issue and should not pass blame onto somebody else. In the example above, you could work out with your colleagues how, as a team, you can help answer the telephones quickly rather than passing blame on to the individual concerned. A customer will not be interested in internal fights, what he or she wants to know is that you are going to help.

Here are some of the problems you might encounter:

Problem	Action I need to take
PRODUCTS OR SERVICES	
Availability	
Quality	
Flexibility	
Ease of understanding	

Problem	Action I need to take
Lack of information	
ORGANISATIONS SYSTEMS AND PROCEDURES	
Ease of use	
Accessibility	
Availability	
Equipment breakdowns	
Communication – in	
Communication – out	
Speed of response	
PEOPLE	
Complaints about individual members of staff	

Figure 4.7 Potential problems that might lead to complaints

Active knowledge

♦ Copy and review Figure 4.7 and add any problems specific to the environment in which you work.

♦ For those points that you have personally encountered, write down in the second column the action you took for the most recent occurrence.

♦ Were you able to involve the right people to help you when required?

♦ Identify sources of assistance for the future.

How to deal with potentially stressful situations

A problem need not create a stressful situation if dealt with properly. A stressful situation will only occur when you, your colleagues, your customers (or any combination of these) are not satisfied with what is happening. This dissatisfaction leads to anger, frustration and a general feeling of wanting to be anywhere but in that situation. Trust breaks down and stress takes its place.

Did you know?

Some doctor's surgeries, local government premises and other outlets put notices up that tell customers:

'We will not tolerate abusive and offensive behaviour towards our staff.'

Active knowledge

There are varying degrees of unwanted behaviour and hopefully you will not be faced with these situations too often. However, to be able to feel confident in what you should do if you are, find out what your organisation's policy is when dealing with the following:

♦ a customer who swears
♦ a customer who is physically aggressive or appears to be about to become so
♦ a customer who shouts loudly
♦ a customer who is offensive.

Stressful situations

Stress might occur at any stage of the problem-solving sequence.

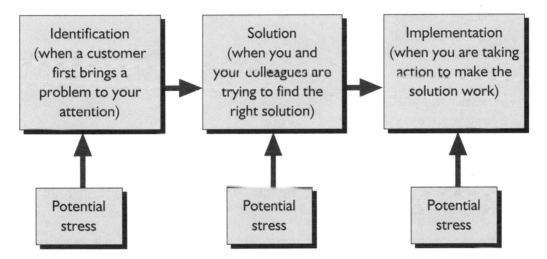

Figure 4.8 The potential for stress to occur

The first step is to recognise when you might be feeling stressed. If you get upset, the likelihood is your customer will follow suit. If your customer is shouting at you, you need to make sure you do not shout back.

You may be feeling stressed as a result of something that is happening in your life that has nothing to do with work, or your journey to work on a particular day may have been difficult, leaving you worn out and unhappy before you even start dealing with customers.

Figure 4.9 Symptoms that might mean you are feeling stressed

Customer service stress test

Now have a go at completing the following stress test. Simply answer yes or no to the following statements:

Statement	Yes	No
I do not worry about the prospect of dealing with unhappy customers		
I know who to go to for help		
I find it easy to find the information I need		
If a customer is late for a meeting or appointment I am flexible		
I am patient with customers		
I am patient with colleagues		
I manage my time effectively		
I enjoy my job		

Figure 4.10 A customer service stress test

These are just some factors which, if you are able to say 'Yes' to, will mean you are well on the way to being able to cope with potentially stressful situations as your own stress levels are kept to a minimum.

Defusing potentially stressful situations

It is better to prevent a difficult situation occurring in the first place, than to have to take steps to cure it. Part of this prevention is recognising the most common mistakes that could cause problems; if you are aware of these you are half way to being able to defuse potentially stressful situations.

There are five common mistakes:

♦ getting the conversation off to a bad start
♦ overloading the customer with too many questions
♦ arguing with the customer
♦ being inflexible
♦ leaving a bad taste in the customer's mouth.

Getting the conversation off to a bad start

If the conversation starts badly there is more potential for your dealings with a customer to get worse. This is especially true where a customer may have been kept waiting before he or she gets to speak with you.

A customer telephones Peter, who works for an insurance firm, to ask some questions about her pet insurance policy.

Peter: Can I help you?

Customer: Yes. I have some questions about my policy. I took it out last ...

Peter: What's the policy number?

Customer: I don't have it handy. You won't need it, my question is simply ...

Peter: Yes, I do need it. I cannot help you without it. Can you go and get it?

Customer: But, my question is simply ...

Peter: OK. Just give me your name.

Customer: Look. If you would just listen to me, all I want to know is ...

Not only did Peter not listen to the customer, but he continually interrupted her. The keys to starting a conversation on the right step are to greet the customer politely by saying who you are and to offer to help, to listen to the customer, ask for his or her name and to sound positive and confident.

A change to the start of the conversation could have prevented a stressful situation occurring. Peter should have allowed the customer to state the question and then ask for the customer's name and/or policy number if required. This approach is more likely to ensure the conversation gets off to a good start.

Peter: Can I help you?

Customer: Yes. I have some questions about my policy. I took it out last month and was wondering if I could change from your Silver cover to your Gold cover?

Peter: Yes. I am sure this would be possible. If you give me your name or policy number, I will be able to check your specific policy conditions.

Customer: Thanks. It's ...

Overloading the customer with too many questions

Asking too many questions will frustrate, confuse and aggravate a customer. Customer service practitioners working with complex or technical products are most likely to fall into this category. Your customer simply wants you to understand and to help, and this does not mean subjecting them to an interrogation.

A customer wants to arrange for her washing machine to be repaired and calls Nneka to report her problem.

Nneka: Can I help you?

Customer: I certainly hope so. My washing machine is making a funny noise. It is still working but I'm frightened it's going to flood the kitchen.

Nneka: What sort of noise is it making?

Customer: A sort of banging noise.

Nneka: OK. What you need to tell me is the make and model, how old it is and when you bought it. Oh, it was from me, I take it?

Customer: I can't remember when I bought it but it's a Washmewell machine. I don't know the model.

Nneka: I'll need the model and the year. What is it? Where did you get it from?

In this scenario, Nneka has asked too many questions at the same time; she has bombarded her customer without pausing for breath. The likely effect is to have a customer who ends up frustrated and upset.

Active knowledge

Rephrase this conversation bearing in mind the following:

♦ Nneka should be reassuring the customer
♦ Nneka should be saying what can be done to help.

Arguing with the customer

When a customer wants to argue, he or she will typically speak loudly, shout and sometimes do all that he or she can to attract the attention of other customers. This angry customer will have a very quick effect on you if you do not deal with the situation properly. You might find yourself making a bad mistake and shouting back.

A customer calls into a garage regarding his car. He speaks to Derek.

Customer: *(shouting)* I can't believe the state of my car! I brought it in for an MOT this morning, collected it an hour ago and got home only to get out of the car and find this enormous scratch all down the passenger side. There are muddy footprints inside on the carpet too. I want the scratch put right, the car valeted and £50 to compensate me for time wasted.

Derek: It's no good shouting at me. I didn't touch your car! I do the services. There's no way it would get scratched here. It must've happened on your way home.

Customer: I don't care who did the MOT. It happened here! How dare you say I'm lying!

Derek: *(shouting)* I don't care what you think. All I am saying is we don't scratch cars or put muddy feet on carpets. You're just trying to get money out of us!

Customer: I'll do more than get money out of you if you're not careful. I'm going to write to the local paper and tell them how awful you are here. You won't get any more customers if I can help it! Let me speak to the manager!

Derek has reacted badly to being confronted with a customer who shouted at him. Derek shouted back and also, without doing any investigation, put the blame firmly on the customer. Whatever Derek might think about the likelihood of his garage being at fault, he needed to take urgent steps to calm the situation down. He could have done this by allowing the customer to let off steam and not getting defensive.

Customer: *(shouting)* I can't believe the state of my car! I brought it in for an MOT this morning, collected it an hour ago and got home only to get out of the car and find this enormous scratch all down the passenger side. There are muddy footprints inside on the carpet too. I want the scratch put right, the car valeted and £50 to compensate me for time wasted.

Derek: I can see you are upset and I would like to help sort this out. I'm pleased you've come back so soon and am sure we can work this out to your satisfaction. Now, I'll go and get the mechanic who dealt with your car and you can show us what you are unhappy about.

Derek has accepted responsibility for the problem even though it was not himself who dealt with the MOT. He has not passed blame on to another member of his team at the garage. This shows he has taken responsibility on behalf of the garage and on behalf of his team. He has expressed empathy but not necessarily admitted liability. The way forward would now be for his colleague to help him explain to their customer what might have happened and to try to help the customer. They can both do this by continuing to ask questions to understand the problem. Derek should involve his manager if necessary.

Being inflexible

Organisations have rules and procedures in place to protect everyone. However, sometimes customer service people need to be able to be flexible. For instance, you need to know when you can adapt rules and regulations in order to maintain goodwill. This is not about breaking the rules so that health and safety are compromised or so that your organisation loses money, but it is about adopting a common-sense approach to knowing when you can be flexible.

Examples of inflexible customer service practitioners:

♦ the car park attendant who will not let you park in a spot allocated for another department, even though it has been empty all week

♦ the cashier who closes the till just as you are about to unload your shopping

♦ the waitress who refuses to serve you breakfast in your holiday hotel because you turn up five minutes late.

All these situations are likely to lead to a degree of stress. What would you do in each of these situations?

Leaving a bad taste in the customer's mouth

We have spoken about the importance of a good first impression. What thought have you given to the last impression a customer has of you and your organisation? Do you leave him or her feeling he or she wants to do business with you again?

A customer goes to collect goods she has ordered from Alison and has proof of identity.

Customer: I am here to collect my parcel.

Alison: Where is your proof of identity?

Customer: Here you go.

Alison: Sign here to acknowledge receipt, please.

Customer: OK. Have you a pen, please?

Alison: Here you are.

Although Alison has been polite, she has not been very welcoming. She has not gone the extra mile to thank the customer for doing business with this organisation. She has not used the customer's name despite knowing it from the documentation. If appropriate it might also be a nice touch to say to the customer 'I hope you enjoy using the ...' or 'I hope to see you again'. Here is how the conversation might have gone:

Customer: I am here to collect my parcel.

Alison: Good morning. I see you have your notification; may I just see it, please?

Customer: Here you go.

Alison: Thank you, Mrs Smart. I just need to see something with your signature on for proof of identity. Many thanks. I'll just go and get it for you. Sign here to acknowledge receipt, please.

Customer: OK. Have you a pen, please?

Alison: Here you are. I hope you enjoy using your ...

Keys to good practice

Defusing a stressful situation

✓ Greet the customer politely.
✓ Ask for their name.
✓ Ask one question at a time.
✓ Wait for the customer to answer.
✓ Listen actively.
✓ Express empathy.
✓ Know when you can be flexible with rules and procedures.
✓ Explain what you can do.

Coping with stress

Naturally, you should make every effort not to let a situation develop to such an extent that you find yourself needing to deal with stress and its impact upon your ability to cope. However, if you do get stressed, here are some hints to get you back on the path to being in control.

If you work in an environment that you find stimulating your energy levels will rise. Do what you can to make your work life more enjoyable and organise it so that it works with you, not against you. Look at the relationships you have with your colleagues. Do you work well together as a team? When you need help from colleagues, do you get it and do you willingly help others? Increase your confidence by developing your knowledge of products or services. Perhaps think about asking for feedback from people you trust as to how well you are performing at work. Give yourself a pat on the back for the positive things you hear and work on those areas that you need to develop. Know where to go for help and do ask for help when you need it.

Figure 4.11 Hints to minimise your stress levels

 Test your knowledge

Ask a friend to try role-playing the following two situations with you.

♦ Imagine you work on a help desk dealing with callers who have problems with personal computers. Ask your friend to call with a problem. Ask questions to identify the exact nature of the problem.

♦ Now try role-playing the scenario with Derek and the garage. Ask your customer to shout and practise your skills at defusing the stressful situation that is building up.

Select the best solution to resolve customer service problems

♦ What your organisation's procedures and systems are for dealing with customer service problems.

♦ How to select the best solution for your customer and your organisation.

♦ What to do if you are unable to help solve the problem.

What your organisation's procedures and systems are for dealing with customer service problems

In dealing with the resolution of customer service problems, you will need to work with your organisation's procedures and systems to help you sort things out. Sometimes, you will not personally be able to help. In these situations, you will need to help your customer understand how he or she might find an appropriate solution.

Remember

'When it comes to service recovery, there are three rules to keep in mind:

1 Do it right the first time.

2 Fix it properly if it ever fails.

3 Remember: There are no third chances.'

Source: Professor Leonard Berry, Texas A & M University

An organisation's systems and procedures are there to protect you, your customers and your organisation. They make sure the needs of everyone are dealt with in an appropriate and successful manner. How many times have you read words similar to the following?

♦ Buy with confidence – satisfaction guaranteed.
♦ It works – or your money back.
♦ If you don't like what you see – tell us.
♦ Your money back – if not totally satisfied.
♦ Our money-back guarantee does not affect your statutory rights.

These statements are all invitations to the customer to return to an organisation if he or she is not entirely happy with the product or service he or she has bought. With this in mind, things go wrong very quickly if on returning, the customer service practitioner does not know how to deal with the customer.

Active knowledge

Knowing in advance what your organisation expects you to do when a customer returns with a complaint will help you to give good customer service.

♦ Find out what guarantees or offers your organisation makes to its customers.

Refresh yourself on the legislation and regulations that may affect your role and the way in which your organisation delivers its products or services (see page 64).

♦ How does this legislation impact on what you are able to do on behalf of customers?

Complaints procedures

Many organisations actively encourage people to contact them with complaints and comments. They go as far as describing in detail what a customer needs to do in order to make a complaint. This shows a willingness to help and to use the information to try to improve customer service in the future. For example, an organisation may describe in its literature or on a website 'How to complain'.

An interactive complaint/feedback form on a company website is an innovative way of hearing customers' complaints

There are also many organisations such as the Citizens Advice Bureau and consumer organisations who will help people to complain. An ombudsman acts independently of the organisation and will step in to investigate a problem as a last resort, i.e. when all other avenues have failed. For example, the financial services ombudsman (www.financial-ombudsman.org.uk) will investigate problems connected with the financial services industry on behalf of customers.

Below is an example of what customers of any service provider are advised to do if they want to make a complaint.

Making a complaint – advice to customers

- ☐ Check whether the organisation has a complaints procedure.

- ☐ If there is no complaints procedure, tackle the problem on the spot. Say why you are unhappy and ask what can be done. If necessary, ask for the name of someone you can complain to.

- ☐ Be clear why you are not satisfied. Was it the way you were treated? Was something faulty? Are you unhappy with a decision?

- ☐ It is usually best to complain in writing. But if you telephone, ask for the name of the person you speak to.

- ☐ Keep a note of this information, with the date and time of your call and what was said. You may need to refer to this later.

- ☐ Say what you want to happen. Do you want an apology? Do you want a different decision? Do you want the proper service that should have been provided in the first place? Do you want them to change the way things are done?

Figure 4.12 A customer complaint checklist

Armed with such advice, it is not surprising that more and more people feel ready and able to make a complaint.

Active knowledge

Find out about your organisation's complaints procedures.

- ♦ What guarantees does your organisation make to its customers for the products or services you deal with?
- ♦ What promises are made concerning what will happen if a customer has a complaint?
- ♦ What (if anything) is the customer required to do when making a complaint?
- ♦ What are your responsibilities to your customers?
- ♦ What are your responsibilities to your organisation?

Dealing with complaints

Once you are prepared for any potential problem a customer may bring to you, your next step is to use the complaints system your organisation has in place for dealing with complaints. If there is no complaints procedure where you work, answering the following questions will help you to understand what role you need to take. You may need to seek guidance from an appropriate person to help you with the answers.

♦ Are you personally authorised to deal with a complaint? If not, who do you need to refer to?
♦ What records do you need to make about the complaint?
♦ What authority do you have, if any, to compensate the customer where appropriate?
♦ What types of compensation can a customer claim?
♦ What information is available to a customer to help him or her make a complaint?

There are many things that might lead to a complaint being made, as shown in the diagram below.

Figure 4.13 With customers ever more ready to complain, what can you add to this list?

It is likely your organisation will have a system for recording complaints. This sort of feedback can be used by organisations to improve the service they offer and can be monitored for trends so that work can be done to make things better in the future. Figure 4.11 illustrates a typical example of what a customer complaint form might look like. It has been completed by a customer service practitioner who has just dealt with a telephone call from a customer who is unhappy about a change to her refuse collection.

Customer complaint/comments	
Date: 28 March 2002	Customer name/details: Greta O'Shea, Manor House, Sea Lane
Description of complaint: new bin men not taking garden refuse away on today's round. Complaints about Council Tax being too high if garden refuse is not collected	
Action taken: Mrs O'Shea very angry. Calmed her down. Listened and explained new Council policy on recycling garden refuse. Asked her if she has seen promotional literature on new service. She had been missed off leaflet drop	
Customer kept informed of progress (include dates and details of action taken): N/A	
Feedback given to colleagues (if necessary): copy of complaint forwarded to team leader and leaflet despatched	

Figure 4.14 Customer complaint/comment form

Case study

Melita is a medical secretary working for an ear, nose and throat (ENT) consultant. When Melita goes on holiday her work is covered by another medical secretary, Wasim. Wasim's main responsibility is to another ENT consultant working in the same practice. Melita knows her colleague will do what he can to ensure customer service is maintained. However, with one person doing two people's jobs, Melita knows from experience that things can go wrong.

As a means of trying to minimise any disruption to service, Melita has introduced a simple complaints form and has discussed with Wasim how this could be used when she is away on holiday. Her colleague is happy to use the form and appreciates it might help everyone.

Melita goes on holiday leaving Wasim to cope as best he can. This means frequently leaving the answer phone on. Soon, a large number of messages and queries are left on the answer phone, including one that says:

'This is the third time I've rung on behalf of my elderly mother who is now really distressed. She has got a letter from your Consultant and doesn't understand why you want to see her back in the clinic. Every time she has telephoned in the past two days the answer phone is on. Now I've tried for her and I can't get through either. Don't you understand how distressing this is? Why isn't there anyone there? If you don't telephone me back by the end of the day, I will personally drive over to the hospital and bang on your door until someone sees me.' On picking up this message Wasim realises he has to prioritise it and deal with it immediately.

Imagine you are Wasim and complete a customer complaints/comment form.

♦ What impact might the system/procedure of completing this form have on preventing this situation occurring again?
♦ What action should he take?

Common customer complaints occur as a result of customer expectations not being met. These are particularly difficult complaints to try and solve as they are not formal complaints. This means you should recognise that a customer does not necessarily need to write to your organisation in order to complain. A passing comment of dissatisfaction made over the telephone or face-to-face should be recognised as a complaint.

Make notes of your customers' queries and complaints.

You should take seriously all instances where you are aware customer expectations have not been met. By recording these and taking any necessary action a cycle of continuous improvement can occur. The next time you hear what appears to be a passing comment such as 'The directions for finding Mrs. Thomas's office are not clear' or 'Why is it I always have to wait on a Friday?' think about recording this so someone can identify whether there is a need to take things forward to improve customer service.

How to select the best solution for your customer and your organisation

Customers should be treated as individuals in order to ensure they feel valued and that their individual needs are respected. When resolving problems, it therefore follows that what might suit one customer by way of a solution, may not suit another. For example, think about a situation where a tour operator needs to cancel a holiday to an overseas destination due to trouble breaking out in that area. The terms and conditions of booking the holiday will cover what the tour operator is obliged to do on behalf of its customer. The solution to this problem might be to offer a full refund to the customer, to rebook the holiday at a later date or to offer an alternative destination on the same date. Three solutions to the same problem. Only by asking the customer, will the tour operator find out which is the best solution.

We have discussed how it is not always possible to give customers exactly what they want every time. You need to consider the impact of every solution on your organisation too. This means you need to balance the needs of your customer with the needs of your organisation. For example, if a customer returns a perfectly good vacuum cleaner made for light use, it would be costly to simply swap it free of charge for a more expensive model suitable for heavy duty use. However, swapping the vacuum cleaner might be what the customer wants. What would you have done? To find out how you approach solution-finding in such circumstances, think about the following questions:

♦ Do you go for the first thing that comes into your head?
♦ Do you ask other people what they might think of your solution?
♦ Do you go for the cheapest/quickest option?
♦ Do you spend ages wondering what path to take?

Now attempt the exercise below:

♦ Join these dots using four straight lines without taking your pencil off the paper.

Did you immediately try to draw a line within the area confined by the nine dots? Only by going outside this area will you solve the problem (see the solution on page 184). This exercise demonstrates how people are often quite narrow-minded when they attempt to solve problems: they pick the obvious route rather than thinking about other more creative ways of doing things. By considering all the options available you might find a better solution.

Finding the right solution

If a problem cannot be solved on the spot, you can consider seeking out the support of colleagues to help you find the best solution. Involving others will not always be necessary. However, just as there is usually more than one solution, two heads are usually better than one.

Remember

There is usually more than one way of solving a problem. Go for the solution that best meets the needs of your customer, your colleagues and your organisation.

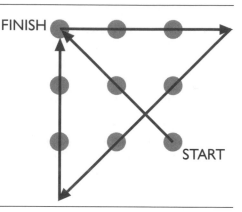

Active knowledge

Think about a complaint or problem you dealt with recently.

♦ How did you set about finding the best solution?
♦ Was your customer happy?
♦ What might you do differently next time?

1 Understand the problem	2 Identify the causes
What is the current situation? What does your customer want? What does your organisation need to happen?	Why/how did the problem happen? Gather all the information you need Gather facts/don't make assumptions

Solution-finding

3 Consider the solutions	4 Select the right solution
Involve your colleagues (if appropriate) Discuss ideas Try not to criticise ideas which seem unusual	Make a decision as to which idea is the right one Balance the needs of your customer with those of your organisation

Understand the problem

At this stage you will probably still have your customer with you. He or she will be talking with you face-to-face or on the telephone, or you might have some form of written communication from your customer. Make sure from what you are hearing or reading, you are absolutely sure of the facts. Customers do not always present you with everything you need to know, so you will need to ask questions such as the following:

♦ Have I fully understood what you are unhappy about; you said you were not happy with ... ?
♦ When did this problem first occur?
♦ Let me see, if I have understood you correctly, you want to ... ?
♦ Please explain to me exactly why it doesn't work.
♦ Who did you speak to?

Identify the causes

To solve the problem you need to identify the real causes, deal with them and then make them right for the future. You can do this by asking more questions such as the following:

♦ What went wrong?
♦ At what stage did it break down?
♦ Please tell me more about what happened.
♦ What should have happened?
♦ Has this happened before?
♦ Who was involved?

Depending on the individual situation, you will need to find out from both the customer and your colleagues what happened, and why. All the time you are asking your questions, you should also be listening very carefully to the responses. Do this non-defensively by not interrupting, not passing blame and not making judgements on what you have heard. You may not find this easy as your natural instincts are probably going to be to protect yourself and your organisation from blame. However, if you listen without making judgement or passing blame you will defuse any potential anger, hurt or confusion that might lead to a stressful situation. Use non-threatening facial expressions and body language. Remember silence is a powerful tool, do not interrupt. Encourage your customer to tell you more. Make probing statements such as 'tell me more about that ...'

Consider the solutions

Armed will all the facts surrounding the problem, you can now start to think about how to solve it. Your knowledge of your organisation's systems and procedures will help you to solve many problems. For example, you will know when you are able to give a refund and when you are not. You will know about your organisation's products and services applicable to your role in order to offer an alternative if necessary.

Where a problem cannot be solved on the spot, try involving your colleagues. Tell them about the facts of the problem and what the customer wants. If you have already thought about a solution, mention that too and ask for an opinion. Seek other ideas and suggestions from your colleagues. This may mean that you end up with three or four possible solutions. In order to decide which one is the right one, it will help if you work out the advantages and disadvantages of each.

Select the right solution

You can do this by writing down the advantages and disadvantages of each solution. These can include the following issues:

- cost: not just money but also risk of losing business
- time: how long will it take to implement the idea/solution? Is this amount of time appropriate for the needs of your customer and your colleagues?
- quality: is your decision a quick fix? If so, is it the right one?
- practicality: will your organisation benefit from sustained and improved customer service?

Case study

Nina is the receptionist at a financial brokerage. She has taken a telephone call from a customer regarding making an appointment with a colleague who is on holiday. Nina decided to draw up an advantages and disadvantages list to help her solve the problem.

Problem: unable to get access to Jane's diary. Customer insisting appointment made now for when Jane gets back	
Solution 1: make appointment now and tell Jane immediately on her return	
+	**−**
Customer happy	Jane might be booked/busy elsewhere. Customer unhappy if expectation not met
Solution 2: negotiate with customer to see someone else	
Customer dealt with even if they don't get their first choice. No risk of double booking. Retain business in my organisation	Jane might be annoyed at loss of customer to a colleague. Lack of first choice might mean customer will go elsewhere

Figure 4.15 Selecting the right solution

As you can see, it still might not be immediately obvious which solution is the right one to take.

- What would you do?
- Which solution is best for the customer?
- Which solution is best for Jane?
- Which solution is best for the financial brokerage?

Nina felt she needed to be honest with the customer and explain the situation. She also wanted to find out how important it was for the customer

Jane instead of another colleague. Nina decided that she needed to offer an appointment with another colleague. That way she did not risk any double booking and she could reassure the customer that her colleague would be able to help. Nina was aware that Jane might not be very happy and made a note to tell her she should leave her diary available next time.

Keys to good practice

Selecting the best solution

- ✓ Ask questions to get all the facts.
- ✓ Listen non-defensively.
- ✓ Check with the customer that you have understood.
- ✓ Take ownership of the problem.
- ✓ Identify the cause.
- ✓ Identify what the customer really wants.
- ✓ Use your organisation's systems and procedures to help select the right solution.
- ✓ Discuss possible solutions with others.
- ✓ Weigh up the advantages and disadvantages of each option.
- ✓ Make a decision bearing in mind the needs of the customer and the organisation.

Keeping your customer in the picture

It is important to remember that while you are trying to find the best solution, your customer is waiting. Sometimes it will take a few days, perhaps longer, to get to the right solution. Make sure you keep your customer updated, this ensures that they do not feel forgotten. Even if you have not quite sorted the issue out, your customer will appreciate you are doing your best and will want to know what you are doing even if the problem is not fully resolved.

Even bad news is better than no news at all. Keeping your customer in the picture also stops unnecessary complaints being made. How many times have you been on the receiving end of customers wanting to know what is happening? This scenario can easily be avoided if you take responsibility for keeping your customer informed.

Keep your customers informed at all times

What to do if you are unable to help solve the problem

You cannot possibly be expected to know everything, or indeed to have the responsibility for dealing with everything your customer wants or needs. Sometimes, you will need to ask for help, and sometimes you will need to suggest alternative options to your customers. This mean you will need to know the following:

♦ where to ask for help and support
♦ possible alternatives to problems
♦ additional information that may be of use to your customers.

Where to ask for help and support

In order to obtain help you will need to know the responsibilities of your colleagues working in other areas of your organisation. You should have a list of contact details (i.e. telephone numbers/addresses) for these people. It will also be useful to know where to find information on websites and product or service leaflets.

Possible alternatives to problems

You should be able to identify similar products or services your organisation offers if you are unable to provide an exact match. Discuss this with your customer and check to see if the alternative is suitable.

Knowing what your competitors offer when you do not provide an exact match may be another option for you to suggest. However, in theses situations you need to know when it is appropriate to mention alternative suppliers to customers. In helping a customer find a solution you may find yourself turning business away from your company. While this is lost business on that occasion, you can actually create goodwill in doing so.

Active knowledge

Find out under what circumstances it is appropriate for you to recommend to a customer that he or she goes to a competitor.

Giving additional information to customers

If a solution does not meet the needs of your customer, you might find that providing extra information will help. For example you might say any of the following:

♦ I know this is not what you originally wanted. However, did you realise that this product is able to ...
♦ Although we are out of stock of the model you need, I can give you this until your order arrives next week.
♦ Only last week another customer told me how much they liked ...

Case study

As an ex-commuter Wayne was pleased not to have to travel too often by train. Occasionally, he had to do so in his new job. His expectation of the train service was pretty low, including the service received at the ticket counter. When he went to buy a ticket to travel to the theatre in London he was surprised to be handed a new timetable with his ticket. He hadn't asked for it and realised these were being distributed because the timetables were changing for the winter.

- ◆ Why was Wayne so surprised?
- ◆ Why was this a good piece of customer service?
- ◆ What could you do in your job to provide information tactfully to your customers before being asked?

Remember

There is nothing wrong in not being able to help as long as you have made your best effort to help. The secret is to be able to tell the customer what you can do, not what you cannot do.

Keys to good practice

When you are unable to help

- ✓ Tell the truth.
- ✓ Don't make excuses.
- ✓ Be positive.
- ✓ Say what you can do.
- ✓ Offer alternatives and seek the agreement of your customer to any alternatives offered.

Test your knowledge

The statements below show some common problems you may face, irrespective of the type of environment in which you work. Think about what is behind the statements and apply them to your own work role. We'll call our frustrated customer service practitioner Damian.

Look at each of the statements and decide what Damian could do to help improve things. Here are some pointers for you to consider:

♦ His organisation's systems and procedures: are they helping or hindering?
♦ His product or service knowledge: is he up to date? If not, what can he do?
♦ Sources of help and assistance: does he know where/what these are?

What else can you think of?

4.3 Implement the solution to customer service problems

♦ How to discuss the proposed solution with customers.

♦ What you need to do to ensure action is taken to resolve the problem.

♦ How to make sure the customer is happy with any action taken.

How to discuss the proposed solution with customers

The problem-solving sequence (Figure 4.2) shows that dealing with customer complaints and problems is a three-step process. In Element 4.1 we looked at identifying the problem and in Element 4.2 you saw that a problem is solved by choosing the best possible solution. However, there would be no point in doing either of these two steps if you do not then take action. This is the focus of this element.

You may have decided upon the solution that you think is the best for the customer, but it is a risk to assume that the customer will always agree with your decision. For example, if a customer wanted to buy a navy blue winter coat and you had run out of that colour, would you automatically assume a red one would be suitable? You would need to find out what your customer wants.

With a more complicated problem you will need to reach an agreement with your customer about the proposed solution and ensure that the solution does meet the customer's needs. This means taking more than one opportunity to keep your customer informed and checking whether your solution is the right one for both the customer and your organisation. Finding the best solution to implement may involve you negotiating with your customer.

What is negotiation?

Think back to when you were much younger and wanted the latest toy for Christmas. How did you set about influencing your parent(s) to buy you this toy? What you were doing without knowing it was negotiating. Have you ever said 'I'll do my homework if you buy me those trainers?' Some may call this bribery, however, it is a form of negotiating.

In your customer service role, negotiating is discussing possible solutions you can offer your customers, hopefully to reach a conclusion everyone is happy with. Negotiation skills are life skills; they work just as well for you in your personal life as they will when applied to your work situation.

Figure 4.16 Successful negotiation

The key to negotiation is to keep it simple. Negotiating follows a five-stage process:

♦ prepare
♦ discuss
♦ propose
♦ bargain
♦ close (make decision).

Prepare

Like everything in life, preparation is the key to success. If you fail to prepare, then prepare to fail! Spending some time in preparing for your negotiation means you will be gathering all the information you need in order to be well informed about what you need to say and do. Doing this will enable you to feel more confident in your discussions with your customer. The following points will help you to prepare yourself to negotiate with a customer:

Assess your customer's expectations:

♦ decide how much information you already have about what your customer wants
♦ decide what action you need to take to seek any extra information
♦ decide what you are prepared to do on your customer's behalf
♦ decide what flexibility you have to change what your organisation usually offers.

Set yourself goals

Setting yourself goals means agreeing with yourself what you are prepared to do and what you are not prepared to do. To do this you need to:

♦ decide what it is essential to achieve
♦ decide which things are just nice to have.

Think what you will say to your customer when you first start to negotiate:

♦ decide what you will say at the start of the conversation.

This is not about the greeting, it is about stating how you wish the conversation to proceed. You should state the facts of the situation as you see them and then check your customer's understanding.

Discuss

You are now ready to start to negotiate. At this stage you will be discussing and agreeing your proposed solutions to the problem with your customer. This will involve a lot of questioning. Use this stage to gather information, clarify the position and test out your customer's reactions. Show your customer you are listening to them. Repeat back from time to time what they say. Be sincere and demonstrate you are serious about sorting out the problem. This is all about developing rapport with your customer. It is important at this stage to ask for your customer's ideas.

Propose

You are now at the stage where you can discuss your proposed option with the customer. Bear in mind that your customer may not accept what you have to say at first hearing, especially if you are sorting out a long-standing complaint. A successful negotiator will at this stage always be thinking back to what he or she decided were the goals that needed to be fulfilled. Equally, your customer will have his or her own firm ideas about how much he or she is prepared to compromise.

Bargain

This is where both parties start to discuss the possible compromises that they are willing to offer. For example:

♦ I'll work late tonight if you work late for me next week.
♦ If you are prepared to wait just one week more I'll be able to get the colour you want.
♦ If you agree to order from us, I will ensure our advertising mentions your involvement.

Having made your statement, expect a discussion to follow until both parties are ready to make a decision on the proposed solution, i.e. to close the negotiation.

Close

This is the end of a successful negotiation. Here you are seeking the agreement of your customer to the way forward. You might say something like:

♦ We've agreed everything else, if you will just accept this, then we have a deal.
♦ What would you like me to do – option A or option B?
♦ Let me summarise what we have agreed ...

When you close, what you are doing is making a statement or putting a question to your customer that requires him or her to say yes or no. If he or she does not, the negotiation simply continues until both of you reach an agreement.

How was it for you?

Think back to the last time you were in a situation where you had to negotiate with a customer.

♦ Was it a good experience for both of you?
♦ At the end, did you both feel you had got what you wanted?
♦ What might you do differently next time?

Not every situation you will be involved in with a customer will mean you need to enter into a full-scale negotiation. This is only necessary where there is no obvious solution and when a certain amount of influencing and persuading is required.

The skills needed to be a successful negotiator

A customer service practitioner needs to be confident that their own knowledge and skills will enable them to enter into a negotiation. This confidence comes from knowing about your products or services, knowing what your organisation expects of you, and from knowing what you are authorised to do without making reference to others. The skills needed to be a successful negotiator are outlined below.

Know what you want

Knowing what you want and why you want it will help your customer to reach a decision, and will also inspire confidence in you. This might be something as simple as knowing that you need to obtain more information, or it may mean thinking about what you need to do in order to keep the customer satisfied with your organisation. Knowing what you want means being specific and having a valid reason for your proposed solution.

Know what your customer wants

Before you start to negotiate you must ensure you know enough about what your customer expects from you and your organisation.

Be fair and honest

Having established your and your customer's expectations, make sure you do not make unrealistic promises. It is pointless proposing a solution that you know will not be possible, as this will only aggravate and frustrate your customer.

Listen

Ensure that you listen carefully to your customer's point of view. Check that the customer has understood any proposed options to solving the problem.

Be friendly

Keep things professional but be friendly. There is no need to be severe in your tone of voice or in your facial expressions simply because you are trying to be assertive. You are allowed to smile at appropriate moments. Negotiation is not about confrontation, it is about both parties reaching mutual agreement.

Have an alternative solution

If you are very clever, you will always keep something up your sleeve with which to reach a compromise if necessary. This means having more than one option; perhaps a first-choice solution and then another one that will still be good for the customer.

Case study

Look at the following situations where negotiation is at work.

1 A customer is very interested in buying a car if the price is right; the salesperson is keen to sell

   This is a classic negotiating situation that will ultimately result in a mutually satisfactory agreement. If the negotiation does not work, the customer will walk away or the salesperson will refuse to sell. The salesperson might start to negotiate by stating that he or she will fit mud flaps to the car if the customer buys at the price quoted.

   Imagine you are the car salesperson.

   ◆ How would you start the conversation?
   ◆ What else might you say to bargain with the customer?
   ◆ What signs would you look for to tell you you were succeeding in getting the right price?

2 A colleague complains to you about your inability to keep your desk tidy. You say 'What about all that equipment I'm storing for you on my desk – I've got no room for my own things!'

   This is a negotiating situation because both parties can discuss how the problem might be solved by reaching a mutually agreeable solution. The desk is untidy because there is simply too much equipment being stored on it. The equipment belongs to the colleague who has complained. By negotiating, the owner of the desk can use the fact that his or her colleague does not like to see it looking untidy by reaching an agreement to store the equipment elsewhere.

Try role-playing this example with a friend. Ensure you bring in all the stages of negotiation.

Active knowledge

1 Think about situations where you might be involved in negotiating with a customer. What would you do in the following situations?

♦ problems occur due to a system or procedure failure
♦ problems occur due to lack of resources (i.e. people, time, money)
♦ human error causes a mistake.

2 Find out what authority you have to negotiate with your customers.

♦ What can you offer?
♦ How much flexibility do you have to change the products or services you deal with?

Case study

Mary has been going to the same hairdresser's for years. During that time she has seen many different hairdressers and she now knows the salon owner well. At her last appointment she was very surprised to be put into the hands of a trainee hairdresser, despite having made her usual booking for her preferred hairdresser, Tina. Mary demanded to see the salon owner, Graeme. Here is a transcript of what was said:

Mary: What's going on? I've been coming here for years and nobody told me Tina was moving on!

Graeme: Tina left unexpectedly. I'm really sorry we didn't phone to let you know.

Mary: So am I. I would've thought I deserved more than to be put into the hands of a junior!

Graeme: I can see you're not happy, Mary. What would you like to happen?

Mary: I want my hair done, of course. By someone who knows what they are doing.

Graeme: Of course, Mary. I can assure you the person we have allocated to you will do a good job for you even though her training is not quite complete.

Mary: That's not good enough. I have an important function tonight and must look my very best.

Graeme: Why don't you give her a go? What I will do is to guarantee I will personally supervise by moving her chair next to mine. If you are not entirely happy afterwards, I will put things right. However, I'm sure that will not be needed.

Mary: That will be fine. Can I check you will personally find the time today to put things right if needed?

Graeme: Yes, that's right. Do we have a deal?

Mary: Yes, I'm happy now.

◆ Has Graeme achieved what he wanted?
◆ Has Mary reached a satisfactory outcome?
◆ Looking at the discussion, where do the five stages of negotiation start and finish?

Problem-solving

Not all problems will need to be approached and solved through negotiations. In most cases what you will be doing is simply discussing options for solving a problem. This involves the following:

Figure 4.17 Solving a problem

Describe what you can do

Describe, in a positive way, what options are available to help your customer. Try to state the benefits or advantages of your proposed solution in order to help your customer make a decision. Think back to the case study at the hairdresser's (page 196). This showed you the stance the salon owner wanted to take, i.e. he wanted to negotiate. Graeme set out to do the following:

♦ keep Mary's business
♦ apologise
♦ reassure Mary that the alternative hairdresser would be supervised
♦ reassure Mary that he would personally intervene in the unlikely event of Mary not being happy.

He balanced the needs of the salon with Mary's needs by not immediately stepping in to do Mary's hair. This would have an impact on customers already booked in with him. Neither did he tell Mary to go and do some shopping and come back when he would fit her in at lunchtime. Neither did he suggest Mary go to the hairdresser in the next village where Tina now worked. These were all options, yet Graeme knew at the outset what he needed to happen, i.e. he wanted to keep the business without compromising other customers' needs

Ask the customer for ideas

Having told the customer what you can do, ask the customer what he or she wants to happen. You must ask the customer for his or her ideas, otherwise you will have no idea what his or her expectations are. For instance, the customer may expect you to do the following:

♦ cancel everything you are doing in order to help
♦ give a full refund
♦ replace damaged goods
♦ repair an item without charging for it
♦ apologise
♦ speak to a manager/supervisor.

Clarify any questions your customer may have

Having discussed proposed options, there are bound to be some questions to deal with. Clarify these and any outstanding issues before agreeing on the action to be taken.

Agree with your customer what you will do and tell them how you are going to do it

Ask for your customer's ideas regarding the action you propose to take. Human nature being what it is, this will make your customer feel involved with the decision and the situation. He or she will feel some ownership of the solution. This helps to calm down even the angriest of customers as he or she will feel they are winning. It also ensures that the customer agrees with the final decision.

Once you have agreed on the best possible solution with your customer, you need to let them know how and when they can expect the action to happen. This will involve you doing the following:

♦ Repeating what action you have decided to take, e.g. 'I will refund your account with the sum of £75 by close of business today. You will also see a credit of £25 on your account as a gesture of goodwill for the inconvenience you have been caused'.

♦ Giving timescales of when the customer's problem will be solved. Break things down in terms of dates and times if more than one action is required.

♦ Confirming the action you will take. Do you need to write to confirm? If so, say when you will be writing

♦ Are other people involved in sorting out the problem? If so, say who else is responsible if you have sought your colleagues' agreement to talk to your customer.

Remember

Keep your customer informed at all times of what you are doing and how their problem is being dealt with.

What you need to do to ensure action is taken to resolve the problem

So many customers complain about their complaints! They say their complaints are not taken seriously and followed through. Customers say that their promises are just not being kept. This, of course, deepens the original problem even more in the eyes of the customer. They are even more upset with you and your organisation than they were when the problem first surfaced.

Customers expect you to do what you have said you will do. It is very important to make sure that you can deliver on the promises that you make, in particular the action that you and the customer have agreed on. This involves monitoring the progress of any action in the following ways:

A complaint that is not handled well can lead to many more problems

♦ making diary notes to check action points have been dealt with

♦ contacting your customer to check they are happy

♦ contacting any colleagues who are involved to check that action points have been dealt with.

Case study

Amazon, the online book shop, promised to deliver a new Harry Potter book to customers who had pre-ordered it by a specified deadline. They promised to deliver it on the same day that shop sales were authorised to begin.

Jeff Bezos – founder and CEO of Amazon.com

This was a tall order – over 250,000 volumes and Amazon and its partner (Federal Express) came very close to achieving it. According to the press, about 3800 people did not get their books on time due to a software problem that misread mailing addresses on some orders. Amazon said that 1.5 per cent of the books did not make it into the expectant hands of Harry Potter's fans on the big day. In other words, the company only scored 98.5 per cent on keeping its promise.

Amazon admitted its mistake, first to its customers and then to reporters who wanted to know how the much-publicised delivery went. Then the company offered to make it up to the customers who received late delivery by giving them full refunds of the purchase price (plus shipping and handling) and they got to keep their books.

The total cost for Amazon's welcome apology was in the region of US$75,000, a sum that would not trouble an organisation of this size too much. However, the underlying gesture is what good customer service is all about: a promise was broken and so Amazon quickly did the right thing at the right time, without hesitation and regardless of short-term costs.

1   If you were a customer service practitioner handling queries about non-receipt of orders, how would you deal with them?

2   What would you need to do in your organisation to ensure you knew about the following:

♦ The promises your organisation makes to its customers?
♦ What your organisation plans to do to recover from poor service delivery?

How to make sure the customer is happy with any action taken

It is very easy to feel as though a complaint is dealt with as soon as you initiate the action, particularly if you work in a busy environment. However, making a courtesy call or a follow-up call to a customer whose problem you are sorting out will strengthen the relationship that customer has with your organisation. This follow-up could be on the telephone or by email or by letter. What is important is that you show an interest. It will also give you the chance to make sure that everything went according to plan. It means you can check with your customer that the action you said would happen has indeed happened to the customer's satisfaction. This will stop another complaint being made if things have not gone quite according to plan Goodwill will continue to grow because you are showing that you care.

The quick guide to service recovery

We have now covered all the stages of the problem-solving sequence and the skills you require to become a successful negotiator. The table below gives you a quick guide that pulls all the information together.

Skill	What it does
Show you are listening	Do not interrupt. What is the customer trying to tell you?
Thank the customer	This shows you are taking the matter seriously and are pleased you and your organisation are being given a second chance to put things right.
Apologise	This does not mean you are admitting liability, it simply acknowledges the problem. Do not get defensive.
Do not pass blame	Accept responsibility on behalf of your organisation and your colleagues. Own the problem – if you do this you show you are going to take action.
Ask effective questions	Get to the heart of the problem. Make sure you have all the facts. Check your understanding is correct.
Explain what you can do	State the action you are going to take. Advise timescales. Keep your customer informed of progress.
Check your customer is happy	Ask 'Are you happy with what I am going to do/with what we have agreed?'
Take action	Just do it! Keep your promises.

Figure 4.18 A quick guide to service recovery

Test your knowledge

Think about recent problems you have dealt with. Consider the following:

♦ how you took action to agree with your customers what would happen to sort the problem out
♦ how you made sure your promises were kept
♦ how you checked with your customer(s) that they were happy
♦ what would you do differently (if anything) next time?

Check your knowledge

1 List three reasons why it is important to resolve customer service problems.

2 What four factors feature in the problem-solving cycle?

3 In your organisation, what are the most frequent causes of customer complaints?

4 How might you check you have understood your customer's problems?

5 A customer complaint form is used to:

   a improve the service an organisation offers

   b blame whoever was responsible for getting it wrong

   c monitor how badly a person is performing

6 Name the four steps to solution-finding.

7 What should you do if you are unable to help solve a problem?

8 Complete this sentence: 'Negotiation is all about ...'

9 Name the five stages of successful negotiation.

10 What do you need to know about before entering into any negotiation with a customer?

11 Why is it important to describe to a customer the action you will be taking to solve a problem?

12 If you are involving colleagues in solving a problem, what must you do to ensure you have their commitment?

13 What is a courtesy or follow-up call?

14 If you don't get things right for your customers, who will?

15 List five reasons why problems might occur.

UNIT 5

Support customer service improvements

Any organisation that aspires to be successful will need to continuously look for ways to improve customer service. Organisations and their employees need to make these improvements and this optional unit will help you do your part. You can help by becoming enthusiastically involved with any changes your organisation decides are necessary in order to improve customer service. You will need to show customers through your behaviour and your actions that you are positive about these changes.

In addition, by listening to customer comments and by taking into account customer feedback, you may have your own thoughts and ideas about how customer service could be improved. You will need to present these ideas to an appropriate person who will be able to judge whether your ideas should be taken forward.

Supporting customer service improvements is a three-stage process:

♦ collect and use customer feedback to identify how customer service might be improved
♦ implement changes to customer service
♦ find out and evaluate what your customers think about these changes.

The elements for this option unit are:

♦ 5.1 Use feedback to identify potential customer service improvements
♦ 5.2 Contribute to the implementation of changes in customer service
♦ 5.3 Assist with the evaluation of changes in customer service.

Use feedback to identify potential customer service improvements

This chapter deals with the first stage in supporting customer service improvements: collect and use customer feedback to identify how customer service might be improved. You need to show how you make sure that comments customers make to you are used to improve customer service. This is important because, if you and your organisation do not listen to customers, another organisation will. By listening and using the feedback you obtain, you will be helping to make sure customer satisfaction remains high. You will be making sure any changes to customer needs and expectations are quickly brought to the attention of your organisation. After all, you are in an excellent position to be able to do this; you deal with customers all the time and they expect you to listen.

WHAT YOU NEED TO KNOW OR LEARN

♦ How the customer experience is influenced by the quality of the service received.
♦ How to gather customer feedback.
♦ How to use customer feedback to identify areas for improvement.

How the customer experience is influenced by the quality of the service received

If a customer does not feel valued, he or she is unlikely to feel any loyalty to an organisation. This experience of not feeling valued might be caused by one or both of the following:

♦ the attitude and behaviour of customer service practitioners
♦ the needs and expectations of the customer not being met.

The customer experience is influenced by the following two key factors:

♦ how you personally deal with customers: the personal service
♦ how your organisation uses its products or services to meet or exceed customer needs and expectations: the material service.

The main reason why a customer will change who he or she does business with is the personal factor, i.e. the wrong attitude or behaviour of one single employee can be all it takes for a customer to go elsewhere. This means you, as the customer service practitioner, have a vital part to play in ensuring the customer experience is what it should be. Every customer service practitioner makes an impact upon the customer experience, and this can be either positive or negative.

The personal service

This relates to what you do and the way that you do it. We have spoken throughout this book about how you can create a positive impression with your customers and how you should look to sustain this throughout your dealings with customers. This positive personal service includes the words you use and the way in which you say them or write them. It is about displaying confidence and showing by your actions that you mean what you say. When dealing face-to-face with a customer, body language is important too. If you say you want to help it must sound and look genuine. This means you have to have the right attitude to your work.

Figure 5.1 Aspects of personal service

Case study

It was November, and Philip (a sales team leader) had booked a meeting room in a hotel for the day. He was meeting with five colleagues who had all travelled long distances. Philip agreed in advance with the hotel that tea/coffee would be required on arrival and again two hours later. He also confirmed all the refreshment details with Warren, the duty manager, when he arrived at the hotel.

Unfortunately the central heating system was not working and the room in the hotel quickly became cold during the meeting. More tea/coffee was required so Philip telephoned through to reception and ordered some more. The receptionist said it would be brought to the room within 15 minutes.

Shortly after this telephone call, the meeting room door opened and Warren walked in looking rather angry and saying 'I understand you have changed your mind; you want more tea and coffee now. I'll bring it to you soon.' Warren then walked out of the room without waiting for an answer, leaving Philip and his colleagues speechless.

◆ Why do you think Warren felt it necessary to check up on the telephone call requesting more tea and coffee?

◆ Bearing in mind the room was cold, what should Warren have done to make it a positive experience?

◆ What could Warren have done to be more proactive?

◆ Was there anything wrong with the words Warren used or the way in which he said them?

◆ List the factors that made this a negative personal experience for Philip.

How was it for you?

Think of a specific time when, as a customer, you were dissatisfied with the service you received.

◆ Concentrate on how you felt.

◆ Think about what the person(s) dealing with you did to make you feel dissatisfied.

◆ List the factors associated with your negative experience that relate to personal service.

We will now look at how Philip's experience changed into a positive one at a different hotel.

Case study

In the light of his experience with the hotel he used in November, Philip cancelled six months' worth of bookings with them. It was now December and time for Philip's monthly review meeting with his sales team. The weather was particularly cold and although the heating was on full, the meeting room in the new hotel was uncomfortably cold.

About an hour into the meeting there was a knock on the door. Philip opened it to find John, the duty manager, with a tray of coffee and tea together with some warm scones and jam. 'I haven't ordered this' said, Philip. John replied that he was aware the hotel's heating system was not coping with the unusually cold weather and that the tea and scones were being made available with the hotel's compliments, i.e. there would be no charge. He said he was also arranging for a couple of fan heaters to be sent to the room.

After John left, Philip smiled at his colleagues while tucking into the delicious scones, and they started to talk about the contrast in service between this hotel and the one they had used the month before.

- ♦ When John decided it was necessary to supply complimentary refreshments, what considerations did he make?
- ♦ List how John used the personal touch to make this experience a positive one for Philip.
- ♦ How easy do you think it was for this second hotel to deliver a positive customer service experience?

How was it for you?

Think about a time when you were very satisfied with the service you received.

- ♦ How did you feel?
- ♦ What personal factors contributed to your satisfaction?

Keys to good practice

Using personal service to make a positive customer experience

- ✓ Always have a positive attitude.
- ✓ Use appropriate words in an appropriate manner.
- ✓ Match your body language to what you are saying.
- ✓ Be courteous.
- ✓ Exceed expectations (within the limits of your authority).
- ✓ Take ownership of issues/problems.
- ✓ Keep your promises.
- ✓ Know about your products or services.
- ✓ Show you are a confident person.

The material service

What you have read about personal service shows you where you have the ability to influence the customer experience. The material service deals with all those things you need from your organisation to support the delivery of excellent customer service. This can include the price, quality, quantity and timing of the following:

- ♦ products
- ♦ services
- ♦ equipment
- ♦ procedures

- support systems
- delivery
- information
- the environment in which the service is delivered.

The material service in Philip's hotel meeting room would include the comfort and suitability of the chairs and tables, the room temperature, the procedures in use to contact the duty manager, the standard of refreshments, the ability of the hotel to follow the agreed contract and the equipment provided in the meeting room.

You may not have a great deal of control over material factors. However, you do have control over the way in which you use them and the way in which you respond to feedback given to you about these material factors.

If you provide an excellent personal and material service the customer experience will be positive, i.e. the customer believes you and your organisation are delivering excellent customer service. You may achieve a 'moment of truth', i.e. a specific milestone when a customer is able to say or think 'That was just what I wanted'. A moment of truth can be also be negative. Remember how just one individual who gets things wrong can badly affect a customer's perception of the quality of service an organisation delivers. On the other hand a positive moment of truth can completely turn around a customer who had previously been dissatisfied.

Some moments of truth are created by the material service you use. For instance, a car-park attendant working in a badly signed multi-storey car park may need to deal with many customers who cannot find their cars. No matter how good the car park attendant is at using his or her knowledge and skills to deliver excellent personal service, customers may still perceive they have paid far too much to park in what turns out to be a car park that causes hassle. The moment of truth here is negative, even though the car-park attendant will have done his or her best to try to win the customer over.

Remember

Positive personal service + positive material service = positive moments of truth.

How to gather customer feedback

Seeking feedback is clearly very important to the success of an organisation. Without feedback, an organisation will not be able to understand customers' changing needs and expectations. The organisation will get left behind, business will be lost and a competitor will step in and take the business.

Feedback is important for the following reasons:

- every customer will have different needs and expectations
- these needs and expectations change over time
- products and services therefore also need to change
- using feedback helps an organisation to show it cares about its customers.

Any changes made to products or services may be as a direct result of feedback or they may occur in anticipation of future customer needs. Think about the mobile telephone industry and how both the appearance and the services available from a handset have changed in the past five years. The personal service you deliver is also something that you can change as a direct result of feedback received.

The case studies about the two hotels (on pages 205 and 206) are examples of how one person can get it wrong and another can get it right. How can the individuals concerned learn to spot opportunities for getting customer service right first time? One obvious way is to listen to customers. What is it that a customer tells you that you should be reacting to in order to support customer service improvements?

Customer feedback can reach you in two key ways:

- Informally when you deal with customers, i.e. when talking or writing to them.
- Formally via systems and procedures your organisation uses to obtain customer feedback.

Methods you can use to gather informal customer feedback

You can obtain informal feedback from customers during your day-to-day dealings with them (see Unit 2 for more information on the following techniques).

Figure 5.2 Methods you can use to gather informal customer feedback

Asking questions

Asking your customers questions is the most direct and effective way of getting feedback on your service. You might say something like the following:

♦ Have I been able to do what you wanted?
♦ Is everything to your satisfaction?
♦ Are you happy with that?

By asking questions you are indicating to your customer that both you and your organisation care about the service offered. Do not forget to listen carefully to the response.

Listening to your customer

As well as listening carefully to the response to your questions, you should also listen for comments a customer might make in passing. If you hear a customer mumbling to another customer while looking less than pleased, this may be an indication that all is not well. You will, of course, only find out what is wrong by asking a direct question, e.g. 'Is there something else I can do for you?' or 'You do not appear to be happy with that. Do tell me if I can do something to help'. Feedback does not always have to be negative. Make sure you also listen out for the positive comments customers make.

Observing customer behaviour

In face-to-face situations you can use your observational skills as a means of gathering informal feedback.

Remember

When observing a customer's body language you should also take account of what he or she is saying. A frowning face might mean your customer has a headache and have nothing at all to do with customer service.

Feedback contained within written communications

There may be opportunities for you to spot feedback in letters or emails you deal with. For instance, when ordering another product a customer might make a comment about how pleased he or she was with his or her original purchase. Alternatively, a customer might express in writing some dissatisfaction with a product or service.

Case study

Albert is Chair of the Brownlands Village Pensioners Society (BVPS). BVPS have a weekly shopping trip to their local superstore, where they also used to enjoy a fish and chip lunch prior to the in-store cafeteria being converted to a coffee shop.

Albert's members have asked him to write to the local superstore to thank the manager for the way in which staff supported Gwenda, who was taken ill while visiting the store. This is what the letter said:

Brownlands Village Pensioners Society
1 The Copse
Brownlands Village
Near Halifax
HF67 1XZ

Dear Sir

As you know, BVPS organise a weekly shopping trip to your store and we are grateful for the support our less able members receive from your staff.

Last week Gwenda Blythe was taken ill suddenly while in your store. She received prompt attention from your first aider who quickly recognised an ambulance was necessary. As a result Mrs Blythe received the help she needed and we believe a serious deterioration in her health was avoided. Please pass on our sincere thanks to all involved

While writing, BVPS miss the fish and chip lunches we used to enjoy after the shopping was completed. Somehow coffee and a croissant just isn't the same!

Yours sincerely

Albert Parsons

Chair BVPS

♦ The purpose of this letter was to thank the store for helping Gwenda. How should the manager use the letter to thank the staff involved?
♦ What else does the letter contain that is useful feedback?
♦ How can the letter be used to support customer service improvements?

When you listen to customers and observe their behaviour, you might also pick up some useful feedback on how you can improve your own performance. Listen out for passing comments about how well (or not) you are doing.

When reading letters or emails from customers, make sure you understand the feelings that are behind the words. If someone has written to you (or your manager) to say they are very pleased with the help you have given, then you should take this as excellent praise for a job well done. It takes time and effort to say thank you; be proud that your customer has told you he or she is pleased.

How was it for you?

Think about a time when you last gave feedback to an organisation or to an individual working in customer service.

♦ What prompted you to give feedback?
♦ What was the response? If it was negative feedback, did you feel you were listened to?
♦ If you have not given any feedback, why have you not done so?

Methods you can use to gather formal customer feedback

Your organisation will have systems and procedures in place to gather customer feedback (see Unit 2 for more information on the following techniques).

Figure 5.3 Formal methods of gathering customer feedback

The variety of methods used will depend on what sort of feedback your organisation wishes to obtain and also on the budget available.

Questionnaires

These are a series of questions put to customers (usually on a form or in a letter) that ask customers about the quality of the service received. A key factor for any organisation to remember when devising a questionnaire is to only ask questions that lead to a response being acted upon. For instance, it would be pointless for a public house to ask the question 'At what time would you like the bar to shut?' if licensing laws state the bar must shut at 10.30pm.

Your involvement with questionnaires might include the following:

♦ collating responses
♦ handing out questionnaires personally to customers who visit your premises
♦ enclosing questionnaires with other written communications to customers.

Telephone surveys

There are two basic types of telephone survey:

♦ the customer is asked questions. These are known as 'ask and answer' surveys
♦ the customer enters into a discussion with the caller.

Ask and answer surveys involve the customer service practitioner reading from a script. That way every customer is asked the same questions, thus ensuring consistency.

Discussion telephone surveys ask exploratory questions enabling detailed feedback to be obtained. The customer service practitioner or interviewer needs to be experienced in listening and he or she will need to probe further. Here is an example of how one of these surveys might sound:

Interviewer:	When you visited the dentist's surgery yesterday, what was your impression of how you were greeted at reception?
Customer:	It was OK. Eventually.
Interviewer:	Could you explain what you mean by eventually?
Customer:	There seemed to be about four receptionists, yet it was a long time before anyone acknowledged I was waiting.
Interviewer:	Were they busy with another patient?
Customer:	No, they were simply talking to each other.
Interviewer:	Is there anything else the receptionists could have done better?

Customer: Yes, after I had gone to the waiting room, it would have been helpful if someone had taken the time to keep me updated as to why the dentist was running so late. And can someone please change those magazines? They are over two years old!

Focus groups

These are meetings run by an organisation for a selected group of a small number of customers (e.g. 8–10). Organisations who choose this method usually have specific questions on an important issue that they want feedback on. Many customers often feel valued or special when they are invited to attend a focus group.

Street surveys

These are used by organisations who wish to seek feedback on a potential customer's buying habits. For instance, a clothing manufacturer might be interested in developing a new line of clothes for females in the 15-to-19-year age bracket to wear out clubbing. In order to seek feedback on what these specific types of customers might be interested in, the manufacturer might employ an agency to undertake a street survey.

Mystery shoppers

These are people employed by an organisation to undertake anonymously the role of a customer, i.e. they will pretend to be a real customer. Results will be collated and given to the organisation as a means of obtaining feedback and what it was like to be a customer.

Comments/suggestion boxes

This is one of the simplest and cheapest methods of obtaining customer feedback. It involves a box being made available in order for customers to drop their suggestions or complaints into it.

 Asking you

You are the person at the sharp end. If you are alert to gathering informal feedback from customers then who better for your organisation to ask than you!

Active knowledge

Looking at both informal and formal methods of gathering customer feedback:

♦ Write down which methods you currently use.
♦ How effective are they at enabling you to obtain customer feedback on their needs and expectations?

How to use customer feedback to identify areas for improvement

Feedback is required to ensure a better understanding of customers' needs and expectations. These expectations are based on a variety of feelings, needs and wants and they change over time.

An example of a change in customer expectations is calling customers by their first name. Only 20 years ago it would have been inappropriate (in the majority of situations) to call a customer by his or her first name, even if the relationship was long standing. Today, many call centre agents will call a customer by his or her first name, despite never having spoken to him or her before. This familiarity is seen by some people as a step too far and by others as a more relaxed way of doing business. Only by asking its customers will an organisation find out if its approach is the right one.

The key questions that need to be answered are the following:

♦ What do customers want?
♦ Is the organisation/department/unit/people providing it?

Of course, there are thousands of ways in which these two basic questions can be asked and you have seen that there are many methods that can be used to seek this feedback.

Remember

Finding out about your customers' needs and expectations is the first step in gathering customer feedback. The next is to make sure something is done with this information.

Using a feedback diary

Earlier in this book we suggested you keep a feedback diary (see page 151). This is particularly useful when you are gathering informal feedback as it ensures you do not forget what you have seen or heard. If time does not permit you to update a feedback diary on the spot, then consider jotting your thoughts down onto a Post-it note and keeping these with your diary until you are in a better position to update it. Figure 5.4 shows an example of an entry in a feedback diary.

Date	Source of feedback	Complaints/compliments	Action taken
28 June	Letter from Albert Parsons, Chair of BVPS.	1. Praise for first aid support and speed of response. 2. Criticism of changeover from cafeteria to coffee shop.	1. Include at next team meeting. 2. Advise district office. 3. Monitor usage of coffee shop.

Figure 5.4 Sample entry in a feedback diary

Using a feedback diary ensures that feedback is captured and not forgotten. It is also useful to be able to record the action you need to take in order to ensure the feedback is used appropriately.

There are three key areas you should look at where feedback could be used to support customer service improvements. Figure 5.5 illustrates some possible areas any organisation will need to think about.

	Possible improvements
SYSTEMS AND PROCEDURES	Upgrade technology. Increase methods of communication between customers and the organisation. Assess competitor activity. Make it easier for customers to complain. Implement a queuing system. Devise a customer satisfaction questionnaire.
PRODUCTS AND SERVICES	Combine services that are very similar. Make information more accessible. Increase variety of stock available all year round.
PEOPLE (employees)	Increase product knowledge. Evaluate customer service training. Recognise achievements. Reward high performing staff. Say 'Thank you'. Introduce an appraisal system.

Figure 5.5 Areas for customer service improvement

Active knowledge

1 Using the three key areas for improvement (systems and procedures, products and services and people), think about what you would personally like to see improved where you work. Include your personal skills and knowledge and your working environment. Make a list.

2 Using this list, think about any feedback you have received that would support your ideas for improvement.

3 Write down why your own thoughts and the feedback you have received from customers make it important for action to be taken.

Sharing feedback

You should decide which is the most appropriate way of sharing feedback with others. The methods available include the following:

- on a 1:1 basis
- informally over lunch
- at a team meeting
- on the intranet/notice board.

It is very important to discuss your ideas with others (e.g. a line manager, supervisor, team leader). This ensures that you are acting within the scope of your authority. For instance, there may already be plans to make improvements that you are unaware of. There may be legal reasons why an improvement would need to be carried out in a certain way. By discussing your thoughts, you will be ensuring that you are playing your part in contributing to the overall perception of the standard of customer service.

Test your knowledge

Think of five negative comments consistently made to you by customers.

1   How did you first learn about these comments – was it by phone, face-to-face or by written communication?

   ♦   Was it easy for customers to give you this feedback?
   ♦   If not, what can you do to show that you and your organisation welcome feedback?
   ♦   How did you react to the comments?
   ♦   What (if anything) did you tell your customers you would do?

2   Thinking about the comments themselves, do they relate to systems, procedures, people or a combination of all three?

   ♦   Is it the personal service or material factors which need addressing?
   ♦   Were the comments made directly about you and your own performance?
   ♦   If so, what do you need to do to address them?
   ♦   In terms of change, where is the biggest need for improvement?

Contribute to the implementation of changes in customer service

This chapter deals with the second stage in supporting customer service improvements: implement changes to customer service. These changes may be in connection with the following:

♦ the products or services your organisation offers
♦ how products or services are supplied
♦ how you and your colleagues behave when delivering products or services.

WHAT YOU NEED TO KNOW OR LEARN

♦ How to present your ideas for change to others.
♦ How to contribute to the implementation of changes to customer service systems and procedures.
♦ How to keep the customer informed of changes.

♦ How to work with others to support changes made by your organisation.

How to present your ideas for change to others

When you are identifying your own ideas for change, you will have gone through a thought process questioning why things need to change at all. This is part of your planning to make a change. Think of it as developing an action plan for supporting customer service improvements. If you work towards drawing up an action plan you can use this to discuss your thoughts and ideas with others. This will mean you and your ideas will have more chance of succeeding because you will be able to explain what the benefits of your ideas will be.

When identifying your ideas for change you will need to consider:

♦ what you are aiming to achieve
♦ what the impact and benefit of any change will be on customer service
♦ what will happen to customer service if a change is not made.

You will also need to identify how you intend making your idea for change happen. This will involve you answering questions such as the following:

♦ Who needs to be involved?
♦ What needs to be done?
♦ What are the costs?
♦ When should the change start?
♦ When should the change be complete?
♦ How will you and your organisation decide if the change has worked?

Case study

Here is an example of a partially completed action plan drawn up by Garry, who works for a firm that designs and installs conservatories. Garry drew up this action plan as he felt not enough attention was being paid to capturing customer feedback.

Proposed change	To write to customers one month after installation, seeking feedback
Impact and benefit	Customer feedback can be used to continuously improve service. Any problem issues can be identified early and resolved. Customer will feel valued
If change not implemented	No customer feedback; no improvements to customer service; problems will not be quickly identified
Who needs to be involved?	Sales Team, After Sales Team, Service Manager
What needs to be done?	Process for sending out letter to be identified by Service Manager
What are the costs?	
When should it start?	
When should it finish?	
How will we know if the change is effective?	

As you can see, Garry has not quite finished.

♦ Imagine you are Garry and complete the rest of the action plan.
♦ Try writing a letter that the conservatory firm could send to customers to seek feedback on the service provided.

When undertaking site visits to talk with customers about their specific requirements, Garry found that, very often, having a conservatory built meant that access to the upper windows, roof and guttering of many properties was prevented.

From his own experience, Garry recognised it was not easy to undertake basic property maintenance once a conservatory was installed. As his firm already had the scaffolding required, it occurred to him that his firm could offer additional after-sales services. These could include roof maintenance and cleaning gutters. The more he thought about it, the more he thought his idea would work. It would provide peace of mind to customers and bring in extra income for the firm for little outlay.

Garry decided he needed to approach the Service Manager, and set about drawing up an action plan to finalise his ideas.

♦ Using the action plan template in the case study above, write up an action plan to support Garry's suggestion.

Active knowledge

Using the three key areas for improvement (systems and procedures, products and services and people) think about what you would personally like to see improved where you work. Select one key issue and write up an action plan.

Once you have an action plan you need to establish who you should discuss it with. This may be your line manager or supervisor, or it may be necessary to seek the agreement of management. Do not forget any colleagues who will need to work with the change. Is it your responsibility to tell them? If so, how would you set about this? Would a team meeting be necessary? Perhaps a one-to-one meeting will be all that is required. The method you choose depends very much on the scale of the change taking place and on how many people you need to tell.

Remember

Face-to-face or telephone communication is likely to make colleagues feel more valued and more involved with the change than an email message or other form of written communication.

How to contribute to the implementation of changes to customer service systems and procedures

You will have your own thoughts and ideas as to what can be done to make improvements to customer service. Similarly, your organisation will also want you to become involved with supporting its own change initiatives relating to the following:

♦ a shift in customer needs and expectations
♦ competitor activities
♦ legal reasons imposing a need to alter systems and procedures
♦ the impact of technology.

For instance, customers might expect longer opening hours, a competitor might start to offer a product or service it did not previously deal with, new legislation might prevent shops from selling certain products.

Active knowledge

1 Think about changes that your organisation has made in the last year. These might include changes to do with the following:

- ◆ products or services
- ◆ systems and procedures
- ◆ staffing changes.

2 What changes have you personally been involved in? Make a list.

- ◆ Why do you think your organisation made the change(s)?
- ◆ What part did you play in supporting the change(s)?
- ◆ How was the customer kept informed?
- ◆ How has customer service improved?
- ◆ What did you and your organisation do to check whether customers liked the change(s)?

If you are involved with implementing a change brought in by your organisation, it is important you do so enthusiastically. This will give the change more chance of succeeding. Treat the change as your own brilliant idea. Many organisations introduce their changes via team meetings or briefings. Employees' behaviour during these events is critical. One person being dismissive of an idea can have a negative impact on the outcome of the whole change process. You need to have an open mind and give the change a chance.

Keys to good practice

Supporting your organisation's change initiatives

✓ Think about the benefit of the change.
✓ Evaluate the impact of the change itself, not the person delivering the message.
✓ Be open and honest.
✓ Participate.
✓ Question to seek clarification when required.
✓ Listen for the positives, not the negatives.
✓ Give it a go.

Case study

Travel Inn, the budget hotel chain, decided to empower its staff to give refunds to customers. Instead of arguing with dissatisfied customers, employees were trained and empowered to solve the problems customers were complaining about.

Customers know they can get their money back if Travel Inn fails to deliver on its brand promise: 'Providing everything you want for a good night's sleep'. In practice, what this means is that customers are getting a 100 per cent guarantee.

Customer service improvements made as a result of the scheme include the following:

♦ at the County Hall Travel Inn, housekeepers identified that rooms could get very hot overnight and so electric fans have been supplied
♦ milk cartons and biscuits are left on reception desks so customers can help themselves when they run out
♦ premises are refurbished according to need rather than as a result of a pre-arranged timetable

1   Imagine yourself in the role of a customer service practitioner who is suddenly asked to talk with customers about the nature of a complaint. What kinds of behaviours and skills would you need to use?
2   What would you do to ensure you gather the customers' feedback effectively?
3   How would you demonstrate to your colleagues that you are enthusiastic about taking on your organisation's change initiatives?

How to keep the customer informed of changes

It is likely that most changes brought about by your organisation will be communicated to customers directly by your organisation. Your part in this is to understand when any change will happen and how your customers will be told about it. The methods of communicating change used by your organisation will depend on the following:

♦ the scale of the change occurring, e.g. the numbers of customers involved
♦ how urgent it is that customers be told
♦ any legal restrictions that might mean the change has to be notified in writing.

Figure 5.6 Keeping customers informed of change

How was it for you?

Think about the last time you were notified (as a customer) about a change.

♦ What method of communication did the organisation choose?
♦ How did you react?
♦ Did you welcome the change? If not, why not?
♦ What would you have liked the organisation to have done differently (if anything) ?

The way in which the financial services industry operates is regulated by bodies such as the Financial Services Authority (FSA). Regulations frequently change, and the customer will constantly need to be advised of any changes. The method chosen would probably be a centralised mailshot to all customers, explaining any changes and listing appropriate addresses and contact details of where a customer can go to make a complaint. This practice of inviting complaints is a means of ensuring that the customer knows who to go to for help; it also helps an organisation continuously improve its customer service.

Remember

Look upon a complaint as an opportunity to improve.

Active knowledge

1 Think about some changes your organisation has introduced.

   ◆ For each one, how were your customers advised of the change(s)?
   ◆ How did you first get to know about the change(s)?
   ◆ What part did you play in helping your customers understand what was happening?

2 Find out now what your organisation's guidelines are in respect of what you need to do to keep your customers informed of changes.

How to work with others to support changes made by your organisation

You are not alone in supporting the need to improve customer service. You will be working with other people with whom you are jointly responsible for making change happen. These other people could include the following:

◆ colleagues
◆ line managers
◆ team leaders
◆ department heads
◆ chief executives

◆ suppliers
◆ supervisors
◆ managers
◆ unit heads.

You will therefore be working as a member of a team. You will need to work positively with the other members of your team to support the changes made by your organisation. Your starting point would be to identify who these people are and how you will work with each other.

Active knowledge

Make a list of people you deal with in connection with making changes to customer service. (These individuals might be external to your organisation or they might be internal.)

   ◆ Put a tick against each individual that you feel you support effectively.
   ◆ Why does your relationship with these people work?
   ◆ For those who do not have a tick, what can you do to improve the relationship?

Many people (both customers and colleagues) find change unsettling. These individuals will do all they can to resist the change. If you work with colleagues who are resistant to a particular change, then it would be helpful if you took the time to talk with them about their concerns. If an organisation decides it is time to make changes, it is unlikely that the employees will be able to alter anything. However, if there is a genuine concern that the change will have a negative impact on customer service, then you and your colleagues need to create a positive statement about why you seriously believe the change is not for the good. You will need to discuss your fears and concerns with an appropriate person. Be specific and express them positively. You may want to include the following:

♦ a brief outline of what you have done so far to make the change work
♦ details of any issues that have arisen from doing this
♦ details of any customer feedback you have
♦ what you suggest as being the way forward.

Similarly, if customers give you feedback that changes are not welcome, then this is valuable information that you need to capture in your feedback diary.

Keys to good practice

Using teamwork to support the changes made by your organisation

✓ Understand why changes are happening.
✓ Help others to understand the impact of these changes.
✓ Participate fully in team meetings held to advise of changes.
✓ Explore differences of opinion in a positive way.
✓ Keep the promises you make.
✓ Accept help when you need it.
✓ Support others when they need it.
✓ Share information and ideas with others as to the impact of the changes.

Test your knowledge

Think about your ideas for improving customer service. Choose one that has been on your mind for some time. Work through the following questions, recording your responses at each stage.

Idea for improvement

♦ Is there anything you can do about it?
♦ Is there anything that stops you from putting your idea into practice?
♦ What do you need to do to gain agreement to your change idea?
♦ Who do you need to go to for support?
♦ What are the advantages of introducing your idea?
♦ What are the risks of doing nothing?
♦ Why is it important to customer service that change happens?

How will you present your idea?

Assist with the evaluation of changes in customer service

This chapter deals with the final stage in supporting customer service improvements: find out and evaluate what your customers think about these changes. This involves checking just how effective the change has been. Evaluating changes to customer service is important, as if you do not do this, your organisation will be making assumptions that customers are happy with any changes, when in reality they may not be.

In order to evaluate changes you will need to ask the following questions:

- Where are we now?
- Where would we like to be?
- How can we get there?
- Have we made it?

WHAT YOU NEED TO KNOW OR LEARN

- Methods you can use to identify any negative effects of changes to customer service.
- How to discuss with others how changes to customer service are working.
- How to discuss with others how negative aspects of change can be resolved.

Methods you can use to identify any negative effects of changes to customer service

Your actions in supporting customer service improvements should follow a path of continuous improvement, as shown below.

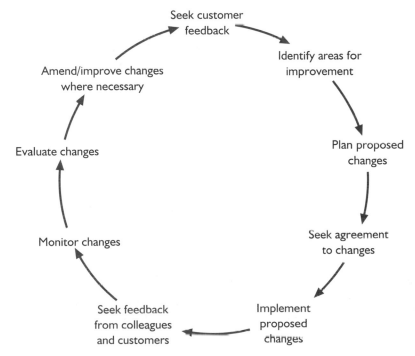

Figure 5.7 A cycle of continuous improvement

It is necessary to monitor the impact of change in order to answer the question 'Have we made it?' It is not sufficient to wait for several months before asking for feedback. You need to think about the following:

♦ When is the right time to start asking for feedback?
♦ Who should be asked?
♦ What method should you use to seek feedback?
♦ What questions should you ask?
♦ How will you use the information you get?

The first step is to find out what your responsibilities are in relation to any change that is being implemented. It may be that your organisation has made arrangements for sending out questionnaires to customers or for telephoning a customer to undertake some formal market research. Some organisations will implement a change and then use mystery shoppers to specifically find out if the change is working. For example, imagine a building society that has invested in a training programme for its employees, aimed to develop a common understanding of how to deal with customers at branch counters. The building society might undertake a mystery shopper exercise to evaluate the success of the training programme. Below are some examples of questions the mystery shopper could answer:

♦ How long were you kept waiting?
♦ If you had to queue, did the customer service officer (CSO) offer an apology?
♦ Was the apology sincere?
♦ How were you greeted?
♦ Did the CSO use your name?
♦ Did the CSO appear interested?
♦ Was their eye contact appropriate?

♦ Was their smile appropriate?
♦ Did you feel rushed?
♦ Did the CSO appear confident?
♦ If so, what did the CSO do to inspire confidence?
♦ Did the CSO meet your needs?
♦ Did the CSO exceed your needs?
♦ Did the CSO anticipate your needs?
♦ If appropriate, did the CSO offer you any alternative products or services?

The above questions are based around the building society's need to continuously improve the service it gives and to evaluate the impact of changes to customer service that it makes.

Mystery shoppers can help evaluate the success of a training programme

Car dealerships often contact customers by telephone or by letter to seek feedback as to how satisfied a customer is with a car service or repairs. This is good practice and is a means of seeking feedback under normal circumstances.

Remember

You should regard evaluating change as an extension of gathering feedback from customers. You and your organisation will be gathering feedback on a specific area of customer service that has been subject to change.

Active knowledge

Locate any questionnaires, letters/emails or details of telephone exercises that your organisation has used in the past nine months to evaluate change. Alternatively, discuss with an appropriate person what systems your organisation has in place for doing so.

- What role did you play in seeking the feedback?
- How did your organisation use the feedback?
- Did the process enable the question 'Have we made it?' to be answered?
- What negative aspects of changes to customer service were identified?

One key role you can play in evaluating change is to listen to customer comments and observe customers' behaviour and body language. For example, if a customer arrives and is dripping wet from a thunderstorm, it would be wrong to assume his or her bad mood has been caused by the changes that have been made to your premises. You would need to ask questions to find out what was wrong. Make sure you record the information or feedback you receive. This will help you to discuss your findings with others. Use your feedback diary to do this.

How to discuss with others how changes to customer service are working

'The greatest brakes on organisational change are satisfaction with the present and the fear of a different uncertain future.'

Sir John Harvey-Jones

Some people can be reluctant to accept change even when it is for the good. However, without change organisations will not survive. If you get into the habit of monitoring customer reactions to change by recording what you see, hear and feel, you will be better placed to discuss with others the impact and benefit of change.

Once you have a series of entries in a feedback diary you can start to look for trends, i.e. are there many customers who are saying the same thing or is the feedback you have an isolated occurrence? What about colleagues you work with? Have they got similar entries in feedback diaries? By discussing your findings with others you can start to work out where change is working and also where further improvements are required. Include in your discussions the impact of the change on your own ability to deliver customer service. If the impact is negative, do not be afraid to mention this. Ensure that you say exactly what is going wrong, i.e. why the change has not been beneficial and what you are doing or intend to do to put it right.

Advantages and disadvantages of the change

There are two main techniques you can use to help you discuss the impact of change. The first is to summarise the advantages and disadvantages of the change. Armed with your list of advantages and disadvantages you will be well prepared to enter into any discussion on the effect of the change. You could also consider the advantages and disadvantages of the change to the following:

- your customers
- your organisation
- your colleagues
- you.

Case study

Craig works as a quality control officer in a factory that packages flowers in presentation boxes for mail order customers. He is also responsible for the office workers who take calls and deal with customer queries. Each Christmas, the company looks to provide some sort of special offer with the aim of increasing business. This year the offer was to provide an extra five blooms with each order, plus offering free postage and packing on all orders over £15. From 1 November, all the adverts reflected this promotion.

Craig asked his colleagues to monitor customer reaction and said that he would be looking to evaluate the promotion in early January.

Patricia from the office and Jean from the packing department promptly started to monitor the promotion by using feedback diaries. After Christmas they got together to list the advantages and disadvantages of running the promotion. Here are the results of Patricia's and Jean's monitoring exercises.

Change: To offer free postage and packing on orders over £15 during the Christmas period plus five extra blooms.

ADVANTAGES		DISADVANTAGES	
Customers	Colleagues	Customers	Colleagues
Increase in orders over £15	None identified	None identified during offer. However, 33 customers registered complaints that P & P should continue to be free after Christmas. Seventy-five customers complained that the five extra blooms were not included	Some colleagues unaware of changes to service offer

ADVANTAGES		DISADVANTAGES	
Organisation	You	Organisation	You
Customers appeared to enjoy getting something for nothing	None identified	Loss of goodwill. Larger boxes needed to accommodate extra flowers.	After Christmas offer ended, some difficulties experienced in explaining P & P now payable

♦ How might Patricia and Jean use the results of their monitoring exercises to discuss their findings with Craig?

♦ What would happen if Patricia and Jean had not made the effort to complete feedback diaries?

♦ Looking at the results of the monitoring exercise, write down how you believe Craig would evaluate the changes to customer service.

SWOT analysis

An alternative method to the advantages and disadvantages approach is to use a SWOT analysis. SWOT stands for:

Strengths
Weaknesses
Opportunities
Threats.

Strengths and weaknesses are usually internal to an organisation whereas opportunities and threats are usually external. In deciding to implement the change to customer service, the flower company in the case study above might well have undertaken a SWOT analysis to decide on the merits of the idea. It might have looked like this:

Change idea: to offer free postage and packing on orders over £15 during the Christmas period plus five extra blooms.

Strengths:	Weaknesses:
Easy to incorporate offer within advertising programme. Matches company's reputation of doing something special at Christmas	Demand might outstrip supply of flowers. Need to communicate plans to staff. Increased quality control required. Need to cover increased P & P costs
Opportunities:	Threats:
Win new customers. Customers may place larger orders to qualify for free P & P	Other flower companies known to be offering free P & P regardless of cost of orders

Figure 5.8 A SWOT analysis

By carrying out a SWOT analysis before the change is implemented, Craig would have the opportunity to identify the following:

- Strengths that he could use to build upon to ensure improved customer service.
- Weaknesses that he could iron out having identified them early on.
- Opportunities that he could later identify as having taken place (or not).
- Threats that he could use to establish whether the change idea was effective enough to deal with the competition.

After the change has been put in place it is equally relevant to do another SWOT analysis to help with evaluating its success.

Active knowledge

Think about a change that you have recently been involved with. Find an appropriate colleague to discuss the change with and draw up a SWOT analysis that shows how you would evaluate the effectiveness of the change.

How to discuss with others how negative aspects of change can be resolved

You have seen how evaluating change can lead to the conclusion that some aspects of a change may be negative and that these need to be dealt with. This is important in order to maintain a good relationship with customers and to ensure that customer service improves. Remember the cycle of continuous improvement (see Figure 5.7, page 227) which has an important stage requiring you to amend and/or improve change where necessary.

Discussing these negative aspects with others becomes much easier if you maintain your feedback diary on a regular basis, as this means you will have facts and figures to support your arguments. You will need to discuss the following:

- customer feedback
- colleague feedback
- supplier feedback
- your own feedback based on findings drawn from research undertaken prior to the change being made, e.g. a SWOT analysis
- your own feedback based on findings drawn from an evaluation of the change after it has been implemented, e.g. an advantage/disadvantage list or a SWOT analysis.

All of this information will enable you to reach a conclusion as to what needs to be done to resolve any negative aspects of change.

Often, a major negative implication of change is cost. This could be cost in terms of manpower or in pure financial terms. This means you might also need to work with your colleagues in establishing a cost analysis. A cost analysis aims to identify how much the change has cost in financial terms and in staff terms. Points you could think about include the following:

- How much staff time has been spent on learning about the change?
- How much staff time has been spent on telling customers of the change?
- Overall, has staff time increased or decreased as a result of the change?
- Have sales increased or decreased?
- Have customer complaints diminished?

The outcome of a cost analysis might be something like the following:

- the change has cost the organisation £X to implement but the number of customer complaints has not gone down
- staff costs have increased by X per cent as there have been costs associated with the training of staff
- the change has not streamlined our delivery times, we are not more efficient, drivers are delivering fewer goods to customers each day, meaning customers are waiting on average 24 hours longer for their orders.

Remember

Just as it is important to identify the positive aspects of change, so too is it important to identify the negative aspects. Both should be based on sound facts and figures.

Case study

Pauline supervises a team of 12 people who work as health and beauty consultants in a large department store. The floor where they are based is in need of renovation and this means considerable disruption will occur for around six months while work is taking place.

Pauline arranges a team meeting with the aim of drawing up a plan to ensure customers are notified of the work and also to make plans to minimise the impact on customers. The team draw up a plan and put it into action. Part of the plan includes the following:

- how to advise customers of the renovation
- maintaining health and safety throughout the course of the works
- minimising any negative impact on scheduled instore promotions
- maintaining the ability to offer an appropriate environment for customers
- how to monitor customer reactions.

One month into the renovation work, Pauline calls a team meeting to discuss how things are going. In particular she is interested to learn what impact the works are having on customers and how the team might improve on the steps they have already taken. This is what the team told her:

- The number of customers staying to have makeovers done instore had decreased from 25 a week to 9 a week.
- There had been 22 complaints from customers who felt the renovations should be carried out overnight.
- One customer had fallen over a cable, badly bruising her shoulder.
- Nine of the 12 consultants found the environment too dusty too work in.
- All the consultants said they felt dirty at the end of their working day.
- Despite displaying posters notifying customers of the works for four weeks prior to commencement, nine out of ten customers said they did not know the work was going to be done.

1 Make a list of all the negative aspects of this change.
2 For each one, discuss with a colleague what you think the impact on customer service has been. In particular, think about what the customer's perception of the department store might be.
3 What would you do to try to improve the situation for the customer?

Test your knowledge

In your own organisation, what opportunities are available to you to support the evaluation of changes in customer service?

Think about the feedback/comments you receive from customers – perhaps use the examples you had for the end of Element 5.1. For these situations, what did you do with the feedback? Did you get involved (with others) in putting in place a change to customer service? What happened? What was the outcome of any discussions you had with colleagues about how the changes were going?

For each occasion when you have been involved with change, whether based on your own idea or on someone else's, think about whether your contribution helped to make the changes effective. What (if anything) would you do differently next time?

Start a feedback diary to ensure you capture comments made by customers. This will help you to contribute to the use of feedback in identifying possible changes, to implement change and then to help with finding out how successful any changes have been.

Check your knowledge

1   What are the three stages of making changes to customer service?

2   Why is it important to continuously improve customer service?

3   What is a 'moment of truth?'

4   List four methods of gathering customer feedback.

5   How can using a feedback diary help you to support customer service improvements?

6   List four ways of sharing feedback with others.

7   What should you consider when identifying a possible change to customer service?

8   List four reasons why an organisation might implement a change to customer service.

9   How might an organisation tell its customers about changes to products or services?

10 What can a SWOT analysis be used for?

11 Why is it important to evaluate changes to customer service?

12 Why should change be undertaken in accordance with organisational guidelines?

13 How should you set about discussing your ideas for improving customer service with others?

14 Why would you set about listing the advantages and disadvantages of changes to customer service?

15 How is the customers' perception of you and your organisation affected by the quality of the service received?

UNIT 6 Develop personal performance through delivering customer service

This option unit will help you take responsibility for your own personal development. It will involve you in identifying the knowledge and skills you need in order to be effective in your role, as well as how your organisation can help you achieve this. You will learn how to carry out a self-assessment of your own performance, identifying your strengths, weaknesses and development needs. You will also need to obtain and use feedback on your own performance in order to develop your customer service skills further.

The elements for this option unit are:

♦ 6.1 Review performance in your customer service role
♦ 6.2 Prepare a personal development plan and keep it up to date
♦ 6.3 Undertake development activities and obtain feedback on your customer service performance.

Review performance in your customer service role

- ♦ How to identify the knowledge and skills you need to be effective in your role.
- ♦ What you can learn from your own experiences as a customer.
- ♦ What you can learn from the impact your own behaviour has in customer service situations.
- ♦ How to carry out a self-assessment of your own performance.

How to identify the knowledge and skills you need to be effective in your role

In order to discover the skills you need to be an effective customer service practitioner you will need to look at the information that is available to you from within your workplace. There are several sources of information as discussed below.

People

Find someone to talk to within your organisation who can help you to find out what you are required to know and understand in your customer service role. This person might be any one of the following:

- ♦ your manager
- ♦ your supervisor/team leader
- ♦ a colleague
- ♦ someone from your human resources or training department.

Documentation

Alternatively, you may have documentation that will tell you what you need to know such as a job/role profile or a job description. Perhaps you have kept some information from when you first applied for your job – does this have the relevant information on it?

Performance reviews/appraisals

If you are in an organisation that carries out performance reviews and appraisals you may have had discussions with your line manager/supervisor that will have included detailed information on what knowledge and skills you require to perform your job.

The following two tables show the skills and knowledge that an effective customer service practitioner might need to know about and/or be able to perform effectively. The actual skills required will vary depending on the nature of your specific role.

Oral communication skills	Written communication skills	Non-verbal communication skills, e.g. body language
Telephone skills	Questioning skills	Listening skills
Decision-making skills	Problem-solving skills	Information-gathering skills
IT skills	Personal development skills	Number skills
Working without supervision	Working with supervision	Working alone
Asking for help	Giving help	Team-working skills

Figure 6.1 A customer service skills tool-kit

In relation to you and your role – knowledge of:	
Products and services	How to use your organisation's systems and procedures
The legislation that affects what you do, e.g. health and safety, data protection, equal opportunities, disability discrimination	The legislation and regulations that affect the way you deliver your organisation's products and services
Industry, organisational and professional codes of practice and ethical standards	Contractual agreements between customers and your organisation
Your organisation's targets and your role in helping to meet them	?

Figure 6.2 A customer service knowledge tool-kit

Active knowledge

1 Copy and amend Figures 6.1 and 6.2 in relation to your own job role:

♦ delete those points that do not apply to you

♦ insert points not included that you think are relevant to your own job role.

2 Discuss your findings with an appropriate person and agree with him or her what you need to know and be able to do to work effectively in your customer service role.

3 What have you learned about your role?

We are all customers

What you can learn from your own experiences as a customer

For a significant part of our lives, we arc all customers, e.g. when buying things, using the telephone, using the Internet or travelling on a plane – all involve a customer relationship.

Case study

Andrea took her shoes in to be heeled in the local mender's. There were no other customers in the shop and both the shoe menders were busy reading newspapers. One eventually looked up and so Andrea went to him and asked for new heels. He asked Andrea when she wanted them back and she replied that she was doing some more shopping which would take about an hour, or she could come back another day. There was no reply.

Instead, Andrea was asked in a rather gruff voice 'Do you know about these marks on your shoes?' 'What marks?' she replied as the shoe mender pointed to the backs of her shoes. Still she couldn't see anything on the shoes but she did notice a look of disbelief on the shoe mender's face.

Andrea wondered why she was being asked about the marks and thought for a moment that the shoe mender was trying to get her to spend more

money and have something else done to her shoes other than get them re-heeled. Then the penny dropped. She asked 'Are you pointing out marks to me so that I don't accuse you of making them when I come back to collect the shoes?' 'Yeah, that's right.' Furious, Andrea took the shoes back and said she would go somewhere else. As she turned to go, the shoe mender said in his gruff voice 'It's my job'. Andrea replied 'It's not the fact that your employer asks you to point marks out, it's the way in which you did it'. The shoe mender shrugged his shoulders and went back to reading his newspaper.

♦ How was Andrea feeling when she first entered the shop?
♦ How do you think she felt when she saw the shoe menders were reading newspapers?
♦ Why did Andrea react in the way she did?
♦ What do you think Andrea learned about customer service from this experience?
♦ If you were Andrea, how would you use this experience to develop your own performance in your customer service role?

Think about all the types of things that happen to you when you are a customer. What can you learn? Below are some questions you might have in your mind the next time you are out shopping or dealing with any situation in which you are a customer.

♦ How did I feel at the start?
♦ How did I feel at the finish?
♦ What did the person say that I particularly liked?
♦ Was anything said that I didn't like?
♦ What about the way in which things were said, i.e. tone of voice?
♦ How did the person behave with me?
♦ What was my behaviour like?
♦ Would I go back again? If yes, why? If no, why not?
♦ What specifically happened during this situation that can help me to learn and develop in my role as a customer service practitioner?

How to use a learning log

The next step is to use this learning in your actions. A learning log is a sort of diary that you use to record your experiences in writing. It is an effective way of putting what you have learned into action. A learning log or diary is an excellent way of developing your own performance. It is not enough to try to remember in your head what happens during your experiences as a customer, you will find you do need to record events. Writing things down in a learning log is a golden opportunity to help yourself develop. On the next page is an example.

Case study

Andrea wrote this entry in her learning log following her visit to the shoe mender's (see page 239). Andrea works part-time in the local café-bar.

Activity – What I did/ What happened	Outcomes – What I learned	Actions – How I will use this experience
Took shoes to mender's. Chap couldn't be bothered to serve me and when he did he wasn't listening to what I was saying. He didn't answer my questions. I felt annoyed at his gruff tone of voice. He didn't explain clearly the reasons for his question about marks on my shoes. I couldn't see them anyway. His manner made me feel as if I had done something wrong. It all annoyed me so I took my shoes back and went to the mender's at the other end of the High Street.	My first impressions of the shop were not very good as the assistants were reading newspapers. The way in which the assistant pointed out the marks was offensive and he didn't give any explanations. His tone of voice also gave me a bad impression. Customers always have a choice. They can take their custom to someone else if I don't get my job right.	Even when I am very busy in the lunch periods I must ensure that as soon as customers walk in the door they are made to feel welcome. I will ensure I give eye contact and help them to a table. If this is not possible I will find a way to acknowledge they are waiting. I will ask a colleague for feedback on my tone of voice when I am under pressure as, in these situations, I may not react in a positive way.

Figure 6.3 Extract from a learning log

How was it for you?

♦ Think back to a time when you had a satisfactory (or even fantastic) customer service experience. Create your own learning log entry that details what happened, what you learned and what you will now do as a result of this experience.

♦ Now do the same for a situation where you were unsatisfied with the customer service you received.

What you can learn from the impact your own behaviour has in customer service situations

In Unit 1 we looked at how establishing an effective relationship with customers is all about your behaviour towards your customers and theirs towards you. You have just looked at the impact people have on you when you are a customer. We are now going to turn our attention to the impact your behaviour has on other people.

What do we mean by behaviour? In simple terms, behaviour refers to everything you do and say. It is important to you in your customer service role because other people will draw conclusions about you, i.e. the sort of person you are, whether they have confidence in you, whether they like you, whether they want to do business with you, etc. These conclusions are based on your behaviour with your customers.

Look back at Andrea's learning log (page 241) and your own. How many of the points that you and Andrea wrote down relate to conclusions based on other people's behaviour?

Face-to-face situations

In face-to-face situations a customer has access to all observable behaviour. They can instantly see what you look like, what you are wearing, how old you are, your facial expressions, your gestures and your body language.

> Face-to-face behaviour = What you look like + What you say + Body language

On the telephone

When you are dealing with a customer over the telephone you are deprived of the ability to see what is happening. The customer will base their judgements about you on what they hear.

> Telephone behaviour = What you say + How you say it

The written word

In addition to situations where you are on the telephone or face-to-face with customers, your behaviour can also be 'seen' through the written word. You may not be present with the customer, but the impact of your behaviour on him or her must still be considered.

> Written communication = What is written + How it is written + How it is presented

What would you think about someone who had sent you a letter or an email that was full of spelling mistakes, was unclear or did not give you the information that you had asked for? You might think that he or she did not care about you. What would that mean in terms of what you felt about the customer service you received from that organisation?

Use the following table to think about what impact certain behaviour has on customer relations:

Behaviour	What is the impact?
Bodily contact and physical position	Notice the effects of: ♦ shaking hands v not shaking hands with your customer ♦ moving closer to someone to discuss something ♦ standing up while your customer is sitting down, i.e. you are in a dominant position ♦ facing the customer from behind a desk, screen or other barrier ♦ facing your customer v sitting next to your customer.
Facial expressions	Notice the effects of: ♦ eye contact v no eye contact ♦ movements of eyes, eyebrows, mouth ♦ frowning v smiling.
Gestures	Notice the effects of: ♦ head nods and shakes ♦ wagging foot/fidgety legs ♦ crossed arms v open arms ♦ hand movements: pointing, clenching, holding.
Voice	Notice the effects of: ♦ loudness v softness ♦ pitch: high v low ♦ speed: fast v slow ♦ silences ♦ interruptions ♦ hesitations.
Clothes and physical appearance	Notice the effects of: ♦ smartness v untidiness ♦ attracting attention through what you wear v blending into the background ♦ smart v casual ♦ clean v scruffy.

Figure 6.4 Significant behaviours that impact upon customer service

How to carry out a self-assessment of your own performance

In order to check how well you are doing in your work you will need to carry out a self-assessment of your own performance. You can then use your self-assessment as a basis for discussion with an appropriate person in your company in order to develop your customer service performance.

Before you start to fill in your self-assessment chart, gather together as much information as you can that will help you gauge your performance. This could include the following:

♦ records of appraisals
♦ notes made following discussions with a line manager, supervisor, colleague
♦ thank-you letters
♦ complaint letters
♦ your memories of conversations people have had with you about what you do and how you do it (feedback)
♦ your experiences on courses, workshops, etc.
♦ your observations of how you think you compare with other people who you respect and who are valued by customers and your organisation.

Completing a self-assessment chart

There are some golden rules to observe when completing a self-assessment chart:

♦ try to be as honest as possible with your responses
♦ don't be too hard on yourself, or too lenient
♦ answer the questions quickly; your first reactions are likely to be the most valuable

 (speech bubble: "What am I like?")

Take time to fill in a self-assessment

♦ the responses you make today may be different to the ones you would give in two months' time
♦ there are no right or wrong answers
♦ remember, you are doing this to help yourself develop.

Below is an example of a self-assessment chart that you could complete to help show where your strengths, weaknesses and development needs lie.

Customer service self-assessment chart for _____

Completed on _____

What are the things that I am doing well? _____

What would I like to do differently? _____

I enjoy these aspects of my job: _____

I would like to change these parts of my job: _____

What do I feel uncomfortable about? _____

My biggest achievement at work this year is: _____

	Mostly true	Not sure	Sometimes true
I create a good first impression with customers	☐	☐	☐
I get regular feedback or comments about my performance	☐	☐	☐
I learn from my experiences inside and outside work	☐	☐	☐
I am patient with customers	☐	☐	☐
People like working with me	☐	☐	☐
I care about other people	☐	☐	☐
I handle difficult customers well	☐	☐	☐
I am good at time management	☐	☐	☐
I work well under pressure	☐	☐	☐
I have no problem making decisions	☐	☐	☐
People understand me	☐	☐	☐
I go out of my way to help customers	☐	☐	☐
I can sort things out for people	☐	☐	☐
My work is accurate	☐	☐	☐
I keep my promises	☐	☐	☐
I understand what I am expected to do in my job	☐	☐	☐
I know all about my organisation's products or services	☐	☐	☐
I know where to go to get help	☐	☐	☐
I understand my organisation's rules and regulations	☐	☐	☐
I take action to develop my own performance	☐	☐	☐
This is the first time I have looked at what I do	☐	☐	☐
I am surprised by what I have put down	☐	☐	☐

Figure 6.5 A self-assessment chart

Your organisation may already have a procedure in place which you could use to carry out your self assessment. Once you have completed your self-assessment chart you will need to think about the reasons behind your responses. For instance, did you find it difficult to write down the things that you do well? Did it take ages for something to come to mind? This may be more because you do not receive feedback (or indeed ask for it) rather than because there is nothing that has gone well recently. What have you put down for the question about obtaining regular feedback? Is it a 'No'?

From both these responses, you could conclude that you have a need in the area of personal development. You need to get constructive feedback from others in your workplace.

Look back to Figures 6.1 and 6.2 on page 238. Ask yourself how good you think you are in each of the areas in the tool-kits. Rank yourself on a scale of 1–6 (where 1 is appalling and 6 is excellent).

You will now have a sound idea of your personal strengths and development needs and can use this to work with an appropriate person to draw up a personal development plan. Element 6.2 will show you how to do this.

Test your knowledge

Review your completed self-assessment chart and pick an area to which you have responded 'sometimes true' or 'not sure'.

6.2 Prepare a personal development plan and keep it up to date

WHAT YOU NEED TO KNOW OR LEARN

♦ What your organisation can do to help you to develop in your customer service role.

♦ How to identify your strengths, weaknesses and development needs.

♦ How to put together a personal development plan.

♦ How to use your personal development plan.

What your organisation can do to help you to develop in your customer service role

We will now look at what you can do with the help and support of others to develop your personal performance. This will help you to build on your personal development work so far. Your organisation might have systems and procedures that help its employees to develop their personal performance. Here are some examples of the support that might be available to you.

Performance appraisals	These are discussions with a line manager or supervisor or some other individual who has responsibility for you. They are usually formal and take place at regular intervals, e.g. quarterly. The outcomes of the discussions usually contribute to an annual report or appraisal that can be used to make recommendations for promotion, pay increases or bonuses.
Feedback	You could ask for feedback from people, e.g. your colleagues, customers or suppliers. Sometimes, people will tell you what they think about you without you having to ask for it. Unfortunately, this is more likely to happen when things go wrong than when things go right.
Coaching	This is specific feedback from someone who can observe you at work and who can give you feedback on your performance. He or she may also encourage you to develop your knowledge and skills by setting personal development objectives.
Resource centres	These are specific places where employees can go to learn about the activities important to the success of the organisation. It may be somewhere where you can access the Internet or it may be a library.
Training courses and workshops	Your company may offer customer service training events at work, or they may send you outside your organisation to receive training.
Study leave/Qualifications	This is time and/or financial support to undertake a customer service qualification.
Watching someone else	This is called work shadowing. You observe someone while they are working. In this way they can act as a role model for you and can answer any questions you may have.

Figure 6.6 What organisations do to develop personal performance

So that you can make the best use of the systems and procedures your organisation might have available to support your development, you should do the following:

♦ use learning logs (see page 240)
♦ use personal development plans (PDPs). These state your personal objectives and what you will do to achieve these objectives (see page 249).

Some organisations will have their own systems in place for using PDPs and learning logs. If so, use them. If your company does not have its own PDP system you can draw up your own. Using a learning log and a PDP will help you to learn in a more efficient way and put your learning into practice in order to improve your personal customer service performance.

Active knowledge

1   Ask your friends and family who are currently in employment to tell you about the PDP system at their workplace. Ask them the following questions:

   ◆ What does their employer do to support their personal development?
   ◆ What systems and procedures are in place?

2   Find out what is available to help you where you work.

   ◆ How does this compare with what happens elsewhere?
   ◆ Are you using all the support that is available to you? If not, why not?

How to identify your strengths, weaknesses and development needs

Element 6.1 looked at helping you to establish what you need to know to be effective in your job. On page 238 you were asked to find an appropriate person and discuss your effectiveness with him or her. You may have covered areas such as the following in your discussion:

◆ communication skills
◆ product and services knowledge
◆ problem-solving skills
◆ decision-making skills.

When you have gathered this information together you need to find out what you are good at and what you are not so good at: in other words your strengths and weaknesses. This will involve discussing your performance against each of the areas identified and reaching an agreement. This discussion will probably take place between you and your line manager, boss or supervisor or another appropriate person.

What you are looking to find out is where your strengths lie and where you have weaknesses in your performance. Just because you have a strength in something, this does not mean that you can sit back and do nothing. There is always room for improvement. Equally, not all weaknesses identified will lead to a development need. A development need relates to an area where any action taken will contribute to an improvement in your customer service performance.

Another way of identifying your strengths and weaknesses is by self-assessment (see page 244). If you have your own ideas about your performance, this will clearly help you discuss it with someone else.

Remember

Gathering all the information together about your own customer service performance before any discussion will help you to:

♦ be better informed
♦ reach an agreement about your strengths and weaknesses
♦ plan what you need to do develop your performance.

Keys to good practice

Preparing to discuss your customer service performance

✓ Ensure you fully understand what you are required to know and do.
✓ Develop this into a list of knowledge and skills.
✓ Use your organisation's systems and procedures, e.g. appraisal system.
✓ Find out all the sources of information available to you.
✓ Use a learning log.
✓ Complete a self-assessment chart quarterly.
✓ Understand what your organisation can do to help you to develop.

How to put together a personal development plan

There is not much point in sorting out your strengths and weaknesses if you do not use this information in some way. The next step is to take some action.

A personal development plan (PDP) is a record of what you intend to do to improve your customer service performance. It could include the following:

♦ your personal objectives: these should be agreed between you and an appropriate person
♦ what you intend to do; the actions you will take
♦ details of any support and resources you will need, e.g. time, access to information
♦ a space for you to record your progress
♦ a target date for completion.

How to access sources of information and support for your learning

How will you get the support you might need to carry out the intentions laid down in your PDP? When looking at your intended actions on your PDP, try asking yourself some questions that will enable you to start to seek help. These questions will be personal to you, but you will need to ask open questions, i.e. questions beginning with Who? What? Why? When? Where? and How?

If some of your development activities involve the need for money then one of your questions will be 'Who is going to pay for this?' Not all organisations will be able to support financially all the development activities that their employees need to take. Some will operate a system of matched funding (where the employee pays a percentage which is then matched by the employer) e.g. you pay half the cost and your employer pays the other half. Other companies will pay all the costs up to a certain limit per year.

To achieve your PDP objectives, it is important that you are able to discuss the following with an appropriate person:

♦ how you will use your learning to improve your performance
♦ how your objectives will impact upon customer service
♦ your own workload
♦ opportunities for learning on the job.

Do not forget that you should be looking to build on your strengths and overcome your weaknesses in areas that are important to customer service. This might mean making some difficult decisions about what to leave out and what to include in your PDP. For instance, you might enjoy and be really good at talking to customers face-to-face, yet not so good at dealing with people over the telephone. You might be tempted to concentrate on further developing your good face-to-face work and leave out your telephone work. You will need to be realistic and only include actions that will ultimately help you improve your customer service performance. You should agree these actions with an appropriate person.

The table below gives you some ideas about sources of information that tell you about your own performance. You could use this as a starting point on your way to creating your own PDP.

Source of information	How it helps you to create your PDP
Learning from experience by completing your learning log regularly	Where your learning log entries relate to a development need, translate them into specific personal objectives.
Performance reviews/annual appraisals	What have you agreed with your line manager? What are your strengths and weaknesses?
Training events/courses/workshops seminars/conferences	Find out about them. How will going to the event help you to improve your performance?
Other people such as colleagues, customers, line managers	What does feedback that you ask for (or that is given to you without prompting) tell you about your performance?
You	How will you use your self-assessment chart?
Learning from others when you are a customer	Your reactions should be recorded in your learning log. How will you use this?
The media	How will you use what you read in newspapers or what you see on TV to develop your performance?

Figure 6.7 Sources of information to help you create your own PDP

Case study

Refer back to Andrea's learning log entry on page 241. Below is an extract from Andrea's PDP showing how she brought her learning log to life by carrying forward the actions she would take as a result of her experiences at the shoe mender's.

Date	Personal objectives	Action points	Support and resources needed	Progress notes	Target date
31 May	Seek feedback from Cynthia on my behaviour during lunch periods	Arrange for Cynthia to observe me on a Friday lunchtime	Cover for Cynthia	Meeting booked with Cynthia to discuss. Date fixed for observation on 15 June and for feedback later that day	6 June
15 June	Maintain eye contact with customers when under pressure Keep customers informed of progress with their snacks	Cynthia to keep an eye on me.	none		
	Develop my knowledge of vegetarian options Learn how to deal with rowdy customers	Discuss with catering team	none	Come in early before shift on a Monday	25 June

Figure 6.8 Andrea's PDP

Looking at Andrea's PDP, you will see it is not yet fully completed.

♦ What is missing?
♦ What do you think happened during her discussions with her boss Cynthia?

Andrea's PDP shows you that in order to construct a customer service PDP you will need to know the following:

♦ how to write personal objectives
♦ how to write about the action you need to take to carry out these objectives
♦ what to think about in terms of the support and resources you may need.

How to write personal development objectives

What you are doing here is setting out your statement of intent. It should be written as clearly as possible so that you and whoever is responsible for you can tell whether or not you have achieved what you set out to do. This is also why you need to set a target date for completion – it focuses the mind!

Look again at Andrea's PDP above. On 31 May she wrote 'Seek feedback from Cynthia on my behaviour during lunch periods'. There is nothing wrong with what Andrea has written. However, it could be improved by her being more specific about what she means by her behaviour. Is she talking about her tone of voice, her body language, etc.? What would you have written?

Similarly, 'Develop my knowledge of vegetarian options' is also fine, but would be further improved if Andrea asked herself 'How will I know if I am up-to-date with the vegetarian options?' In the action column she could add more than 'Discuss with the catering team'. She could talk in terms of doing this regularly and asking a colleague to test her. The table below gives some examples of development needs, showing how they might be written as personal objectives.

Development need	Personal objective
Find out about health and safety issues affecting my role	Attend half-day health and safety workshop run by our training team within the next 3 months
Dealing with difficult customers	Discuss with my line manager which aspects of dealing with difficult customers I need to develop
Product and services knowledge	Achieve my P & S Certification by the end of October
Competitor activities	Visit Emm & Co and Newtons in the High Street to find out what they offer to their customers. Complete my learning log with my impressions by end of November

Figure 6.9 Turning development needs into personal objectives

Active knowledge

Imagine you need to know and understand more about each of the points listed below (i.e. they are your development needs).

- ◆ Operating equipment.
- ◆ Problem-solving.
- ◆ Establishing rapport with customers.
- ◆ Recording telephone conversations.
- ◆ Managing your workload.
- ◆ Dealing with sensitive issues.
- ◆ The Data Protection Act
- ◆ The knowledge and skills you require to do your job.

Taking each point in turn, write them down in the form of a personal development objective.

Each objective should state specifically what you will do and should be written very clearly to enable you to show someone else that you have achieved your objective. Do not forget to include a date for completion (or review).

How to use your personal development plan

The hard work is now done. Do not waste it by not implementing the action points listed on your PDP. The progress notes column now comes into play (see page 251). Think about what you need to do to check up on how well you are doing. This might include the following:

- ◆ booking regular meetings to discuss things with your line manager
- ◆ negotiating changes to your PDP that are needed due to factors outside your control affecting your plans
- ◆ seeking feedback from others.

Discussions with your line manager

This will include discussions on what is going well with your plan as well as what is not going so well. This is sometimes referred to as evaluating and reviewing your development activities. Issues you will talk about will include the following:

- ◆ what you have learned
- ◆ how your actions have helped you to achieve your personal development objectives
- ◆ how you will use this to improve customer service in your organisation
- ◆ any difficulties you have faced (see negotiating changes)
- ◆ what further support you might need
- ◆ what you will do next.

Negotiating changes to your PDP

Sometimes, through no fault of your own, you will be unable to achieve some of your personal objectives. This sometimes happens when the plans you agree are affected by organisational changes outside of your control, e.g. cuts in budgets, staff changes, company take-overs or job role content changes. Also things like long-term staff sickness may find you covering for a team member and therefore doing things you had not expected to do when you originally agreed the content of your PDP.

Negotiation is an important part of the PDP process

At times like this you will need to negotiate with your line manager, or other appropriate person, alterations to your personal development objectives. Go into any negotiating discussion with information regarding why you need to change your personal objectives and what you believe is the right way forward. If the other person disagrees with what you are saying, for instance, he or she might not fully appreciate the impact of team changes upon you, you might need to reach a compromise. This means being prepared to listen to the other person's point of view, talking it through and coming to some sort of agreement that suits both of you in the end.

Seeking feedback from others

You will not be able to fully review your PDP without first seeking feedback on your performance. We will cover how to use and receive feedback in this context in Element 6.3.

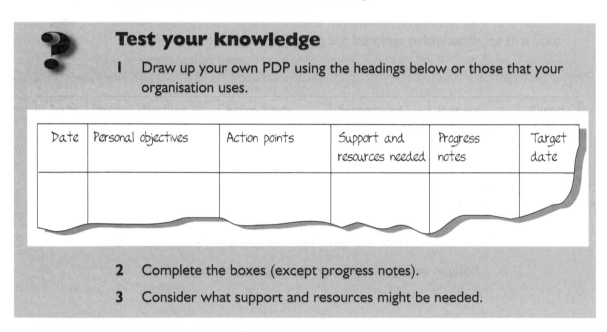

Test your knowledge

1   Draw up your own PDP using the headings below or those that your organisation uses.

Date	Personal objectives	Action points	Support and resources needed	Progress notes	Target date

2   Complete the boxes (except progress notes).

3   Consider what support and resources might be needed.

6.3 Undertake development activities and obtain feedback on your customer service performance

Undertake development activities and obtain feedback on your customer service performance

♦ Ways of ensuring you carry out your development activities.
♦ How to use day-to-day experiences to develop your own performance.
♦ How to obtain and use feedback about your own performance.

Ways of ensuring you carry out your development activities

The type of development activity you might undertake will fall into one of two categories:

♦ off-the-job learning
♦ on-the-job learning.

OFF-THE-JOB DEVELOPMENT ACTIVITIES	ON-THE-JOB DEVELOPMENT ACTIVITIES
Reading, e.g. library books, quality newspapers, magazines, periodicals	Asking for help from a colleague or other appropriate person
Attending courses, training events, workshops, seminars, conferences	Asking for feedback from colleagues, line managers, supervisors, customers, etc.
Searching the Internet for information	Observing someone else perform a task or doing their job
Using a multi-media package, e.g. CD-ROM	Observing someone else for a period of time (work shadowing)
Completing a self-assessment chart to regularly review your progress	Using work manuals, guides and handbooks to train yourself
Achieving professional qualifications	Being coached by someone at work
Performance reviews with an appropriate person	Taking on new and challenging tasks
Learning from your experiences as a customer	

Figure 6.10 Off-the-job and on-the-job development activities

Remember

You can use a learning log to record customers' problems and how you dealt with them. This way you will use what you have learnt to improve your customer service performance.

If you have written sound personal development objectives, and agreed with an appropriate person the support and resources you require, then it is down to you to make sure you carry out your actions and achieve your goals. You should not necessarily expect someone to be checking up on what you do all the time.

Keeping on track with your PDP

Look at your PDP from time to time and use the progress column to record how you are doing. Always remember to put the date on the form and to be honest about your progress. If you have not been able to make the progress you had hoped for, perhaps due to sickness or team changes, then do not panic. Discuss the situation with an appropriate person and work out between you how to move forward.

Consider also using a diary system as a reminder for the major milestones in your PDP. Book in advance a series of appointments/meetings (e.g. for the next three months) with whoever is responsible for discussing your performance with you.

How to use day-to-day experiences to develop your own performance

In Element 6.1 we looked at how you can use learning logs to help you to learn from your own experiences as a customer (see page 240). You can now take this process a step further by adopting the same learning log approach with your own customers.

Try to review what happens when you deal with customers

Look at what you do with your own customers that will help you to develop your own personal performance. You can use the following statements to help you review what happens when you deal with customers:

♦ The customer liked it when …

♦ The customer didn't like it when …

♦ The customer smiled at me today and this made me feel …

♦ I dealt with a difficult customer and this made me feel …

♦ The customer was happy because I …

♦ The customer was unhappy because I …

♦ I was able to answer the customer's questions and this meant …

♦ I did not know what to say to the customer and this meant …

♦ I was not sure how my organisation would wish me to help my customer and this meant …

Active knowledge

Not all the points on the review list above may be relevant to you and your customer service role. Think about the types of activities you are involved with. e.g. dealing with equipment, operating machinery, following instructions, etc.

♦ Add any questions to the review list above that will help you learn from your day-to-day experiences.
♦ Draw up your own list of questions to think about and keep it with your learning log.

Using your review list

Once you have drawn up your list of points to help you review what happens when you deal with customers you will need to use it. For example, look at the first point in the review list on page 256:

♦ The customer liked it when I …

Here you would need to examine what happened to make you think that the customer was satisfied with the way you dealt with him or her. Did you receive a thank-you letter or were you thanked face-to-face? Did the customer simply give you a broad grin that made you feel that you had done well? Did the customer recommend you to someone else?

By completing your responses to all the points included on your own personalised review list, you can see that you are identifying what you did that went well and what you did that did not make a good impression. You should then think carefully about the nature of each incident in order to identify what you did that made the difference between good and bad customer service. You will need to look for specific actions that you took that made the difference for the customer. When you have done this you can complete your learning log.

Case study

Below is an extract from Andrea's learning log completed after her Friday lunchtime shift at the café-bar. Here you can see how Andrea has learned from experience and used this learning to improve her customer service performance.

Activity – What I did/ What happened	Outcomes – What I learned	Actions – How I will use this experience
I was taking an order from a group of local businessmen who use the café-bar frequently. We were having a chat. I didn't notice that sitting at the next table were two women who had come in for a snack. The two women walked out making quite a fuss as they left. I heard one of them say 'She's too busy chatting the men up to serve us. We won't come here again.'	I was doing a good job making the regular customers welcome; we were talking about a conference they had been to. I had failed to balance the time I was spending with the regulars with the needs of other customers. I felt very embarrassed as the women left and too upset to even try to stop them leaving. I must not appear to have favourites and I have learned to be more aware of what is going on around me.	I can stop this happening again by simply observing customers more frequently and being aware of their body language. I must take special note of when customers come in. I did not know how to approach the women to try to calm them down and will find out what I can do to get more confidence in dealing with difficult situations.

Figure 6.11 Extract from Andrea's learning log

Remember

When you are a customer and when you deal with customers you can use these experiences to improve your personal performance.

How to obtain and use feedback about your own performance

Much of what we have said so far in this unit has seen you reflecting on what you do. It is important that you also obtain other people's views about your customer service performance. In other words you need feedback.

What kind of feedback do you need?

In the context of this unit, you are looking to improve your customer service performance. In the broadest terms this will include asking for feedback about the following:

- your strengths and weaknesses
- your behaviour with other people, e.g. customers, colleagues, suppliers, managers, etc.
- your progress with your customer service development objectives.

Sometimes, you will be given feedback without having to ask. Perhaps your supervisor observed you doing something exceptional on behalf of a customer. After the customer has left, your supervisor might come over to you and tell you specifically what it was you did that was impressive. Equally, you might have done something, albeit unwittingly, that upset a customer. Your supervisor might also take the opportunity to tell you about this.

Many people work for months without receiving feedback from anyone. It is therefore vital that you take the initiative and ask for feedback yourself.

Who do you ask for feedback?

How many times have you been asked by a friend to tell him or her what you think of their new hairstyle or their new outfit? Not wanting to hurt their feelings, you may have been tempted to say 'You look fantastic' when what you really wanted to say was 'It makes you look ten years older'. This is not the sort of feedback you need in your job.

What you need is someone you can trust to give you feedback that is going to help you to develop; someone who can give you open and honest feedback and not just tell you things they think you want to hear. Appropriate people who might be able to give you feedback include the following:

Always give honest feedback

- your manager
- your supervisor
- your team leader
- your colleagues
- your N/SVQ assessor
- your mentor
- individuals from your training department
- individuals from your human resources department.

Whoever you choose, you will need him or her to do the following:

What a person giving feedback will need to do

Planning your feedback meeting

Think about what kind of situation you would want to be in to receive your feedback. Do you want to set up a one-to-one meeting? If so, who will be responsible for finding somewhere where you can talk in private? Surprising someone with a request to give you feedback just as they are about to leave for the day is not a good idea. Think about giving as much notice as possible to the person you have asked to give you feedback. Equally, the date you set for the meeting itself should be on a date that is mutually convenient for you and the other person involved.

Decide how long the meeting will last. You may be told this, but if not, sticking to an agreed timescale will help both of you to control what is happening during the feedback session and demonstrates that you are using time efficiently.

When setting the meeting up, say what it is you specifically require feedback about. Remember, in the context of this unit you need feedback on your progress with your customer service development objectives. This will include asking for feedback on your strengths and weaknesses and your behaviour with other people.

You could try to narrow things down a little and concentrate on one or two areas at each feedback session. You could think about what you believe are your weaknesses and ask for feedback on one particular area, e.g. prioritising your workload, handling difficult customers or goal setting. When looking at your behaviour with other people, again make it easy for both of you. Narrow it down and select one or two areas you believe are important to receive feedback about, e.g. non-verbal communication (body language), assertiveness or team skills. You will then be able to concentrate on improving and developing your customer service in bite-sized chunks.

If you do decide to be very specific about the areas you want feedback on, always give your selected person the chance to add anything else at the end. He or she may do so anyway, but, if they do not, it is courteous to mention you would like to hear anything else they have to say.

Remember

Getting the planning right will help to ensure that you get the most from the feedback meeting or discussion.

How to receive feedback

The way in which you deal with receiving feedback is important because what you hear is likely to be a mixture of good things and the not so good. In other words, you will hear both criticism and praise.

How was it for you?

1   Think about a time when someone told you something nice about what you do.

   ♦ How did this make you feel?
   ♦ What, if anything, did you say to this person?
   ♦ What did you learn about yourself?

2   Now think about a time when someone criticised you.

   ♦ How did you react?
   ♦ Did you try to change what you do or how you behave as a result of this feedback?

It is not always easy to sit down and listen to someone telling you about what they think of your personal performance, whether you are being praised or criticised. Remember that the other person has given their time in order to help you. He or she wants you to succeed. You are obtaining important information, but it will be of no use to you unless you receive it in a positive manner. This means not letting your feelings get in the way.

Keys to good practice

Responding positively to personal feedback

✓ Listen without interrupting.
✓ Ask for explanations if you do not understand what is being said.
✓ Ask for specific examples of when you have done what is being discussed.
✓ Value the feedback you have been given.
✓ Ask how the person providing the feedback would expect you to behave in future.
✓ Thank the person providing the feedback.

After the meeting

After the feedback meeting you will need to reflect on what has been discussed. You may end up thinking 'I didn't realise I was that good' or 'I'm surprised to learn that I need to improve my product knowledge'. Either way, you will need to take action. If you feel the individual concerned was not suitable to give you feedback, your action could include finding someone else to discuss the matter further with and give you some additional feedback.

At the end of the process it is up to you what you make of the feedback. Think of it as information for you to use in assessing yourself. Try to avoid thinking 'I'm useless' or 'I'm fantastic'. Instead, think of the following:

◆ What have I learned from this?
◆ How will I use this information?
◆ How can I use this feedback to help me improve my customer service performance?

You should be thinking about the impact and benefits of your intended actions on your customers, colleagues and your organisation. Finally, do not forget to update your PDP and (if applicable) your learning log.

Case study

Ed has nearly finished his three-month probationary period for his new job in a call centre. He is responsible for answering customer queries relating to the renewal of household insurance policies. As part of his training he was able to discuss with the call centre trainers exactly what it was that he needed to do to be effective in his role. This included the following:

Communication skills

♦ Communicate in a clear, polite and confident manner.
♦ Use the call centre standard greeting.
♦ Follow internal guidelines for responding to calls.
♦ Convey relevant and accurate information to customers.
♦ Use customers' names.
♦ Avoid using jargon.
♦ Keep customers informed of progress.

Product knowledge

♦ Demonstrate an understanding of household insurance products.
♦ Know where to find information.

At the end of his three-month probation, Ed knew he would be having a discussion with his line manager in order to obtain feedback on his progress.

♦ What would you recommend Ed does to prepare himself for the feedback session?
♦ How can Ed find out about his strengths and development needs prior to the feedback session?
♦ What tips on how to deal with receiving feedback would you give to Ed?
♦ How can Ed ensure he continues to develop his personal performance through delivering customer service?

Check your knowledge

1   How can you identify what knowledge and skills you need to be effective in your role?

2   What can you do to help yourself learn from your own experiences when you go shopping?

3   Name the three headings used in a learning log.

4   Why is your behaviour so important in customer service situations?

5   List five things you can do to review your personal strengths and development needs.

6   Name three top tips for writing effective personal development objectives.

7   Personal development objectives cannot be changed once they have been agreed with an appropriate person. True or false?

8   What are the benefits of using a Personal Development Plan?

9   What do you need to consider when planning a feedback meeting?

10   Why is it important to ask questions when you receive feedback?

11   'Feedback is always about what I did wrong.' True or false?

12   What should you do after receiving feedback?

UNIT 7 Promote additional products or services to customers

It does not matter how successful an organisation is at delivering customer service; it will fail if it does not also ensure its products or services keep up with or exceed the pace of change. This is because customer expectations change and technology changes. Therefore, products and services need to change in order to reflect this and you, as the customer service practitioner, need to ensure you play your part in promoting additional products or services to customers

Organisations need to advise customers about the variety of products or services that are available. If this does not happen, another organisation will soon come to the attention of a customer who might have used your organisation had he or she known that the product or service was available from you.

You must not force customers to buy things they do not really want or need. That is wrong, unethical and potentially damaging to both your customer and your organisation. You should promote additional products or services on the basis of providing customers with appropriate information in order that they may make an informed choice or decision.

In order to work through this option unit your role must therefore involve you with promoting additional products or services that are new to your customers, and encouraging customers to make more use of products or services they have used before. This means you will be providing information to customers by following organisational guidelines or by creating your own opportunities to encourage the use of additional products or services by responding to customer comments.

The elements for this option unit are:

♦ 7.1 Identify additional products or services that are available
♦ 7.2 Inform customers about additional products or services
♦ 7.3 Gain customer commitment to using additional products or services.

7.1 Identify additional products or services that are available

◆ How the use of additional products or services will benefit customers and your organisation.

◆ Ways of keeping your product or services knowledge up to date.

◆ How to match your products or services to your customers' needs.

◆ What you can do to spot opportunities to offer customers additional products or services.

How the use of additional products or services will benefit customers and your organisation

Before you can understand how products or services will benefit your customers, you will need to know the range of products or services your organisation offers, what type of customer they might suit and how to spot opportunities to encourage their use.

You must not encourage someone to think about buying a product or service that does not match his or her needs. By understanding what motivates customers you will understand how your customers will benefit from your additional products or services.

Customers buy for their own reasons

Do not assume that you know what a customer wants or needs. Do not assume that people will buy your products or services instead of going elsewhere simply because you believe they are the best.

Being the best is not good enough. Each customer will have personal reasons for committing to an additional product or service. These include financial reasons as well as the less logical factors of emotion, e.g. ego, fear or guilt. Your job is to find out the real reason for buying, in order for you to match a relevant product or service to each customer.

Customers are not usually concerned about you

A customer is not going to worry too much about any sales targets you need to reach. He or she is more likely to be concerned about what will make life easier or give value for money.

Customers do not buy products or services

Your customers buy benefits and solutions. The product or service is the wrapping paper around the special package inside – the solution – that is going to be of benefit to him or her. Customers buy what the product or service will do for them and how it will make them feel.

People do not like high-pressure selling techniques

Telling a customer about a product or service they do not want or need will not do you or your organisation any favours. Furthermore, if you continue to try to press unwanted information onto a customer you may end up losing the customer for good.

By understanding your customers' expectations and needs you will be successful in promoting additional products or services. The most effective technique for doing this is to make it easy for customers to buy.

Ways of keeping your product or services knowledge up to date

Both customers and your organisation stand to benefit when relevant additional products or services are brought to the attention of customers.

Over time you will become very familiar with the products or services you work with, and it will become second nature for you to discuss these with customers. When you are new to your job, there are many sources of information you can use to find out about your organisation's products or services.

Figure 7.1 Sources of information about products or services

Active knowledge

Locate your own main sources of information about the key products or services you deal with.

♦ Write down anything about the products or services which is new information for you.

♦ How will you use this new knowledge to promote additional products or services?

Try to find out about any additional products or services

Some of the additional products or services that may be of interest to customers may not be so familiar to you. It is therefore important that you familiarise yourself with products or services that you do not deal with so frequently. For example, a person working in a shoe shop will be very familiar with the range of shoes on offer, but perhaps less so with the types of shoe cleaner that might be offered to a customer. Someone working in a travel agency would need to know about the types of insurance on offer as well as how to book a holiday for customers.

Key product or service	Additional product or service
Ladies' leather boots	Special leather cleaner. Shoe horns. Matching handbag
Boosters for dogs at the vets	Claw clipping. Dental hygiene
Package holiday	Travel insurance. Destination guide book
Bus fare	Concessionary travel for senior citizens
Car purchase	Mud flaps. Spoilers. Upgraded audio system
Chiropractic treatment	Neck support pillows. Lumbar rolls. Vitamins and minerals

Figure 7.2 Opportunities to offer additional products or services

When to offer additional products or services to customers

You need to check what your organisation's procedures and systems are for promoting additional products or services, in order to make sure it is appropriate to suggest a customer thinks about buying something extra. There are many reasons for this, including the following:

♦ Your organisation is unlikely to welcome being tarnished with the reputation of being involved with hard-selling. Hard-selling occurs when customers are faced with an employee who simply will not let go. So keen is he or she to get the customer to commit to buying that the customer ends up saying 'yes' simply to make this employee go away.
♦ Your organisation may want to promote a specific range of products or services at a particular time of year, e.g. Christmas decorations to go with the purchase of a Christmas tree, barbeque sauces to go with the purchase of charcoal, clotted cream to go with the purchase of scones.
♦ Legal reasons may restrict the promotion of certain products or services to individuals, e.g. alcohol to under-18-year-olds.

Active knowledge

By talking with a colleague or other appropriate person, find out what your organisation's systems and procedures are for the promotion of additional products or services to customers.

What you need to do to if you are unsure about any new products or services

New products or services are constantly introduced and existing ones are altered in order for your organisation to keep ahead of the competition, provide variety for their customers, comply with legislation and ensure the product or service is safe.

It is vital that you show you are confident when discussing with customers any new or additional products or services. Make sure you know the following (refer back to Unit 2 for more information):

♦ as much as you can about the product or service
♦ any sources of assistance if you need help
♦ where to find out more information if required.

When an organisation introduces a new product or service you will need to make sure you do your research before you start to introduce it to customers. To make sure you keep up to date you will need to be proactive. Do not wait for somebody else to tell you; make the time to seek out the information yourself.

Keys to good practice

Keeping your product or service knowledge up to date

✓ Do a frequent check on the validity of the information you have.
✓ Have the most recent information readily available or accessible.
✓ Ask colleagues.
✓ Check your organisation's newsletters/website/intranet/updates/in-house magazine.
✓ Always look for ways to improve your knowledge of products or services.
✓ Think about things you read in the press or see on the TV and how they might affect the products or services your organisation offers.
✓ Listen to customers' questions and queries and update your knowledge for those you cannot answer easily.

How to match your products or services to your customers' needs

Once you have found out about any additional products and services your company offers, you will need to know how to use this knowledge. You need to make sure you know what your customers' needs and expectations are in order to effectively match what your organisation can offer them by way of a solution.

In order to be successful in doing this you need to get to the heart of a customer's problem or to the heart of their specific interests. You can do this by demonstrating that you are confident, have a thorough knowledge of your product and services and by asking the right questions. Do not forget to listen carefully too. You will then be well placed to think about which additional products or services might support your customer's needs and wants.

Benefits that motivate customers to buy

In order to match your organisation's products or services to your customer's needs you will be asking questions to find out what it is he or she wants.

As you ask questions, listen carefully for responses that indicate cost/quality is the most important factor

The ten most common benefits a customer will look for when making a purchase are shown in Figure 7.3.

It is useful to look at how products or services might help certain types of customers. The table overleaf details some products or services suitable for the benefits shown in Figure 7.3 and then suggests people who might be interested in them.

Figure 7.3 The ten most common customer benefits

Notice that we have talked in terms of benefits not features. A **feature** describes what a product or service does. A **benefit** describes how that feature can help a customer.

Product/service	Benefit	Suitable for
Car phone (handsfree)	Safe to use, legal	Travelling salespeople, any car driver
Solar roof panels	Eco-friendly, save money	Environmentally friendly consumers
Surge-protected extension lead	Peace of mind	Personal computer users
Four-wheel drive car	Safe in all weathers	People in rural communities
Left-handed scissors	Convenience	Left-handed people
Armchair with built-in footrest	Comfortable	Hard-working people, people who enjoy relaxing
Four-course luxury meal	Enjoyable	People who have something to celebrate
Hearing aid	Convenience/flexibility	The hard of hearing
Dishwasher	Save time	Large families
High-interest-earning bank account	Earn more money	Savers
Internet shopping	Convenience	Busy people, people with disabilities
Private medical insurance	Peace of mind	Self-employed people

Figure 7.4 Products, benefits and customers

Active knowledge

Draw up a table with the headings shown below.

Product/service	Benefit	Suitable for

♦ Write down five key products or services you deal with, together with any additional products or services you offer alongside in the product/service column.

♦ Think about the benefits of each and record them in the middle column.

♦ Decide what type of customer each product might be suitable for and record these thoughts in the final column.

♦ What do you need to do to ensure you are thinking about the benefits of your products or services when you deal with customers?

How was it for you?

Think of the individuals you have bought from when you wanted to buy a certain product or service. Include those times when someone tried to tell you about something additional to what you originally wanted. Make a list of what was good or bad about your experiences.

What you can do to spot opportunities to offer customers additional products or services

In order to spot opportunities to offer customers additional products or services you will need to know and understand the key products and services you deal with. Alongside this you will need to know and understand which additional products and services might meet the needs of customers who buy your key products and services. Working through this unit will already have helped you to establish this information base.

In addition, you will also need to develop rapport with a customer. Without your ability to establish rapport and develop the relationship between the customer, yourself and your organisation, it is unlikely a customer will want to listen or to be told about additional products and services. In order to develop rapport you need to show you are sincere by doing the following:

♦ maintaining eye contact
♦ listening
♦ responding to questions and queries
♦ thanking your customer when appropriate.

If you do this, your customer will feel valued. If your customer feels valued, he or she will be more likely to listen to what you have to say about additional products or services.

The next step is to listen for opportunities to help a customer further. There are often opportunities for a customer service practitioner to offer additional products or services when a customer buys a key product. Some of these opportunities might come about by the practitioner listening carefully for chance comments a customer might make in passing, such as the following:

♦ in a shoe shop the customer murmurs to herself 'My handbag won't match these boots.'
♦ in the vet's, the dog owner says to the vet 'My dog gets taken for walks on grass all the time, his claws do not get worn down very quickly; they're rather long.'
♦ in the travel agency, the holidaymaker says to his partner 'I've always wanted to go to Singapore, but I don't know very much about what places to visit.'
♦ while having chiropractic treatment, the client says to the chiropractor 'I've never been able to find a pillow that gives me a comfortable night's sleep.'

These comments are all clear signals that the customer might find an additional product or service helpful. You should offer some advice or information as to what you and your organisation can do to help. Do so in a non-threatening way; be helpful and considerate and have a relaxed approach. Any attempt to force something on your customer that is not needed or relevant will soon be recognised by your customer as an attempt to use hard-sell techniques.

Keys to good practice

Spotting opportunities to offer customers additional products or services

✓ Know about your products or services.
✓ Develop rapport with your customers.
✓ Listen out for chance comments.
✓ Identify the best solution to your customers' needs.
✓ Offer advice and information on how you might be able to offer further help.
✓ Adopt a relaxed style.

Test your knowledge

A new member of staff, Sinead, will be working with you soon. This will be Sinead's first job since leaving school and you are aware she has no prior knowledge of the products or services you deal with. To help Sinead settle in, you decide to draw up a list of the key products or services she will need to become familiar with. Do this now by completing the following table:

Key product or service	Who suitable for	Features	Benefits	Relevant additional products or services

♦ Who will you need to go to for help (if you need it) to complete this table?

♦ How will you decide which products or services you need to include?

♦ What do you need to do to ensure you accurately describe the features and benefits of each?

♦ How will you set about identifying any additional products or services?

Inform customers about additional products or services

WHAT YOU NEED TO KNOW OR LEARN

♦ What factors influence customers to use your products or services.

♦ How to choose the right approach to tell your customers about additional products or services.

♦ How much information to give your customers to help them make their decision.

♦ How to encourage customers to ask questions, and then to give them appropriate answers.

What factors influence customers to use your products or services

Customers buy benefits not products

A definition of the word benefit is 'anything that brings about an improvement' or 'something that enhances well-being or helps assist someone to obtain an advantage'. If a customer is introduced to an additional product or service, he or she will form an impression as to whether or not this new information is of interest and benefit to him or her. Look at the table below which illustrates some examples of how an individual customer might perceive a benefit. Consider how one customer's opinion as to whether something is a benefit or not, might differ from another customer's opinion.

Benefit	Examples of a customer's possible perception of a benefit
Helps make a positive impression	Fashionable brand jeans v nondescript pair. Contact lenses v glasses
Helps make life easier	Laser eye surgery v contact lenses. A wheelchair v not going out. A mobile telephone v a landline. Ready-cooked meals v home cooking. Auto-defrost fridge v manual defrost
Cheaper	More money to spend on something else v possible loss of quality
More expensive	Less money to spend on something else v possible increase in quality

Figure 7.5 A customer's perception of a benefit

Active knowledge

Think about five key products or services you deal with. For each one compile a table similar to Figure 7.5 by listing how customers interpret their benefits.

What a customer perceives as a benefit can also be something so personal to the individual that only he or she knows the reason.

Figure 7.6 Influences affecting customers' perceptions of benefits

Many people never move bank accounts; not because it is difficult to do so, but because the account was the first one he or she opened after leaving school.

External influences on customer needs

There are external influences that affect your customers' wants and needs. These will change over time.

Spending power

Think about your own spending power; how has this altered with the passage of time? Customers may get a new job with an increased salary and this may alter where they buy their products or services. Customers lose jobs too; this may adversely affect their ability to spend money on anything but essential products or services.

Economic climate

What is currently happening to interest rates? Is it better to be a borrower because interest rates are low, than a saver where money earns very little interest? Have worldwide events affected global stockmarkets to such an extent that consumer spending is restricted?

Fashion

Changes in fashion will have a different impact upon different age groups. What is cool now will possibly be out of date in a few months' time. Think about how changes in fashion impact upon the products or services you deal with.

Media promotions

If you work in an organisation that promotes its products or services by way of newspaper, magazine, television or radio adverts, or on posters, billboards and the Internet, then you will find certain products or services will be high on people's agendas to buy, in line with the timing of the adverts. Think about the run-up to Christmas and how the nature of television adverts changes during November/December. Have you noticed increases in adverts for toys and CDs?

Lifestyle changes

People retiring earlier, increased numbers of people working from home and decreased time to socialise all influence where a customer chooses to buy his or her products or services and whether he or she is able to buy less or more of what your organisation offers.

How to choose the right approach to tell your customers about additional products or services

Choosing the right time

Getting the timing right to tell your customers about additional products will be critical to achieving the result you want. In some situations you will get a clear signal that tells you the time is right. In these situations, the decision is almost made for you. After all, why let the customer leave without showing you care enough to help further?

In other situations, you may need to trust your instincts as to whether the time is right. This is much more difficult, but your ability to do so will improve with experience. You need to be watching out for or listening for signs that indicate something more is required from you. A puzzled face might tell you the customer requires more information. Alternatively, it might mean a customer is mulling over in their head the impact of moving forward with a product or service. They may have lots of questions that they are afraid to ask you for fear of looking silly. You will not know unless you ask questions to seek clarification as to what is required. When doing this, assess the individual needs of your customer.

For example, some customers will have done their homework by researching your product range (and that of your competitors) on the Internet or from a brochure. Others will come to you with little background information or even on the spur of the moment. By asking questions to find out your customer's needs you will be able to establish how much information you need to give. This is sometimes known as recognising a customer's personal buying behaviour.

Keys to good practice

Choosing the right time

✓ Create a friendly and courteous environment.
✓ Listen and watch for signals.
✓ Ask appropriate questions to seek the information you require.
✓ Communicate in a clear, polite and confident way.
✓ When the customer responds in a positive way, carry on by discussing the product or service in terms of benefits rather than technical features.
✓ Have a supply of product or service information literature readily available.
✓ Check that the customer has understood the benefits of the additional product or service.

If your timing is wrong, the customer will soon let you know. Listen out for phrases such as the following:

◆ I can't afford that.
◆ I've got all I need.
◆ I'm only looking.
◆ That's no use to me.
◆ I'm not interested.
◆ Maybe I'll think about doing that next year.
◆ I'm in a hurry.
◆ I bought one of those last time I was here.
◆ My husband/wife/mother/father/partner needs to see it before I make my mind up.

The above are all ways of saying 'No. Not right now, thank you'. Respect your customer's choice to walk away, providing you have given your customer an adequate opportunity to make an informed decision.

How was it for you?

Think about a time when you were given some information about an additional product or service you did not want or need, and tried to stop the customer service practitioner from doing so.

- ◆ How did you feel?
- ◆ How did you manage to say no?
- ◆ What did the customer service practitioner do after you made it clear you were not interested?

Choosing the right method

As well as getting the timing right, you also need to decide what method you should use to introduce the additional product or service to your customers. Remember that your organisation may be doing something itself to promote a new or enhanced product or service. Anything you do should therefore link in to your organisation's promotion of its products or services.

As always, you should be aiming to communicate in a clear, polite and confident way. You should be looking at the means of communication your customer has used and following that example. For example, if a customer has written a letter, it is likely that the customer's preferred means of communication is by letter.

Many customers will tell you how they wish to be contacted. For example, a letter might say 'You can call me between 11.00am and 3.00pm.' 'Please reply by email.' 'I'll call in to see you next Tuesday.'

Below are some tips on choosing the right method if the customer does not state a preference.

At the point of service

You would choose to talk with a customer (face-to-face or on the telephone) in the following circumstances:

- ◆ when a customer gives you a clear signal that an additional product or service might be of benefit
- ◆ when your organisation asks you to promote a specific product or service
- ◆ when you spot an opportunity to offer an additional product or service.

By post

If a customer has not visited your place of work, you could write enclosing literature you wish to them to see. This is particularly useful if the information is detailed and requires the customer to have the opportunity to have time to look at it. Some organisations have sophisticated systems that track information relating to customers' purchases. For example, if a customer has a loyalty card with a supermarket, when it is used, information captured from barcodes will show the supermarket what products the customer buys. If there is a trend for purchasing organic fruit and vegetables, the supermarket could undertake a mailshot to all customers with this trend to inform them of a new range when appropriate.

By telephone

Using the telephone to promote additional products or services when you are not already engaged in conversation with a customer might be thought of as cold-calling. This falls into the hard-sell area that is unlikely to be successful. However, if you are talking to a customer about something as a matter of course and you listen out for signals indicating that something additional is required, then discussing an additional product or service over the telephone would be entirely appropriate.

By email

Using email will ensure a speedy introduction to a customer. It is also cheap. However, consider whether such an email might be perceived as being junk mail and therefore be deleted before being opened.

Websites

Your organisation will take the opportunity to update its website regularly to bring to the attention of customers any new or enhanced products or services. Often a customer will be directed to a 'what's new' page.

Active knowledge

If your organisation has a website, review it now to find out how new or enhanced products or services are brought to the attention of customers.

♦ How can you use this information to promote the use of additional products or services?

How much information to give your customers to help them make their decision

We have said that you need to treat customers as individuals and to recognise that everyone has their own personal buying behaviour. When making a major purchase (e.g. a new television or car) or becoming involved with a new service (e.g. digital television or private health insurance) some people will want to do a great deal of research before even approaching an organisation. Others will not want the bother of doing any research, either through lack of time or because they trust an organisation to provide accurate, reliable and appropriate information.

It is your job to make sure the customer has as much information as he or she needs to make an informed decision about an additional product or service. To do this you should consider your individual customer's personal buying behaviour; he or she may be a slow buyer or a fast buyer.

Slow buyers

Give those customers who require a great deal of information the time to reflect on what you have said or written about. This means you will be allowing them to buy in their own time. The customer will not feel pressured and will be more likely to think about the advantages and disadvantages of what you are offering.

Too much information? Or just enough?

This is important because a slow buyer's concern (and therefore motivation) is being in control of the final decision and of having the ability to think things through in a logical way. They do not respond well to pressure and will actively resist being forced into making a decision.

Slow buyers will shop around, if only to confirm that a decision made is indeed the right one. Do not be surprised if a customer appears to want your additional product or service, but then leaves the shop or ends a telephone call without saying yes. The customer may require a little more time to shop around to justify saying yes to your product or service. In these situations you need to make sure a customer knows how to get back in touch with you, and you should let them leave armed with the appropriate literature.

Slow buyers often need to seek the opinion of a partner in order to make a joint decision. Very often the customer will also call you back or visit you again to go over some of the details. This is all perfectly fine; your role is to provide relevant, accurate and appropriate information about additional products or services. If you do this, the rest is down to the customer to make a decision.

Fast buyers

For those customers who buy quickly, you should remember that these individuals tend to be people who enjoy power and authority and are motivated by being in charge. If you present a lot of detailed information he or she may become bored or even frustrated. For this type of customer you could try summarising the details of your additional product or service.

It is very important to continue to provide accurate and relevant information to fast buyers. If you do not, a purchase will be made that may not be appropriate, causing loss of goodwill and damaging the relationship your customer has with you and your organisation.

How to encourage customers to ask questions, and then to give them appropriate answers

You need to be well prepared for your discussions with customers. Put yourself in their shoes. If you have got to the stage of suggesting an additional product or service to your customer, you will already have done some or all of the following:

♦ asked questions to clarify the customer's needs
♦ thought about the types of products or services your customer is interested in
♦ thought about your customer's apparent personal buying behaviour
♦ put yourself in the customer's shoes to understand what he or she might be wanting you to do
♦ chosen an appropriate method of communication.

Assuming you have not been asked to stop discussing the additional product or service, the next step is to make sure your customer feels comfortable enough to ask you questions that might make the difference between the customer walking away or actually buying the product or service. Using effective communication skills will enable you to create a positive relationship with your customers. The relevant communication skills for encouraging customers to discuss products or services with you include the following:

♦ asking questions
♦ effective listening.

As a means of encouraging questions you should be alert to signs that your customer needs further clarification. Such signs may include looking puzzled, frowning or staring into space. If you see this happening, try saying the following:

♦ Have I explained that properly for you?
♦ Is there anything else I can tell you about the product?

On the telephone you will need to listen out for long periods of silence that may indicate you have 'lost' your customer's train of thought. You would need to check this carefully as he or she may simply be listening intently to what you are saying. You could try saying the following:

♦ I am not sure if I have explained that enough. Can I give you any more information?
♦ There's a great deal of information to absorb here. Would you like me to go over it again?

When you are in a situation where your customer appears to understand fully, you should still give him or her the opportunity to ask questions. In this way you will show you are willing to discuss the additional product or service further. You could try saying the following:

♦ How do you feel about that?
♦ Is that what you are looking for?
♦ Do you agree that having X will help you with Y?

A customer will feel more able to ask you questions if you show you are interested in him or her. You can do this by demonstrating that you are listening effectively to what he or she has to say. This applies whether you are on the telephone or face-to-face with a customer. To show you are listening you can ask a specific type of question that will help you to gain a better understanding of what your customer is thinking, as well as encouraging him or her to ask you questions. These are called clarifying questions and confirming questions.

Clarifying questions

In order to increase your understanding of what the customer wants, you may need to ask a question to clarify things, such as the following:

♦ You say that you are not sure about visiting the clinic in the evenings. Are there any days in the week when you could do so?
♦ You say that evenings are very difficult for you. What would be a good time of day for you to visit?
♦ You said you have had problems with a similar product before. Would you mind telling me a bit more?
♦ I understand now is not a good time to discuss this. When would be more convenient for us to talk?

All these questions could be asked in response to something a customer has said. By asking a clarifying question you are creating an opportunity for your customer to open up the discussion.

Confirming questions

Instead of asking questions to clarify what a customer has said, you could try stating your understanding and checking this back with the customer, as shown in the examples below:

♦ You seem to be interested in finding out more about our savings accounts. Am I right?
♦ The property-finding service would seem to be just what you need. Is that correct?
♦ I have told you about our new service being launched next week. May I put you on our mailing list?

Confirming questions require a 'yes' or 'no' answer or a response which encourages further discussion.

Keys to good practice

Encouraging customers to ask questions

✓ Maintain regular eye contact.
✓ Let the customer ask you questions.
✓ Sound friendly and positive.
✓ Listen to what the customer says.
✓ Use silence as a means of letting your customer think.
✓ Have product or service information readily available.
✓ Take your time.
✓ Watch for signs that your customer wants to ask questions.

Case study

Ruth left a beauty salon based in a hotel to set up her own business. This has now been running for six months and Ruth is delighted with the number of

customers who regularly use her services. She wants to offer additional products or services to her customers as most seem to return for the same treatments.

Her range of products and services includes the following:

♦ aromatherapy massage
♦ facials
♦ manicures and pedicures
♦ eyelash tinting
♦ eyebrow shaping
♦ high-quality skin care products
♦ a range of nail varnishes.

1 Should Ruth match an additional product or service to the key treatment(s) her customers use?
2 What would be the advantages of doing this?
3 What would be the disadvantages?
4 What methods could Ruth use to advise her customers about the range of products or services she offers?
5 When would be the most appropriate time to inform her customers of additional products?
6 How can Ruth encourage her customers to discuss her full range of products and services?

Test your knowledge

1 Try role-playing this scenario with a friend or colleague.

   ♦ Imagine you are trying to encourage your friend to rent a room in your house or flat. You want your friend to take the room furnished but he or she would prefer to rent it unfurnished.
   ♦ Why might it be important to you for the room to be rented furnished?
   ♦ Why might it be important for your friend to rent the room unfurnished?

2 Now ask your friend to start a conversation with you which enables you to practise your listening skills and also to practise your ability to describe in a positive way the features and benefits of renting a room which comes complete with furniture, TV etc.

7.3 Gain customer commitment to using additional products or services

WHAT YOU NEED TO KNOW OR LEARN

♦ What to do if your customer shows interest in additional products or services.

♦ Ways of referring customers to alternative sources of information if you are not responsible for dealing with the additional products or services they want.

♦ What to do if your customer shows no interest in additional products or services.

What to do if your customer shows interest in additional products or services

Having identified the customer's needs or expectations and clarified any problems, you will now be in a position to know whether or not you have a customer who is interested in your additional products or services. We will now look at what you can do to gain commitment from your customer to buying the additional product or service. This may involve providing further information or it may involve you taking action to ensure the product or service is made available to your customer.

There are differing degrees of showing interest. Some customers will buy on the spot, others will say more time is needed to think or to discuss the matter with friends or family. Others will want more information. The important thing to remember is to aim for some sort of commitment at each stage. If a customer says he or she needs time to think, you should seek his or her agreement to contact him or her again by a certain date

Similarly, if a customer requests more information, you should agree with him or her to send some information though the post or to get a colleague to contact him or her. What you have striven to do in both these situations is to promise to take action (which will help move the customer closer to making a decision, and therefore closer to a sale) and you have sought agreement from your customer that this action is acceptable.

Checking your customer's interest

While you are in discussion with a customer, take the opportunity to ask for his or her opinion as you go along. This is often described as taking your customer's buying temperature, as it is a means of testing out whether he or she remains interested. You can do this by saying the following:

♦ How does this fit with what you need?
♦ What do you think about having the ability to do X?
♦ What do you like most about what I have just shown you?
♦ If you decided to go ahead, what would you need to do in order to take this idea further?

You then need to respond with accurate and sufficient information to ensure your customer remains interested. Always discuss additional products and service in terms of the benefits it will bring to your customer. Many customer service practitioners make the mistake of jumping in too quickly and bombarding the customer with too much information, as the example below demonstrates.

Financial advisor: How important is your long-term financial security to you?

Customer: I guess it's quite important. At the moment though, I do not have a pension or any life-assurance policies.

Financial advisor: OK, let's talk more about this. Let me tell you about the benefits of having an X pension. (The financial advisor launches into a full-scale presentation about pensions and life assurance.)

What the financial advisor has failed to do is to continue to check out just how interested the customer is in having a pension or life-assurance policy.

The conversation should have gone like this:

Financial advisor: How do you feel about not having a pension?

Customer: It's a bit of a worry actually.

Financial advisor: What problems will this cause you?

Customer: I may not have sufficient savings to maintain or improve my standard of living when I reach retirement age.

Financial advisor: What about life assurance? How do you feel about not having any?

Customer: Not too worried about that. I have no dependants.

By checking out the customer's interest in the second version of this conversation, the financial advisor has found out that a pension may be relevant, but life assurance not so appropriate for this particular customer. This is very important in the financial services industry as to mis-sell would lead to serious legal implications.

Let us assume you have reached the stage where your customer has confirmed he or she is interested in the additional product or service. What happens next is often referred to as closing the sale. This is the end of the buying process when a customer agrees to purchase.

How to close the sale

So far, you have done the following:

◆ opened a discussion with your customer that has included the promotion of additional products or services
◆ asked questions that helped to identify your customer's needs
◆ presented the features and benefits of the product or service
◆ checked your customer's understanding
◆ checked your customer's interest.

The final part of this process will be to close the sale.

Closing techniques

There are many ways a customer service practitioner can bring to a conclusion his or her discussions with customers about an additional product or service. Closing the sale involves you in using a variety of techniques to secure your customer's agreement to the purchase of the additional product or service.

Direct close: here you would simply ask for the order when you are sure your customer is happy with the purchase:

'I will go ahead now and arrange for this order to be completed.'

Assumptive close: if you are sure your customer is interested, you could try making an assumption that they are going to say yes by saying:

◆ This will solve all your problems when you have it installed.
◆ When would be the best time to deliver?
◆ Will a choice of four colours be enough?

Alternative close: this technique gives your customer the choice between two alternatives, both of which have been chosen by yourself:

◆ I'll arrange for it to be delivered next Tuesday, or would Friday suit you better?

Figure 7.7 Closing techniques

♦ Would you prefer the blue or the black one?
♦ Would you like me to post this to you or will you collect?

Deal/concession close: here you bring to the attention of the customer any special offers that might be available. Salespeople use this technique when they feel they need to demonstrate to a customer that a purchase gives value for money, or that the customer is making a smart choice by going ahead:

♦ Order today and you will get 10 per cent off.
♦ If you place the order by Friday I will be able to add an additional pack to your order for free.

Make sure you do not come across as a high-pressure salesperson if you use this technique.

Converting on objections: an objection can turn out to be a very strong buying signal. For instance, if you have established that an objection relates to a stated delivery time you can turn this around:

♦ 'You say that you want to order this from us but are concerned about our discount given for bulk purchases. If we can work out a compromise would you be happy to place an order today?'

Negotiated close: this involves you striking a bargain with a customer:

♦ 'If I find out I can reduce the price by 10 per cent, will you place the order today?'

Time-driven close: using this technique, a salesperson brings to the attention of the customer any relevant time-based information that may impact upon a decision to buy:

♦ I need to tell you that prices are going up next week.
♦ The model you have selected will be withdrawn at the end of March.

Advantages/disadvantages close: this technique involves you pointing out to your customer what the advantages and disadvantages are in relation to him or her saying yes to your product or service. If dealing face-to-face with a customer you can list these on a piece of paper with a **+** on one side and a **–** on the other.

Active knowledge

1   Discuss with a colleague which of the techniques on pages 287–8 are relevant to you and your role.

2   Write down which techniques you use now.

   ♦ For each one, write two or three statements that you could use when attempting to close a sale.
   ♦ Practise using them and decide which are the most effective.

Points to remember about closing a sale

Closing techniques are not enough to secure a sale: it does not matter how successful you are at using the closing techniques, the other parts of the buying process also need to be effective. If your ability to develop rapport and your product or service knowledge are not up to date, then you are unlikely to secure a sale because your customer will not have confidence in you, your organisation or the product or service.

Be prepared for rejection: if you are in a sales role you will need to get used to rejection, i.e. customers who say no.

The more you promote, the more you will sell: selling is a numbers game; the more you promote additional products or services, the more you will sell.

Close when the customer is ready to buy: the right time to close the sale is when the customer is ready. This does not necessarily mean at the end of a conversation. Sometimes a customer will indicate that he or she wants to move forward after only a short time in discussion. When this happens you should seek commitment there and then, providing you are sure the customer is basing his or her decision on sound and sufficient information.

There will be more than one chance to close the sale: there will be several occasions during your discussions when a customer is ready to buy. There will also be many opportunities for you to close the sale.

For instance, if a customer says no now, it does not follow that he or she will still be saying no in ten minutes' time. Providing you have done your best to explain the benefits of a product or service, you could turn the no into a yes.

A customer's resistance is natural: you should expect a degree of resistance from customers. The customer will often be thinking about the consequences of the additional purchase. For instance, he or she could be thinking the following:

♦ Am I getting value for money?
♦ I've done without for years. Do I really need this?
♦ Are they as reliable as you are making out?
♦ I've seen one cheaper in a shop down the road.
♦ What other alternatives are there?
♦ What happens if I say no?

All these thought processes that may occur during the closing stages will cause your customer to hesitate. You might detect this hesitation in his or her voice. What your customer is looking for is some reassurance from you that the decision he or she is about to make is the right one.

Customers may not say yes even when they want to: sometimes a customer will wait for you to actually ask him or her if they wish to make

Figure 7.8 Points to remember about closing a sale

the purchase. If you fail to ask, you may lose a customer who was ready to say yes.

How to ensure your organisation reacts promptly to the customer's agreement

Having obtained a decision from your customer to take up the additional product or service, you will need to ensure it is actually delivered. Sometimes this is simple as you will be able to deal with it yourself at the point of sale by literally handing over the product to your customer, e.g. shoe cleaner with a pair of shoes. At other times you might need to involve colleagues or suppliers, e.g. travel insurance with the purchase of a package holiday or a vet referring a customer to a veterinary nurse to have a dog's claws clipped. You will need to communicate exactly what it is your customer has agreed to buy to any other people involved with the delivery of the product or service. This might be via the telephone, by fax, letter or email. Choose whichever method will be supported by your organisation, and also bear in mind how fast you need other people to react to your request.

Sometimes it might be necessary to make a diary note to follow up actions you have asked to be done by colleagues or suppliers. Likewise, your organisation might have a system that requires you to contact the customer to check delivery has been made or to check he or she is satisfied with the additional product or service.

Active knowledge

Find out what your organisation's systems and procedures are for ensuring prompt delivery of additional products or services.

Case study

Dominic works in telesales for ExcitingExperiences4U. This firm specialises in promoting gift packages to companies who wish to congratulate or provide an incentive for employees. The gifts are also used as part of team-building events. The range of gifts he deals with includes the following:

♦ a Ferrari for a day
♦ race round Brands Hatch
♦ health-farm packages
♦ hot-air-balloon rides
♦ bungee-jumping
♦ trips on the Orient Express
♦ West End theatre breaks.

Bad weather last year meant the hot-air-balloon rides were not popular. In an effort to promote this service, Dominic has been asked to offer the balloon trips at half price to all companies booking a gift in the next two months. He has also been asked to telephone the companies he deals with to advise them of the offer.

- ♦ How should Dominic prepare for the telephone calls?
- ♦ What benefit is there to Dominic's customers?
- ♦ How can Dominic identify his customers' needs?
- ♦ Where interest is expressed, what could Dominic say to close the sale?
- ♦ What does he need to do to ensure that companies buying a gift package get what they want?

Ways of referring customers to alternative sources of information if you are not responsible for dealing with the additional products or services they want

When you enter into a discussion with a customer, you may find that his or her needs fall outside the particular products or services you deal with. In cases where you are unable to help, you will need to refer the customer to somebody else or to an alternative source of information.

A good place to start with identifying who can help is to log all customer comments or queries where you were unsuccessful in helping your customer. You can review this list periodically and find out what you might have said to a customer that would have helped him or her to get what he or she wanted.

When passing a customer on to other people in your own place of work, you need to ensure your customer does not feel as if he or she is being passed around unnecessarily. You can do this by ensuring that your customer knows who you are passing him or her on to and why. It is very frustrating for customers to spend time talking with one individual, only to be told minutes later that he or she does not deal with what they want. This can happen when a telephone call has been misdirected or when a customer has misunderstood what you do. You need to make a decision as to how long you will let your customer talk before you explain that you are going to transfer him or her to a more appropriate person.

You have a number of choices to make when passing a customer on to somebody else, these include the following:

- ♦ contact the other person/company yourself and explain what it is the customer wants
- ♦ take the customer to see the other person
- ♦ give the customer the contact details and ask him or her to contact the other person
- ♦ give the customer product or service information leaflets/brochures that show the contact details.

Active knowledge

Make a list of the products or services that customers ask you about but which you do not deal with.

♦ Which of the above methods would be the most appropriate to use?
♦ What are the reasons for your choices?

Sometimes you might be aware of an alternative organisation which could help your customer when you cannot. This organisation may or may not be a competitor of yours. While you should always be helpful, sometimes it may not be appropriate to recommend other organisations. Find out now what the policy is where you work.

Keys to good practice

Referring customers to alternative sources of help

✓ Know who to go to for help.
✓ Keep up-to-date telephone contact lists.
✓ Keep and update a query log.
✓ Know how to operate the telephone system to transfer a call.
✓ Know when it is appropriate to take a customer to see another person.
✓ Tell the customer what you are doing.
✓ Tell the customer why you are passing him or her on.
✓ Keep the customer informed of progress.
✓ Remain positive and confident.

Case study

Imran works in a small town library and finds he is frequently asked for advice about matters that do not relate to the borrowing of books.

Conscious of the need to be helpful and to create a good impression of the library, he started to record queries in a log. In a quiet moment, Imran then set about researching the information he would need to be able to answer similar queries in the future. Here is an excerpt of the entries in his log.

Date	Query	Who to refer to
23 April	Temporary wheelchair hire	Local Red Cross Branch
1 May	Refuse collections over Easter	Council Cleansing Department
5 May	Town trails	Tourist Information Officer – Civic Hall
17 June	Disposal of fridge freezer	Council Cleansing Department
19 June	NHS dentist	Try Mr Greene's practice in Bedale Road

♦ Why is it good customer service to help people with information about products or services you do not normally deal with?

♦ How can Imran ensure his research is accurate?

♦ Can you see any dangers in Imran passing this type of information on to customers? If so, what are they?

♦ How should Imran balance the time he spends with customers answering queries that are not library-related, with those customers who come to the library to borrow books?

What to do if your customer shows no interest in additional products or services

When the customer appears not to want to take up your offer, the first thing to remember is a no might not mean a definite no.

Figure 7.9 Customer reservations

These are actually clear buying signals because what the customer is really saying is not no, but something like 'I have reservations but there might be something you can do about that.' You should therefore look on these apparent 'no' statements as opportunities to question your customer a little more to find out if you can compromise or help them with further information.

Overcoming customer reservations

During your discussions with customers, some will have reservations about what you are saying. These reservations may occur for many reasons, including the following:

♦ the customer cannot spare the time to listen
♦ the customer is not convinced about the benefits
♦ the customer feels under too much pressure to say yes
♦ the customer has misunderstood you
♦ the customer needs time to think
♦ the customer cannot afford to spend any more money.

When you spot a customer who has reservations you need to bear in mind that different emotions may be at work. He or she may be experiencing feelings of:

♦ frustration
♦ anger
♦ irritation
♦ confusion
♦ worry
♦ fear.

He or she might suddenly start to behave in a different way. Be aware of your own body language and what you are saying. Remain calm, positive and confident. The golden rule when dealing with a reservation (whatever it might be) is that you should never openly contradict the customer. Contradicting the customer puts him or her in the wrong frame of mind for buying. Do not forget that he or she may have simply misunderstood what you have said. In order to deal with customer reservations you should do the following:

Listen to the reservation: resist the temptation to interrupt the customer. Do not step in and say things like 'No! You're wrong! I've got one myself and I'm really pleased with it.' Instead, keep quiet and listen. Listening to what your customer has to say will show that you care and that you are interested in his or her concerns. It also gives you breathing space to think about how you are going to deal with the reservation.

Check that you have understood the reservation: if you start to get a little worried about your customer's reaction, this may affect your ability to listen effectively. By checking that you understand the customer, you will also be clarifying the extent of his or her concerns. It may turn out to be a trivial reservation and something you can deal with easily.

Figure 7.10 Dealing with customer reservations

Give an answer: once you have fully understood your customer's reservations you can take steps to answer them. Your response will depend on whether the reservation is a misunderstanding by the customer, disbelief in what you have said, or a product or service disadvantage.

When the reservation is based on a misunderstanding you should accept responsibility for this even if you do not consider it to be your fault. Then provide the information that will clarify the situation before moving on to test out your customer's level of interest.

If you are dealing with a customer who does not believe what you have said, you should respond in a non-threatening way by talking about his or her feelings and restating the benefits of using the additional product or service.

For a customer who feels your additional product or service is less attractive than something he or she can get elsewhere, i.e. it has a disadvantage, you will need to restate the advantages of doing business with you and the benefits of the product or service. This means you need to be very sure of the key selling points of your products or services.

Active knowledge

Working with a colleague, think of the five most common reservations your customers raise. List these below and work out what you can try saying to overcome them.

The five most common reservations	What I can say to overcome them
1.	
2.	
3.	
4.	
5.	

Finally, remember you will not succeed in creating interest where there genuinely is none. Do not worry about this. Just thank the customer for his or her time and move on.

Remember

Customers buy benefits and solutions. The more you promote benefits and solutions, the more you will succeed.

Test your knowledge

Promote the benefits of an activity to a friend or colleague. Practise the following:

◆ identifying any reservations
◆ overcoming these reservations
◆ gaining commitment to moving forward.

Check your knowledge

1　Why is it important to promote additional products or services to customers?

2　List six of the benefits that motivate a customer to buy an additional product or service.

3　What is the difference between a feature and a benefit?

4　People buy products and features. True or false?

5　How can you identify opportunities for promoting additional products or services?

6　What are the key communication skills that you will need to be successful at promoting additional products or services?

7　Name five key factors that influence your customers to buy from your organisation.

8　During which situations would you use clarifying or confirming questions?

9　How can you encourage customers to ask you questions about additional products or services?

10　Describe three closing techniques.

11　How can completing a query log help customer service?

12　What are the benefits to your customer and your organisation of keeping your product or service knowledge up to date?

13　What are the five steps for dealing with customer reservations about using additional products or services?

14　What do you need to consider when giving customers information about additional products or services?

UNIT 8

Process customer service information

This option unit looks at those customer service roles that deal with a significant amount of customer information. The information you handle may include information about new and existing customers.

Sometimes you will personally be involved in asking your customers questions in order to obtain information. At other times you will be providing information. Alternatively, your organisation may have systems and procedures for capturing information, such as questionnaires or email surveys.

Without accurate, up-to-date, accessible and reliable information, customer service will suffer. This means the way in which you handle information will be vital to the success of your organisation and to your own performance. Customer satisfaction is also directly related to the way in which you use information.

The elements for this option unit are:

♦ 8.1 Collect customer service information
♦ 8.2 Select and retrieve customer service information
♦ 8.3 Supply customer service information.

8.1 Collect customer service information

♦ Why correct handling of customer service information contributes to efficient customer service.

♦ What you can do to ensure that customer service information is accurate and relevant.

♦ Where to store information so that it is accessible to appropriate individuals.

Why correct handling of customer service information contributes to efficient customer service

Everybody relies on accurate and reliable information. Both internal and external customers will want to know they can trust the information they are provided with. Similarly, you too will want to know that the information you provide to customers can be trusted. Teamwork is essential to making this happen.

Without accurate, up-to-date and accessible information, the whole customer service operation in your organisation will suffer. You will not be able to provide customers with the information they require and your organisation will not have the appropriate information to support the achievement of its aims.

How was it for you?

Think back to occasions when a customer service practitioner gave you inaccurate information.

♦ How did you feel?
♦ What impression did this give you of the organisation you were dealing with?

If information is accurate and reliable, you and your colleagues can work in an environment where everyone knows that what they are being told or what they are reading is trustworthy.

Figure 8.1 The impact of trustworthy information on customers

Dealing with accurate and reliable information helps you to avoid
irritating your customers with inaccurate information. Passing on
inaccurate information is not only detrimental to customer service, it can
also be dangerous. Imagine what would happen if you worked in an
environment that involved knowing about safety procedures (e.g. for an
airline). If the safety manual you used was not up to date, the
consequences could be fatal.

What you can do to ensure customer service information is accurate and relevant

There may be occasions when you are required to collect new customer
service information or to amend existing records. This might be for the
following reasons:

♦ when customers advise you of a change in personal circumstances (for
instance a change of address)
♦ when customers advise you of a change to a regular order
♦ when customers provide you with additional information that you or
your organisation has requested
♦ when customers give you instructions about a new order

- when customers make a complaint or say thank you
- when customers provide feedback on a product or service.

Active knowledge

Make a list of the main types of situation in which you collect customer service information. For each one:

- Which information do you find the most difficult to obtain from customers? Why is this?
- What do you do to ensure the information is accurate?
- How do you know whether the information you record is relevant?

Note-taking

To help ensure you collect accurate information, you will find it helpful to take notes. Most people need to take notes when listening to a customer conversation or perhaps directly afterwards. This ensures that important points are not missed, especially when interruptions are likely to occur. You may also find note-taking useful when reading long correspondence. By writing down key points yourself, you may find this helps you to focus on the key points of written communications. Notes help you to remember what was agreed with a customer, what action needs to be taken and by whom. This is all part of maintaining a reliable customer service.

You can update records from your notes at a later date if necessary. Alternatively, your organisation might have a computer system for automatically recording updates to customer records while the practitioner is talking with the customer. The accuracy of the information you collect is very important, therefore your note-taking needs to be very efficient.

Keys to good practice

Efficient note-taking

✓ Record relevant customer details, e.g. name, reference/account/order numbers.
✓ Detail your name, contact details and date.
✓ Show what action is required and by whom.
✓ Indicate critical points, e.g. use highlighting or underlining.
✓ Be legible.
✓ Be easy to understand by yourself and others.
✓ Be brief and specific; only include relevant and important points.

Using bits of paper for your note-taking is a recipe for disaster; they soon look like bits of rubbish and may get accidentally discarded. To help you record accurate notes it may be useful to have a stock of specially prepared note-taking forms, as shown below.

Notes of discussion with   _____

Taken by _____

Date _____

Key points _____

Action to be taken and by whom _____

Records updated by _____

Figure 8.2 A sample note-taking form

Confirming the accuracy of the information you have collected

Having made your notes or collected information, it is a good idea to check back the accuracy of what you have done. If you fail to do this, you run the risk of working with information that is useless because it is inaccurate.

When collecting information from a customer you can check the accuracy of the information by repeating the key elements back to your customer. Think about any parts of the discussion you have had difficulty in understanding. If you have had trouble, then it is likely someone else will have trouble too. Clarify these doubtful areas in order to make sure your information is accurate. This can be something as simple as asking a customer to clarify the spelling of a name or a place. It could be about checking a date. You might need to check numbers. If you are in any doubt, check.

Active knowledge

Ask a colleague, team leader, supervisor or other appropriate person what systems and procedures your organisation has for collecting and recording customer service information.

Case study

Qaalfa works on the helpdesk for a charity. He deals with queries from individuals and businesses who are involved with fund-raising for the charity. Most of the calls he has been getting recently involve people seeking information about a marathon that the charity is associated with. Here is a transcript of a conversation he had with Chloe, who is the Sponsorship and Promotions Manager of IT4U, a website design firm that has recently moved into the area where the marathon is being staged.

Chloe: Hi. I'm from IT4U. You may know we have recently moved in at the business park. We are very interested in becoming involved with the marathon. Can you please tell me what opportunities there are?

Qaalfa: I can send you some sponsorship forms but you have to raise £750 before we can accept your entry.

Chloe: No. I'm not wanting to run myself. I'm interested in what my company can do to help.

Qaalfa: Sorry. What you mean is your company might want to become involved with some form of sponsorship. Is that right?

Chloe: Yes. Now what opportunities are there? We would, of course, want our name to be mentioned during the event in some way.

Qaalfa: What did you say your name was?

Chloe quickly became disillusioned. Qaalfa had failed to listen properly and was wasting her time. She told him she would find out the information she needed in some other way and put the telephone down.

Qaalfa soon realised he had lost a potential sponsor through not listening properly. He became annoyed with himself and soon learnt that he could not give out the right information if he did not first ask the right questions to collect the information he needed.

The information Qaalfa failed to seek himself included the following:

♦ details about IT4U; location, number of employees, what they do. Even the spelling of the company name would be worth checking
♦ how IT4U found out about the marathon
♦ what IT4U wanted to achieve by becoming involved with the event
♦ what their budget was
♦ what advertising they would expect from a financial commitment
♦ whether involvement could be achieved by employees of IT4U helping on the day.

Imagine yourself in Qaalfa's position.

♦ Using the list above, write down the questions Qaalfa might have asked Chloe.
♦ How might he check back the accuracy of the information he had collected?

Where to store information so that it is accessible to appropriate individuals

There is little to be gained from having large amounts of information if it cannot be found easily by those who need to use it. Do not let your efforts go to waste by being disorganised about where to store information once it has been obtained.

You must also ensure that you take steps to maintain confidentiality when dealing with any information that is sensitive. Sensitive information is not just that which is personal or of commercial interest to a competitor. Any information about a customer is potentially sensitive in that a customer has a right to privacy. Leaving address details lying about could mean a breach of privacy.

What you are aiming for is to store information in such a way as to prevent it from theft, fraud, interference, unauthorised access and accidental loss. Your organisation will have ways of helping you to do this, especially if information is stored on computer.

Active knowledge

1 Find out what your organisation's guidelines are for the storage of information using the following:

   ♦ manual systems, e.g. filing cabinets
   ♦ computerised systems.

2 What role do you play in ensuring the security of information when you are not at work?

3 What role do you play in ensuring information is not accidentally lost?

Keys to good practice

Storing information

✓ Return any sensitive documents to their source as soon as possible.
✓ Make sure notes you have taken are not left lying around.
✓ Tidy your workspace when your period of work is finished.
✓ Follow your organisation's guidelines.
✓ Ensure you file papers in the correct place when using a manual

Test your knowledge

While watching a TV news bulletin or listening to the news on the radio, take notes about what you hear. Do this for a two-minute period while videoing or tape-recording the news bulletin.

1 Play the recording back and compare it against the notes you made.

♦ How accurate were your notes?

♦ What kind of information (if any) did you leave out?

♦ Was it information which you found boring?

♦ Or was it information which you did not understand?

♦ If you found it difficult to take notes, was it because you were easily distracted?

♦ If so, what distracted you?

2 Now make a list of what you did well.

♦ How will you use this to help you accurately record customer service information?

♦ What about your areas for improvement? Make a list of what did not work so well (e.g. 'I became distracted by noises from another room' or 'I couldn't write fast enough to keep up with what was being said.'

♦ Discuss with an appropriate colleague what you can do to improve on these areas.

Select and retrieve customer service information

WHAT YOU NEED TO KNOW OR LEARN

♦ Why it is important to respond promptly to requests for information

♦ How to select the information needed

♦ How to retrieve the information needed

Why it is important to respond promptly to requests for information

Your customers will be asking for information for a reason. These reasons are many and varied and may include the following:

♦ to find out about a product or service

♦ to update existing information

♦ to replace out-of-date information

♦ to compare what you and your organisation offer with a competitor organisation.

Sometimes a buying decision will be made on the basis of the information you supply. In these situations, the impression you create by the way in which you deal with the request will have an impact on your customer's decision to make the purchase.

Figure 8.3 Reasons for responding promptly to requests for information

If you take days to respond, your customer might have gone elsewhere, i.e. to a service provider who is more responsive. If you send the wrong information this frustrates your customer and delays the receipt of the information. Even where you act promptly, you may still be in the hands of a third party as to whether or not your customer receives the information in a reasonable time. If you rely on the postal service to send information, think about the impact of the Christmas holidays and other bank holidays.

Remember

If you fail to supply information promptly to an external customer, a competitor will be waiting to do so.

How to select the information needed

In order to help customers and other people, you will need to be able to identify the right information in response to requests made. This means you need to fully understand what the customer or other individual wants.

When dealing with verbal requests for information (e.g. on the telephone or face-to-face) you should listen carefully and confirm your understanding of what is required by summarising the key points back to the person you are dealing with. Do not worry about repeating back information or asking for more clarification. It is much better to be sure that you have fully understood your customer in order to provide him or her with reliable information. This information also needs to be relevant to his or her needs. You will only identify the relevance of the information you intend to provide if you understand your customer's needs. Make sure you know why the information is required and when it is required.

Case study

Katrina works as a personal assistant to the Managing Director of a clothes manufacturer. She has been asked to provide her boss with full details of the travel arrangements that need to be made for a forthcoming series of wedding fairs taking place in hotels across the UK.

This is the email her boss sent her:

Please sort out the travel times for this year's Spring Wedding Fairs. I will be going to the Bristol, Birmingham, Cardiff, Edinburgh, Leeds and Southampton events. I want to travel first class.

Katrina thought about what she needed to know and realised her boss had not given her enough information in order for her to research the information required.

♦ What questions should Katrina ask her boss to help her get the right information?
♦ How might Katrina demonstrate to her boss that she is thinking about the needs of her boss and the needs of the organisation?

Having identified what information is needed, you might need to do some research to obtain it. To do this you need to know the sources of information available to you.

Figure 8.4 Sources of information

Active knowledge

If you have Internet access and/or a company intranet, take a look at your organisation's website and/or intranet.

- How will it help you provide relevant information to others?
- Identify new ways in which you can use the intranet or your organisation's website to access information on behalf of others.

If you do not have a company intranet or access to the Internet, identify where in your organisation you have access to company information and access to information that will help you to provide relevant information to others.

- Identify ways in which you can use these sources of information to respond to requests for customer service information.

Keys to good practice

Selecting relevant information

- ✓ Listen or read carefully the request for information.
- ✓ Check your understanding of the request.
- ✓ Ask questions to avoid making assumptions.
- ✓ Understand why the information is required and when it is required.
- ✓ Know the sources of information available to you.
- ✓ Keep any information databases/filing up to date.
- ✓ Use only up-to-date information on products or services.
- ✓ Check your stocks of product or service leaflets/brochures regularly.

How to retrieve the information needed

The way in which you find the information you need will depend on where and how it is stored. Think about the types of information you frequently need to find and then ensure you know exactly where to find them.

- Keep an up-to-date list of contact details for other people within your organisation in order to be able to easily reach them to request information.
- Identify whether any security systems are in use that you will need to know about in order to access the information.
- Know how to operate the computer system.
- Keep manual filing systems in effective order.
- Keep your own workspace tidy and well stocked with information leaflets.
- Identify helpful websites (if appropriate to your role).

The key to the successful retrieval of information is to be organised. Having a comprehensive knowledge of your sources of information and how to access them will mean you can efficiently respond to requests.

Test your knowledge

Think back to a time when you were unable to promptly provide customer service information.

♦ Why was this?
♦ What stopped you acting promptly?
♦ What effect did this have on your own self-confidence?
♦ Did your organisation lose business because of this?
♦ Or was there loss of goodwill and trust?
♦ Were mistakes made?
♦ Overall, what was the impact upon your customer(s)?
♦ What was the impact upon your colleague(s)?

Take steps now to put right anything that prevented you from responding in the appropriate manner.

 ## Supply customer service information

WHAT YOU NEED TO KNOW OR LEARN

♦ Why it is important to maintain confidentiality when dealing with customer service information.
♦ How to select the most appropriate way to supply information to customers.
♦ How to ensure the information you supply is accurate and sufficient.
♦ How to confirm your customers have received and understood the information you supply.

Why it is important to maintain confidentiality when dealing with customer service information

During all of you customer service work you should remember the need to protect your customer and your organisation's interest when processing information. The loyalty and goodwill built up between service providers and customers will be destroyed if there is a breach of confidentiality. Trust will be broken and the customer/service provider relationship will be badly (and sometimes terminally) affected.

There is legislation in place that is designed to protect the privacy of the individual. It is important for you to know about this since in your role you will have access to a great deal of information about customers.

The Data Protection Act 1998

When dealing with the processing of information you are likely to be operating in an environment where yourself or other individuals will have asked the following questions:

♦ Why is this information being collected?
♦ How is it going to be used?
♦ Who will have access to it?

The Data Protection Act 1998 established eight enforceable principles of good practice that you need to know about when dealing with the processing of personal customer service data.

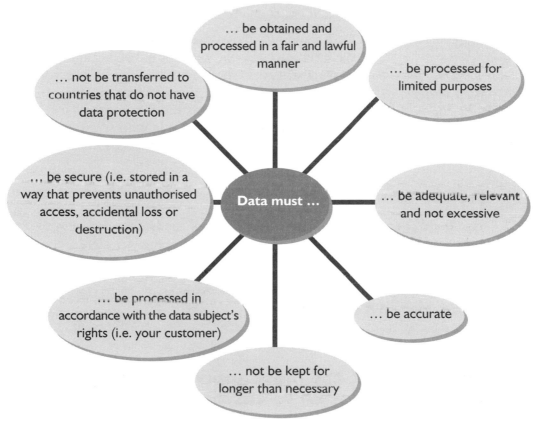

Figure 8.5 The eight principles of good practice when processing personal data

Personal data covers both facts and opinions about customers and applies to information supplied or stored in computerised, manual or any other formats.

The Act covers the processing of information relating to individuals including obtaining, holding, using or disclosing information. Some of the systems and processes your organisation has in place that deal with the collection and supply of information may have been designed or amended in order for the processing of customer service information to comply with the Act. The Act gives the customer rights to the following:

- to be informed when the data is being processed
- to a description of the details being held
- to know the reason why the data is being processed
- to know who the data may be disclosed to.

Always consider how the way in which you pass information on to others is going to impact upon your ability to maintain confidentiality

Sensitive information

The Act now makes it clear that information concerning race or ethnic origin, political persuasion, religious or philosophical belief, trade union membership, health or medical condition and sexual orientation may not be collected and processed unless your customer has given his or her explicit consent.

On a day-to-day basis there may be some information passed between colleagues or between different departments that should not be seen by everyone. Respect for the privacy of individuals must be maintained. If the information is commercially sensitive then the fewer people who know about it, the less likely it is to fall into the wrong hands.

Active knowledge

Find out if your organisation has its own code of conduct for dealing with information in order to comply with the Data Protection Act 1998 and to maintain confidentiality.

- What do you need to do to ensure you work within organisation guidelines and best practice?

How to select the most appropriate way to supply information to customers

The information you have selected and retrieved needs to be given to your customers in a way that best meets the customers' needs and also in a way that ensures it is fully understood.

There are two types of information you may handle: information about customers and information for customers. The type of information alone may influence how you decide to supply the information. However, there are also other factors that you need to consider when you supply information to your customers; the method you choose will be influenced by a combination of the following:

- your organisation's needs and guidelines
- any legal restrictions
- your customers' needs and expectations.

Supplying information in writing

You should supply information in writing, e.g. letters, emails, memos, faxes, leaflets or posters in the following circumstances:

♦ when a permanent record is required
♦ when the impact of a professionally produced poster or leaflet is appropriate
♦ email can be used if this is supported by both your technology and the customer, and where the quantity and sensitivity of the information are appropriate.

Supplying information using the spoken word

You should supply information using the spoken word, e.g. face-to-face conversations, telephone conversations or meetings in the following circumstances:

♦ when information is readily accessible and the customer has requested you speak with him or her
♦ for information that can be easily understood
♦ when you need to discuss the information with your customer.

Ask yourself why the information is required and who needs it. Your answer may help you to determine your method of communication.

Speed of response?

♦ Does the customer require the information urgently?
♦ How long will it take you to select and retrieve the relevant information?
♦ Are there any organisational standards in terms of time for responding to customer requests?

Level of technology?

♦ Have you and/your customer access to email?
♦ Is email appropriate for the type of information required?

How much information?

♦ The quantity of information to be supplied might mean that certain forms of communication are inappropriate.

Impact?

♦ If the information you are supplying is required to make an impact, you should consider how attractive it is visually to the reader.
♦ It should also visually match the product or service you are promoting.

Confidentiality?

♦ If the information you are supplying is sensitive or should only be accessed by certain individuals, you should select your method of communication appropriately.
♦ emails are not the most secure means of communication.

Figure 8.6 Points to consider when supplying information to customers

Costs?

♦ The quantity of information to be supplied might impact upon your decision.

♦ Think about postage and telephone costs and how these influence what you are handling.

Organisational guidelines?

♦ Your organisation may have its own standards for responding to requests for information. For example, there may be standards relating to speed of response and the method you choose in relation to cost.

Active knowledge

Find out if your organisation has standards or guidelines for supplying information to customers.

♦ How will these standards or guidelines (if any) impact upon the method you choose to supply information to customers?

How to ensure the information you supply is accurate and sufficient

Having selected the most appropriate method to supply the information, you must ensure that what you supply is fit for purpose. In other words, is the information you are supplying going to meet (or exceed) the needs of your customer? Will he or she understand it? Is it going to make the right impact? Is it accurate? Is there enough information?

If you can answer these questions with a 'yes', then you are doing your best to ensure that the customer gets the information he or she needs.

If you need to write to customers you should ensure your that letters/emails follow your organisation's guidelines. A sloppy letter or email will quickly create the wrong image. Here are some hints and tips to improve your writing skills in situations where you are supplying detailed information.

1 Remind yourself of the following:

   ◆ who your reader(s) will be
   ◆ why the information is required
   ◆ what the reader needs and expects from you.

2 Prepare an outline

   Try making a note of all the key points you need to include. Think about the impact you need to make. Think about your introduction, which will set the context of the communication. The middle will set out all the information you need to put across. The ending will include any points you wish to re-emphasise, together with details of any action that needs to be taken.

3 Style

   The style you use should focus on the needs of the reader. Make sure you use language appropriate to the reader and keep well away from jargon or abbreviations that will be confusing to customers. Use short sentences and paragraphs. Concentrate on being clear and concise.

If you are using email as your means of communication, you should also follow these additional guidelines:

♦ check that email is the most appropriate method to supply the information

♦ remember that emails are not necessarily confidential

♦ give the message an appealing subject line that encourages the reader to open it

♦ keep the message concise

♦ consider including a summary of the key points at the end

♦ do not type in capitals; the reader might think you are shouting

♦ do not type in all lower case; just because you are using email it does not mean the grammar rule-book can be thrown away

♦ read through your message and do not rely on the spell checker.

Keys to good practice

Checking if information will meet customer needs

✓ Answer all the customer's questions or queries.
✓ Provide enough information.
✓ Enclose relevant supporting literature.
✓ Use appropriate language that is free from jargon.
✓ Ensure that information is current.
✓ Check for spelling mistakes.
✓ Check any figures/dates are correct.

How to confirm your customers have received and understood the information you supply

When you supply customer service information you will have done so on the basis that you have understood why the customer wants the information and what he or she specifically needs information about. You will then have matched these needs with the information you select to provide.

If you are speaking with a customer, you can ask your customer if you have given him or her the information he or she needs by saying the following:

♦ Have I given you all the information you need?"
♦ Does that answer your queries?
♦ This is the information I have found for you. Let me know if I can help further.

If you are dealing face-to-face with a customer, watch also for any visual signs that you have not supplied the appropriate information. Your customer might actually say so or he or she might look a little confused.

How was it for you?

♦ What action, if any, did you take when you were last given some information that you did not understand?
♦ How did you feel?
♦ What impression did you have in your mind of the organisation and the people you were dealing with?

If sending information to others, perhaps through the post or by email, you will need to consider whether it is appropriate to follow up with a courtesy call to check that you have supplied what was required. This will not always be the right thing to do; you will need to judge each situation on its own merits.

Active knowledge

By asking an appropriate person, find out in what circumstances you are required to check whether customers have understood and received written information you have supplied through the post or by some other form of written communication.

Test your knowledge

Imagine a friend has asked you to give him or her some information that he or she knows you can help with.

♦ Role-play with your friend how you would supply this information.
♦ Think about the most effective method.
♦ Think about what you would need to help you put the message across effectively.
♦ How will you check that your friend has understood the information you give?

Check your knowledge

1   Why is the correct handling of customer service information important to your organisation?

2   Why do customers need you to respond promptly to requests for information?

3   What might happen if you fail to respond to a customer request for information?

4   List three ways in which accurate and reliable information can impact upon a customer.

5   Complete this sentence: The correct storage of information aims to prevent ...

6   When you supply information to others, what are the two key things you need to know about the information required?

7   Name four key sources of information.

8   What must you do to ensure that the sources of information you use are accurate and reliable?

9   What rights does the Data Protection Act 1998 give to customers?

10 How can you ensure that you maintain customer confidentiality when handling information?

11 List four key points you should consider when supplying information to customers.

12 In what circumstances might you choose to give a customer information verbally?

13 When should you give a customer information in writing?

14 How can you check if the information you have selected will meet your customers' needs?

Useful addresses

Commission of Racial Equality
Elliot House
1-12 Allington Street
London
SW1E 5EH
www.cre.gov.uk

Data Protection Commissioner
Wycliffe House
Water Lane
Wilmslow
Cheshire
SK9 5AF
www.dataprotection.gov.uk

Customer Contact Point
Equal Opportunities Commission
Arndale House
Arndale Centre
Manchester
M4 3EQ
www.eoc.org.uk

The Office of Fair Trading
Fleetbank House
2-6 Salisbury Square
London
EC4Y 8JX
www.oft.gov.uk

The Institute of Customer Service is the professional body for customer service professionals and also sets the standards for national vocational qualifications in customer service. Individuals working towards or holding an SVQ or NVQ in Customer Service can join the Institute at different levels of membership. As well as professional recognition, membership brings opportunities to keep up to date with developments in customer service and access to the experience and support of other customer service professionals.

2 Castle Court
St. Peter's Street
COLCHESTER
Essex
CO1 1EW

Telephone: 01206 571716
Fax: 01206 546688
Email: enquiries@instcustserv.com
www.instituteofcustomerservice.com

Fit for the Future is the UK's national best practice campaign. For free independent advice on who to speak to regarding best practice issues, call the free helpline on 0870 600 2513 or visit **www.fitforthefuture.org.uk**.

Fit for the Future
CBI
Centre Point
103 New Oxford Street
London
WC1A 1DU
Email: fitforthefuturequeries@cbi.org

Index